Cross Index Title Guide
to Classical Music

Cross Index Title Guide to Classical Music

Compiled by STEVEN G. PALLAY

Music Reference Collection, Number 12

Greenwood Press

New York • Westport, Connecticut • London

Library of Congress Cataloging-in-Publication Data

Pallay, Steven G., 1930-
  Cross index title guide to classical music.

  (Music reference collection, ISSN 0736-7740 ; no. 12)
  Includes index.
  1. Titles of musical compositions—Bibliography.
2. Music—Bibliography. I. Title. II. Series.
ML113.P34 1987   016.78'043   86-25723
ISBN 0-313-25531-8 (lib. bdg. : alk. paper)

Library of Congress Catalog Card Number: 86-25723
ISBN: 0-313-25531-8
ISSN: 0736-7740

First published in 1987

Greenwood Press, Inc.
88 Post Road West, Westport, Connecticut 06881

Printed in the United States of America

The paper used in this book complies with the
Permanent Paper Standard issued by the National
Information Standards Organization (Z39.48-1984).

10 9 8 7 6 5 4 3 2 1

Contents

Introduction

As in most fields, there is an information explosion occur-ring in music. A confusing array of titles are continually appearing in print, on records and on tapes, as well as being heard daily on the airwaves. Often it is difficult to identify compositions that are commonly known by popular names but generally listed in some other form as standardized entries in textbooks and encyclopaedias and record, tape and library catalogues.

Nicknames such as "Alleluia Symphony" or "Turkish Concerto" are commonplace and sometimes date back centuries. Others have more recent origins, and some pieces have even acquired a number of popular titles over the years. Simply stated, the purpose of this fully cross-indexed guide is to enable the user to trace the "true identity" of a particular work.

The main section of this book, the "Title-Composer Index," lists each work multiple times, under variant names, and provides the composer's last name. For each entry, an arrow indicates the title under which the piece is most likely to be found in reference works or catalogues:

Music for radio <- Saga of the prairie / Prairie journal:
    COPLAND
Prairie journal / Saga of the prairie -> Music for radio:
    COPLAND
Saga of the prairie / Prairie journal -> Music for radio:
    COPLAND

The title of a piece from a larger work is given in round brackets following the main title:

Gloria concertata -> Salve morale e spirituale (Gloria):
    MONTEVERDI

Where there is more than one alternate title, either original or translated, they are divided by a slash:

Schweizer-Sinfonie / Swiss symphony -> Symphony, string
   orchestra, no. 9, C minor: MENDELSSOHN

As initial articles are disregarded in all languages (a,
an, the, der, die, das, ein, eine, le, la, les, un, une, il,
gli, lo, las, los, etc.), such titles are given in an invert-
ed form in the alphabetization:

King shall rejoice, The <- Wedding anthem: BOYCE
Villanella rapita, La -> La villanella riconosciuta:
   CIMAROSA

When two or more titles are identical, the alphabetical or-
der is determined by the composers' names:

Prometheus -> Die Geschöpfe des Prometheus: BEETHOVEN
Prometheus <- Poem of fire: SKRIABIN

Except for Slavic languages, standard titles are given
mostly in the vernacular, but their popular titles appear
usually both in English and in their language of origin.
   It should be noted that straightforward translations of
foreign titles are excluded (Le nozze di Figaro - The marriage of Figaro: MOZART); however, the guide incorporates
the English title if it deviates from the original form:

Titus -> La clemenza di Tito: MOZART

Vocal compositions known by their titles rather than their
first lines, but catalogued under the latter (Evening hymn
-> Now that the sun hath veiled his light: PURCELL) - a
source of frequent confusion - are also fully listed; however, excerpts from large-scale vocal works, such as opera,
operetta and oratorio arias, are not. In part due to their
sheer numbers, these fall outside the limited scope of this
book; they will be covered separately in a forthcoming vol-
ume.
   In choosing uniform entries (or "conventional titles," as
they are called in library terminology), I have basically
followed the provisions of the Anglo-American Cataloguing
Rules; modifications occur mostly in form entries (concertos,
quartets, sonatas, etc.) where I have disposed of the uni-
versal plural form recently adopted in the revised second
edition of these Rules.
   An alphabetical "List of Composers," with their full names
and life dates, follows the main section of this book.
   I have made extensive use of numbering systems for composers whose works have been documented in thematic catalogues,
employing the standard abbreviations (H. numbers, K. numbers,
S. numbers, etc.); the bibliographic descriptions of these
publications are given in an appendix, the "Key to Catalogue
Numbers," following the composers' list.

The principal sources consulted in preparing this guide,
which are listed in the last section, may also serve as aids
for locating printed editions and recordings of a work, as
well as biographical and bibliographical information about
composers.

Students and professionals, record collectors and devotees
of trivial pursuits, concert goers and librarians will dis-
cover more than one use of this Guide. It will provide an-
swers to such diverse questions as: Who is the composer of
The Violence of Love? Who, beside Mozart, has written a Jupiter symphony? How many Canticles has Britten composed?
Does Cowell's fourth string quartet have a popular title? In
which language other than English is Gottschalk's Battle Cry
For Freedom known?

No such index can possibly claim to be complete, but this
one represents most major composers, from Josquin Deprès to
Penderecki - 220 in all, and over 6000 entries - and it is
hoped that it will be found useful by an ever growing army
of music fans.

Title-Composer Index

A l'infant -> Concerto, violin & string orchestra, op. 7, no. 1, D minor: LECLAIR

A Montevideo -> Symphony, no. 2: GOTTSCHALK

Abaris <- Les Boréades: RAMEAU

Abbé de l'Attaignant, L' <- Die Theaterprobe: DANZI

Abdelazer <- The Moor's revenge: PURCELL

Abegg variations -> Thème varié sur le nom Abegg, piano, op. 1: SCHUMANN

Abencérages, Les <- L'étendard de Grenade: CHERUBINI

Abend, Der, D. 221 <- Temora: SCHUBERT

Abendempfindung <- An Laura: MOZART

Abendlied / Schlummerlied -> Schlaflied, D. 527: SCHUBERT

Abendlied der Fürstin, D. 495 <- Der Fürstin Abendlied: SCHUBERT

Abendständchen, D. 265 <- An Lina: SCHUBERT

Abgebrannte Haus, Das -> Die Feuersbrunst: J.HAYDN

Abraham and Isaac <- Canticle II: BRITTEN

Abraham Lincoln symphony -> Symphony, no. 10: HARRIS

Abschied, D. 475 <- Wallfahrtsarie / Lunz: SCHUBERT

Abschiedsgesang -> Die Stunde schlägt:BEETHOVEN

Abschiedssymphonie / Farewell symphony -> Symphony, M. 45, F# minor: J.HAYDN

Absente et présente -> Séraphine: GRÉTRY

Acanthe et Céphise <- La sympathie: RAMEAU

Accedo ad te mi Jesu <- Dialogus inter Deus et hominem: COUPERIN

Ach bleib bei uns, Herr Jesu Christ /Schübler chorales -> Chorale prelude, S. 649: J.S. BACH

Actéon changé en cerf -> Symphony, K. 75: DITTERSDORF

Actus tragicus -> Gottes Zeit ist die allerbeste Zeit, S. 106: J.S. BACH

Ad nos ad salutarem undam -> Fantasie und Fuge über den Choral Ad nos ad salutarem undam, organ: LISZT

Adagio, piano trio, D. 897, E♭ major <- Notturno, op. 148: SCHUBERT

Adagio cantabile, string quartet, double bass & piano <- The innate: IVES

Adagio Solenne, organ (arr.) <- Cantique: ELGAR

Adam and Eve -> Eden: ROSENBERG

Adelaida di Borgogna <- Ottone, re d'Italia: ROSSINI

Adelaide concerto -> Concerto, violin, K. Anh. 294a: MOZART

Adelia <- La figlia dell' arciere: DONIZETTI

Adelina Senese <- L'amore segreto: SPONTINI

Adieu, L' / Farewell waltz /Valse de l'adieu -> Waltz, piano, op. 69, no. 1, A major: CHOPIN

Adieu, L' -> Lieder ohne Worte, op. 85 (No. 2): MENDELSSOHN

Adieu a Varsovie, L' -> Rondo, piano, op. 1, C minor: CHOPIN

Adieu coranto / A toy -> Coranto, keyboard instrument, H.
    40: GIBBONS
Adieux, Les /The farewell -> Sonata, piano, op. 44, E♭ ma-
    jor: DUSSEK
Adieux, Les -> Concerto, piano, op. 110, E major: HUMMEL
Adieux, Les -> Reverie sur un motif de l'opéra Roméo et
    Juliette: LISZT
Adieux sonata, Les -> Sonata, piano, no. 26, op. 81a, E ma-
    jor: BEETHOVEN
Adieux sonata, Les -> Sonata, harpsichord, K. 206 (L. 257) E
    major: D. SCARLATTI
Adina <- Il califfo di Bagdad: ROSSINI
Ádventi ének -> Veni, veni Emmanuel: KODÁLY
Adventures of Mercury, The -> Mercure: SATIE
Aeolian harp etude / Harp etude / Shepherd boy etude ->
    Etude, piano, op. 25, no. 1, A♭ major: CHOPIN
Africa <- Fantaisie, piano & orchestra, op. 89, G minor:
    Saint-Saëns
Africaine, L' <- Vasco de Gama: MEYERBEER
After Delacroix -> Symphony, no. 6: ANTHEIL
After the Battle / Ballade / Left alone -> Forgotten:
    MUSORGSKY
Agachadas, Las <- Shake-down song: COPLAND
Agarista -> Gl'ingami felici: A.SCARLATTI
Age of anxiety, The <- Symphony, no. 2: BERNSTEIN
Age of gold, The -> The golden age: SHOSTAKOVICH
Agitation -> Lieder ohne Worte, op. 53 (No. 3): MENDELSSOHN
Agnes -> Von Ida, D. 228: SCHUBERT
Agnus Dei -> L'Arlésienne (Suite, no. 2(Intermezzo; arr.)):
    BIZET
Ah seek to know <- Vauxhall songs : J.C.BACH
Ah, why shou'd love <- Vauxhall songs: J.C.BACH
Aimable lazure, L' -> Pièces de clavecin, 4. livre, 20.
    ordre (Les cherubins): COUPERIN
Air on the G-string / Aria of the fallen angels -> Suite,
    orchestra, S. 1068, D major (Aria): J.S.BACH
Air russe -> Moments musicaux, piano (No. 6): SCHUBERT
Air russe <- Schöne Minka: WEBER
Airplane sonata -> Sonata, piano, no. 2: ANTHEIL
Ajax et Ulisse qui se disputent les armes d'Achille -> Sym-
    phony, K. 84: DITTERSDORF
Ajo nell' imbarazzo, L' <- Don Gregorio: DONIZETTI
Ala and Lolly -> Scythian suite, orchestra: PROKOFIEV
Alassio -> In the south: ELGAR
Albergo del giglio d'oro, L' -> Il viaggio a reims: ROSSINI
Album leaf -> Meditation: MUSORGSKY
Album leaf -> Songs, op. 38 (Daisies; arr.): RACHMANINOFF
Album leaves /Feuillets d'album -> Pièces brèves, piano:

FAURÉ
Album of miniatures -> Les saisons: ALBÉNIZ
Album sonata -> Sonata, piano, A♭ major: WAGNER
Alceste <- Le triomphe d'Alcide: LULLY
Alceste in Ebuda <- Olimpia: PAISIELLO
Aldimiro <- Favore per favore: A. SCARLATTI
Aldous Huxley in memoriam -> Variations, orchestra: STRAVIN-
    SKY
Alessandro <- Roxana / Alexander in India: HÄNDEL
Alexander in India / Roxana -> Alessandro: HÄNDEL
Alexander's feast <- The power of music: HÄNDEL
Alexander's feast concerto -> Concerto grosso, C major:
    HÄNDEL
Alfred (Overture) <- Tragic overture / Dramatic overture:
    DVOŘÁK
Alfred, König der Angelsachsen <- Der patriotische König: J.
    HAYDN
Alhambra, The -> La vega: ALBÉNIZ
Ali Baba <- Les quarante voleurs: CHERUBINI
Alimelek / Die beiden Kalifen / Aus Scherz ernst -> Wirt und
    Gast: MEYERBEER
All for you -> Songs, op. 57 (Only you): TCHAIKOVSKY
All men are brothers -> Symphony, no. 11, op. 186: HOVANESS
All the way around and back -> Scherzo, piano, 4 hands,
    winds, bells & violin: IVES
Allegretto, violin & piano <- Allegretto in the style of
    Boccherini: KREISLER
Allegretto, violin & piano, G minor <- Allegretto in the
    style of Porpora: KREISLER
Allegretto in the style of Boccherini -> Allegretto, violin
    & piano: KREISLER
Allegretto in the style of Porpora -> Allegretto, violin &
    piano, G minor: KREISLER
Allegretto quasi andante, piano, K. 61a, G minor <- Bagatelle,
    piano, K. 61a, G minor: BEETHOVEN
Allegro, piano, op. 46 <- Concert allegro / Concert solo:
    ELGAR
Allegro appassionato und Adagio -> Concertstück, violin &
    orchestra, op. 84, F minor: BRUCH
Allein Gott in der Höh' sei Ehr / Leipzig chorales -> Chorale
    prelude, S. 662; Chorale prelude, S. 663; Chorale prelude,
    S. 664: J.S.BACH
Alleluia symphony -> Symphony, M. 30, C major: J.HAYDN
Alles tönet, schallt und singt <- Frühlingskantate / Spring
    cantata: TELEMANN
Alma brasileira -> Chóros, no. 5: VILLA-LOBOS
Alma Dei creatoris <- Offertorium de B.V. Maria, K. 277:
    MOZART

Alma redemptoris mater <- Marian motets: DEPRÈS
Alman, keyboard instrument, H. 36 <- The king's jewel:
  GIBBONS
Alman, keyboard instrument, H. 34 <- A toy / Adieu coranto:
  GIBBONS
Almira <- Der in Krohnen erlangte Glücks-Wechsel: HÄNDEL
Als ich sie erröten sah, D. 153 <- Die entfernte Geliebte:
  SCHUBERT
Als Luise die Briefe ihres ungetreuen Liebabers verbrannte
  <- Unglückliche Liebe: MOZART
Alskande, Den -> Rakastava: SIBELIUS
Also sprach Zarathustra <- Zarathustra: R.STRAUSS
Alster overture / Ein musikalischer Spass / A musical joke
  -> Suite, orchestra, Fll, F major: TELEMANN
Altenberg-Lieder -> Orchester-Lieder, op. 4: BERG
Altrhapsodie -> Rhapsody, alto, men's voices & orchestra,
  op. 53: BRAHMS
Alvila, L' -> L'amazone corsara: A.SCARLATTI
Am Erlafsee -> Erlafsee, D. 586: SCHUBERT
Am Geburtstage des Kaisers, D. 748 <- Constitutionslied /
  Am Namensfeste des Kaisers / Geburtstags-Hymne: SCHUBERT
Am Grabe <- Grabgesang: BRUCKNER
Am Grabe Anselmos, D. 504 <- Bei dem Grabe Anselmos: SCHUBERT
Am Namensfeste des Kaisers / Constitutionslied / Geburts-
  tags-Hymne -> Am Geburtstage des Kaisers, D. 748: SCHUBERT
Am schlummernden Strom / Side by side -> Songs, op. 73 (We
  sat together): TCHAIKOVSKY
Am Tage aller Seelen, D. 343 <- Litanei auf das Fest aller
  Seelen: SCHUBERT
Amant jaloux, L' -> Les fausses apparences: GRÉTRY
Amante combattuto dalle donne di punto, L8 <- La giardiniera
  fortunata / Biondolina: CIMAROSA
Amante disperato, L' / Il marito geloso -> Il marito dis-
  perato: CIMAROSA
Amanti comici, Gli <- La famiglia in scompiglio: CIMAROSA
Amanti in cimento, Gli <- Il geloso andace: SPONTINI
Amants de Corinthe, Les -> Briséis: CHABRIER
Amants magnifiques, Les <- Variations sur des thèmes de
  Lully: JOLIVET
Amants magnifiques, Les <- Divertissement royal: LULLY
Amazones, Les <- Le fondation de Thèbes: MÉHUL
Amazzone corsara, L' <- L'alvilda: A.SCARLATTI
Ambrosian hymn / Hymnus Ambrosianus -> Symphony, no. 3:
  MILHAUD
American centennial march / American festival march ->
  Grosser Festmarsch, orchestra: WAGNER
American festival march / American centennial march ->
  Grosser Festmarsch, orchestra: WAGNER

American intermezzo -> La diva de l'Empire: SATIE
American muse -> Symphony, no. 10: SCHUMAN
American overture, An -> When Johnny comes marching home:
  HARRIS
American overture -> Overture, op. 42, B♭ major: PROKOFIEV
American quartet -> Quartet, strings, no. 12, op. 96, F
  major: DVOŘÁK
American requiem / Fliederrequiem / A requiem for those we
  love -> When lilacs last in the door-yard bloom'd: HINDE-
  MITH
American suite -> Suite, piano, op. 98, A major: DVORAK
American symphony -> Symphony, no. 2: ANTHEIL
Amerindian legend -> Izi: VILLA-LOBOS
Amor contrastato, L' / La bella molinara -> La molinara:
  PAISIELLO
Amor di Circe con Ulisse -> Circe: CIMAROSA
Amor ingegnoso, L' <- La giovane scaltra: PAISIELLO
Amor mio, L' <- L'arcano del core: DONIZETTI
Amor perfetto, L' -> Il servo padrone: PICCINNI
Amor volubile e tiranno, L' W- Dorisbe: A.SCARLATTI
Amor vuol sofferenze <- Il cioè / La finta frascatana: LEO
Amore e virtù <- Il trionfo della virtù: A.SCARLATTI
Amore innamorato -> Psiche: A.SCARLATTI
Amore segreto, L' -> Adelina Senese: SPONTINI
Amore vendicato <- Apollo e Dafne: PAISIELLO
Amori di Paride con Enone, Gli -> Paride sull' Ida: CALDARA
Amoroso, L' -> Concerto, violin & string orchestra, R. 271,
  E major: VIVALDI
Amors Macht, D. 339 <- Amors Zauber: SCHUBERT
Amors Zauber -> Amors Macht, D. 339: SCHUBERT
Amour au berceau, L' -> Pièces de clavecin, 3. livre, 15.
  ordre (Le dodo): COUPERIN
Amour conjugal, L' -> Céphale et Procris: GRÉTRY
Amour et gloire -> Charles de France: BOIELDIEU
Amour et la musique, L' -> La barcarolle: AUBER
Amour fugitif, L' -> Anacréon: CHERUBINI
Amour peintre, L' -> Le sicilien: LULLY
Amours badins, Les -> Pièces de clavecin, 4. livre, 24.
  ordre (La divine Babiche): COUPERIN
Amours d'Henri IV, Les -> Gabrielle d'Estées: MÉHUL
Amphitryon <- The two Sosias: PURCELL
Amusements d'Apollon, Les -> Sonata, violin & harpsichord,
  op. 25, no. 4, E minor: CORRETTE
An Cidli -> Furcht der Geliebten, D. 285: SCHUBERT
An das Vaterland -U Tantum ergo, D. 461: SCHUBERT
An der Bahre -> Totengräberweise, D. 869: SCHUBERT
An der schönen blauen Donau <- Donauwalzer / Blue Danube
  waltz: JOHANN STRAUSS

An der Wolga <- Mon salut!: JOHANN STRAUSS
An die Frauen <- Ode to women: J.HAYDN
An die Freunde -> Symphony, no. 2, op. 46, C major: PFITZNER
An die Harmonie -> Gesang an die Harmonie, D. 394: SCHUBERT
An Elisa -> Trost, D. 97: SCHUBERT
An Emma, D. 113 <- Emma: SCHUBERT
An Franz Schubert -> Geheimnis, D. 491: SCHUBERT
An Laura -> Abendempfindung: MOZART
An mein Klavier, D. 342 <- Seraphine an ihr Klavier / Schubert an sein Klavier; SCHUBERT
An Wasserflüssen Babylon / Leipzig chorales -> Chorale prelude, S. 653: J.S.BACH
Anacréon <- L'amour fugitif: CHERUBINI
Analinda, L' -> Le nozze con l'inimico: A.SCARLATTI
Andalusian dance /Danse andalouse -> Las mollares: GLINKA
Andante, piano, K. 57, F major <- Andante favori: BEETHOVEN
Andante favori -> Andante, piano, K. 57, F major: BEETHOVEN
Andromède sauvée par Persée -> Symphony, K. 76: DITTERSDORF
Ange de Niside, L' / Daila / Elda / Leonora -> La favorite: DONIZETTI
Angel of death / Asrael -> Symphony, no. 2, op. 27, C minor: SUK
Angéla <- L'atelier de Jean Cousin: BOIELDIEU
Angelus ad pastores <- Christmas motets: G.GABRIELI
Angiolina <- Il matrimonio per susurro: SALIERI
Ani -> Symphony, no. 23, band, op. 249: HOVANESS
Anima del filosofo, L8 <- Orfeo ed Euridice: J. HAYDN
Antar <- Symphony, no. 2, op. 9: RIMSKY-KORSAKOV
Animal sonata -> Sonata representativa, violin & continuo, A major: BIBER
Années de pèlerinage, 2. année <- Italy: LISZT
Années de pèlerinage, 2. année (Après une lecture de Dante) <- Dante sonata: LISZT
Années de pèlerinage, 2. année (Sonetto 47 del Petrarca; Sonetto 104 del Petrarca; Sonetto 123 del Petrarca) <- Petrarca sonnets: LISZT
Anniversario della liberatione di Roma dal terremoto <- Donna che in ciel: HÄNDEL
Annunciation cantata -> Kleine geistliche Concerte (Sei gegrüsset, Maria): SCHÜTZ
Anthem -> The dove descending breaks the air: STRAVINSKY
Anthems, op. 79 -> Spruche: MENDELSSOHN
Anthropos -> Symphony, no. 2: COWELL
Antretter serenade / Finalmusik -> Serenade, K. 167a (185) D major: MOZART
Antwort auf die Frage eines Mädchens -> Vergiss mein nicht: J.HAYDN
Apfelfest, Das -> Jabuka: JOHANN STRAUSS

Apocalyptic symphony -> Symphony, no. 8, C minor: BRUCKNER
Apollo e Dafne <- La terra è liberata: HÄNDEL
Apollo e Dafne -> Amore vendicato: PAISIELLO
Apothéose, L' <- Chant héroïque: BERLIOZ
Apothéose de Corelli, L' -> La Parnasse: COUPERIN
Appalachia <- Variations on an old slave song: DELIUS
Apparenza inganna, L' <- La villeggiatura: CIMAROSA
Appassionata -> Sonata, piano, no. 23, op. 57, F minor:
  BEETHOVEN
Appassionata -> Lieder ohne Worte, op. 38 (No. 5): MENDELS-
  SOHN
Apponyi quartets -> Quartet, strings, no. 70, op. 71, no. 1,
  Bb major; no. 71, op. 71, no. 2, D major; no. 72, op. 71,
  no. 3, Eb major; no. 73, op. 74, no. 1, C major; no. 74,
  op. 74, no. 2, F major; no. 75, op. 74, no. 3, G minor;
  J.HAYDN
Apprensivo raggirato, L' <- Il matrimonio raggirato: CIMA-
  ROSA
Aquarelles -> To be sung of a summer night on the water
  (arr.): DELIUS
Arabesque, bassoon & piano <- Carignane: IBERT
Ararat -> Symphony, no. 14, band, op. 194: HOVANESS
Arbor sonata /Mondschein Sonate /Moonlight sonata / Sunset
  sonata -> Sonata, piano, no. 14, op. 27, no. 2, C# minor:
  BEETHOVEN
Arbre enchanté, L' <- Le tuteur dupé: GLUCK
Arca di Noè, L' -> Quartet, strings, no. 6: MALIPIERO
Arcano del core, L' -> L'amor mio: DONIZETTI
Archduke trio / Erzherzog-Trio -> Trio, piano & strings,
  no. 6, op. 97, Bb major: BEETHOVEN
Archipelago<- Rhumba: ANTHEIL
Ardeatine caves, The / Le fosse Ardeatine -> Symphony, no.
  9: SCHUMAN
Arevakal -> Concerto, orchestra, no. 1, op. 88: HOVANESS
Aria di passaglia -> Arie musicali, 1. libro (Così mi dis-
  prezzate): FRESCOBALDI
Aria mit 30 Veränderungen, harpsichord, S. 998 <- Goldberg
  variations: J.S.BACH
Aria of the fallen angels / Air on the G-string -> Suite,
  orchestra, S. 1068, D major (Aria): J.S.BACH
Ariadne's lament / Il piano d'Arianna -> Concerto a quattro,
  string orchestra, op. 7, no. 6: LOCATELLI
Arianna, L' -> Lamento d'Arianna (Aria): MONTEVERDI
Arie musicali, 1. libro (A piè della gran croce) <- Madda-
  lena alla croce: FRESCOBALDI
Arie musicali, 1. libro (Begli occhi io non provo) <- La
  lancione: FRESCOBALDI
Arie musicali, 1. libro (Così mi disprezzate) <- Aria di

passacaglia: FRESCOBALDI
Arietta con variazioni, piano, A major -> Variations, piano,
    H.XVII,2, A major: J.HAYDN
Arietten op. 82 <- Italienische Liebeslieder: BEETHOVEN
Arietten, op. 82 (Dimmi, ben mio) <- Hoffnung: BEETHOVEN
Arietten, op. 82 (T'intendo, sì, mio cor) <- Liebesklage:
    BEETHOVEN
Arioso <- The maiden's seasons: SIBELIUS
Arise, my muse <- Ode for Queen Mary's birthday [1690]:
    PURCELL
Aristophanic suite -> The wasps (Suite): VAUGHAN WILLIAMS
Arjuna -> Symphony, no. 8, op. 179: HOVANESS
Arlecchino <- Die Fenster: BUSONI
Arlésienne, L' (Suite, no. 2 (Intermezzo;arr.)) <- Agnus
    Dei: BIZET
Armida abbandonata <- Dietro l'orme fugaci: HÄNDEL
Armidoro e Laurina -> Il ritorno di Don Calandrino: CIMA-
    ROSA
Arnstadt prelude -> Prelude and fugue, organ, S. 546, C
    minor: J.S.BACH
Arpeggio caprice -> Caprice, violin, op.1, no. 1, E major:
    PAGANINI
Arpeggio etude -> Etude, piano, op.10, no. 1, C major:
    CHOPIN
Arpeggio etude -> Grandes études de Paganini, piano (No. 4):
    LISZT
Arpeggione sonata -> Sonata, violoncello & piano, D. 821, A
    minor: SCHUBERT
Arsinoe -> La verità nell' inganno [1727]: CALDARA
Artaserse / Sehnsucht -> Leiden der Trennung, D. 509: SCHU-
    BERT
Arte del violino, L' (Concerto, no. 12, D major (Capriccio))
    <- The labyrinth / Il laberinto armonico: LOCATELLI
Arte dell' arco, L' <- Variations on a theme by Corelli:
    TARTINI
Article of faith -> Credendum: SCHUMAN
Artik <- Concerto, horn & string orchestra, op. 78a: HOVA-
    NESS
Artinis -> Vahakn, no. 5: HOVANESS
As Celia's fatal arrows <- The unhappy lovers: HÄNDEL
As I slept, I dreamt / Ich schlief -> Variationen über die
    Arie Ich schlief, da träumte mir: QUANTZ
Ascensão -> Symphony, no. 2: VILLA-LOBOS
Ascension, L' <- Meditations symphoniques: MESSIAEN
Ascension oratorio / Himmelsfahrt-Oratorium -> Lobet Gott in
    seinen Reichen, S. 11: J.S.BACH
Asklepios-Walzer, orchestra <- Pikanterien-Walzer: LEHÁR
Asrael / Angel of death -> Symphony, no. 2, op. 27, C minor:

SUK
Assyrian dance -> A trip to Syria: GRIFFES
Astre de nuit, L' -> La sentinelle: HUMMEL
Astuzie feminili, Le <- How to get your way with men with-
out them finding out / The ladies' game: CIMAROSA
Asyle, L' -> Zelmar: GRÉTRY
At the ball -> Songs, op. 38 (In the din of the ball):
TCHAIKOVSKY
At the open window / New hopes -> Songs, op. 63 (I opened
the window): TCHAIKOVSKY
At twilight <- Nocturne: FIBICH
Atelier de Jean Cousin, L' -> Angéla: BOIELDIEU
Atlantische dansen, piano & orchestra <- Concerto, piano,
no. 2: BADINGS
Atropo -> Symphony, no. 10: MALIPIERO
Au temple de l'amour -> Les pellerines (La marche): COUPERIN
Au tombeau -> Sonata, violin & continuo, op. 6, no. 7, F
minor: LOCATELLI
Aubade -> Feuillets d'album, op. 19 (Les champs): BERLIOZ
Aucassin et Nicolette <- Les moeurs du bon vieux temps:
GRÉTRY
Audite principes <- Christmas motet: G.GABRIELI
Auf dem Anstand / Hornsignal-Sinfonie -> Symphony, M. 31, D
major: J.HAYDN
Auf der Bruck, D. 853 <- Auf der Brücke: SCHUBERT
Auf der Brücke -> Auf der Bruck, D. 853: SCHUBERT
Auf einen Kirchhof, D. 151 <- Im Kirchhof: SCHUBERT
Auferstehungs-Symphonie / Resurrection symphony - Symphony,
no. 2, C minor: MAHLER
Aufforderung zum Tanz <- Le spectre de la rose: WEBER
Aurora's wedding -> The sleeping beauty (Selections; arr.):
TCHAIKOVSKY
Aus das Vaterland -> Symphony, no. 1, op. 96, D major: RAFF
Aus der Kinderzeit (Schlummerlied) <- Wiegenlied: WOLF
Aus der Werkstatt eines Invaliden / From an invalid's work-
shop -> Sonatina, wood-winds & brasses, no. 1, F major:
R.STRAUSS
Aus Heliopolis, D. 753 <- Helipolis: SCHUBERT
Aus Heliopolis, D. 754 <- Heliopolis / Im Hochgebirge:
SCHUBERT
Aus Holbergs Zeit <- Holberg suite: GRIEG
Aus Scherz ernst / Die beiden Kalifen / Alimelek -> Wirt
und Gast: MEYERBEER
Auschwitz oratorio -> Dies irae: PENDERECKI
Austrian quartets / Österreichische Quartette / Viennese
quartets /Wiener Quartette -> Quartet, strings, K. 168, F
major; K. 169, A major; K. 170, C major; K. 171, E♭ major;
K. 172, B♭ major; K. 173, D minor: MOZART

Autumn /L'autunno / Concerto, op. 8, no. 3, F major -> Il
  cimento dell' armonia e dell' inventione (No. 3): VIVALDI
Automne, L' -> Symphony, no. 7, op. 63: LAJTHA
Autunno, L' / Autumn / Concerto, op. 8, no. 3, F major ->
  Il cimento dell' armonia e dell' inventione (No. 3):
  VIVALDI
Avak (Symphony) <- Symphony, op. 65, no. 2: HOVANESS
Ave Maria -> Méditation sur le premier prélude de Bach:
  GOUNOD
Ave Maria / Hymn to the Virgin -> Ellens Gesang, D. 839:
  SCHUBERT
Ave Maria, no. 3 <- Sposalizio / Trauung / Geistliche Ver-
  mählungsmusik: LISZT
Ave nobilissime creatura <- Marian motets: DEPRÈS
Aventure de garnison, Une -> Le baiser et la quittance:
  MÉHUL
Axur, re d'Ormus -> Tarare: SALIERI

Babar, the elephant -> Histoire de Babar, le petit élé-
  phant: POULENC
Baba-Yaga -> Legend, op. 29: RIMSKY-KORSAKOV
Babi Yar symphony -> Symphony, no. 13, op. 113: SHOSTAKOVICH
Bach variations -> Variationen und Fuge über ein Thema von
  Bach, Piano: REGER
Bachianas brasileiras, no. 2 (Toccata: O tremzinho do caipi-
  ra) <- The little train of the Brazilian countryman:
  VILLA-LOBOS
Bagatelle, piano, op. 59, A minor <- Für Elise: BEETHOVEN
Bagatelle, piano, K. 61a, G minor -> Allegretto quasi an-
  dante, piano, K. 61a, G minor: BEETHOVEN
Bagatelles, piano, 4 hands (arr.) <- Kleine Blasmusik /
  Little wind music: KŘENEK
Baiser et la quittance, Le <- Une aventure de garnison:
  MÉHUL
Bajazet -> Tamerlano: VIVALDI
Bal, Le / The ball -> Jeux d'enfants (Galop): BIZET
Bal masqué, Le -> Gustave III: AUBER
Ball, The / Le bal -> Jeux d'enfants (Galop): BIZET
Ballade -> Mélodies, op. 2 (L'origine du harpe): BERLIOZ
Ballade / After the battle / Left alone -> Forgotten: MUS-
  ORGSKY
Ballade, piano, no. 1, op. 23, G minor <- Polish ballade:
  CHOPIN
Ballade, piano, no. 2, op. 38, F major <- La gracieuse:
  CHOPIN
Ballade, piano, op. 10, no. 1, D minor <- Edward ballade:
  BRAHMS
Balle il bronzo -> Il pescatore: DONIZETTI

Ballnacht in Florenz -> Prinz Methusalem (Selections; arr.):
  JOHANN STRAUSS
Ball-Scenen, op. 109 <- Kinderball, op. 109: SCHUMANN
Balmont songs -> Poems: STRAVINSKY
Bamboula <- Danses des nègres: GOTTSCHALK
Bananier, Le <- Chanson nègre: GOTTSCHALK
Band song, The -> The orchestra song: SCHUMAN
Banjo, The -> Grotesque fantasie: GOTTSCHALK
Banjo song -> I got plenty o' nuttin': GERSHWIN
Banquet infernal, Le -> Scherzo, piano, no. 1 op. 20, B mi-
  nor: CHOPIN
Barbe-bleu <- Ritter von Blaubart und seine Sechste: OFFEN-
  BACH
Barbier de village, Le <- Le revenant: GRÉTRY
Barbiere di Siviglia, Il <- La precauzione inutile: PAISI-
  ELLO
Barcarolle, La <- L'amour et la musique: AUBER
Barcarolle -> Nuits d'été (L'isle inconnue): BERLIOZ
Barcarolle -> Sonata, harpsichord, K. 429 (132) A major: D.
  SCARLATTI
Bardo sonata, piano, op. 192 <- Sonata, piano, op. 192:
  HOVANESS
Bargain broken, A -> The Canterbury guests: PURCELL
Barrikaden-Lieder -> Freiheits-Lieder-Walzer, orchestra:
  JOHANN STRAUSS
Barone deluso, Il / La sposa in contrasto -> Il due baroni
  di Rocca Azzurra: CIMAROSA
Baronessa stramba, La -> I matrimoni in ballo: CIMAROSA
Bartholomew fair -> Here's that will challenge: PURCELL
Baryton trios -> Divertimenti, H.XI: J.HAYDN
Baseball cantata / Casey at the bat -> The mighty Casey
  (Cantata): SCHUMAN
Basler concerto -> Concerto, string orchestra, D: STRAVIN-
  SKY
Bas-relief <- La reine Nefertiti: CASTELNUOVO-TEDESCO
Bataille, La / Die Belagerung Belgrads / The siege of Bel-
  grade -> Contretanz, K. 535: MOZART
Battell, The (The march before the battle) <- The Earl of
  Oxford's march / My Lord Oxenford's maske: BYRD
Battle cry of freedom <- Le cri de délivrance: GOTTSCHALK
Battle galliard, The -> The king of Denmark's galliard:
  DOWLAND
Battle of the Nile, The <- Nelson-Arie / Pindarick ode: J.
  HAYDN
Battle symphony -> Wellingtons Sieg: BEETHOVEN
Battle hymn of the Republic -> Voices of freedom: FINE
Bauern-Kantate / Peasant cantata -> Mer hahn en neue ober-
  keet, S. 212: J.S.BACH

Bauernkirchfahrt, Die / Die Pfauenkirchfahrt -> Sonata, 3
  violins, 2 violas & continuo, Bb major: BIBER
Bauernsinfonie / Dorfmusikanten-Sextett -> Ein musikalisch-
  er Spass, K. 522: MOZART
Bavarian dances -> From the Bavarian highlands (Selections;
  arr.): ELGAR
Bays in petticoats -> The rehearsal: BOYCE
Bear, The / L'ours -> Symphony, M. 82, C major: J.HAYDN
Béarnais, Les <- Henri IV en voyage: BOIELDIEU
Beati omnes qui timent Dominum <- Wedding anthem: PURCELL
Bee's wedding, The / Spinnerlied / Spinning song -> Lieder
  ohne Worte, op. 67 (No. 4): MENDELSSOHN
Beethoven variations -> Variationen und Fuge über ein Thema
  von Beethoven, 2 pianos: REGER
Beethoven variations -> Variations sur un thème de Beeth-
  oven, 2 pianos, op. 35: SAINT-SAËNS
Beethoven variations -> Etudes basées sur un thème de
  Beethoven, piano: SCHUMANN
Begräbnislied -> Nun lasst uns den Leib begraben, D. 168:
  SCHUBERT
Begrüssung <- Humboldt cantata: MENDELSSOHN
Beherrscher der Geister, Der <- Rübezahl:WEBER
Behold, I bring you glad tidings <- Christmas anthem: PUR-
  CELL
Bei dem Grabe Anselmos -> Am Grabe Anselmos, D. 504:
  SCHUBERT
Beiden Freunde von Salamanca, Die -> Die Freunde von Sala-
  manca: SCHUBERT
Beiden Kalifen, Die / Alimelek / Aus Scherz ernst -> Wirt
  und Gast: MEYERBEER
Belagerung Belgrads, Die / The siege of Belgrade / La bat-
  aille -> Contretanz, K. 535: MOZART
Belief / Faith -> Lieder ohne Worte, op. 102 (No. 6): MEN-
  DELSSOHN
Bell anthem -> Rejoice in the Lord alway: PURCELL
Bell quartet / Quinten-Quartett / Erdödy quartets -> Quar-
  tet, strings, no. 77, op. 76, no. 2, D minor: J.HAYDN
Bell symphony -> Symphony, no. 2: KHACHATURIAN
Bella greca, La -> I matrimoni impensati: CIMAROSA
Bella Italia -> Wo die Citronen blüh'n: JOHANN STRAUSS
Bella molinara, La / L'amor contrastato -> La molinara:
  PAISIELLO
Belle Helène, La <- Helen of Troy: OFFENBACH
Bellezza e cuor di ferro / Matilde e Corradino -> Matilde di
  Shabran: ROSSINI
Bellona-Polka, orchestra <- Die Kriegsgöttin: JOSEPH STRAUSS
Bells, The / Les cloches -> Sonata, harpsichord, K. 328
  (L.s. 27) G major: D.SCARLATTI

Bells of Moscow, The -> Morceaux de fantaisie, piano, op. 3
   (Prélude): RACHMANINOFF
Bells of Yale, The <- Chapel chimes: IVES
Bells of Zlonice, The -> Symphony, no. 1, op. 3, C minor: DVOŘÁK
Beneath a shady willow <- The dream: HÄNDEL
Bendita sabedovia <- Ur: VILLA-LOBOS
Benedicta es caelorum regina <- Marian motets: DEPRÈS
Bénédiction papale -> Urbi et orbi: LISZT
Benedictus mass -> Mass, D. 452, C major: SCHUBERT
Beni Mora <- Oriental suite: HOLST
Béniowski <- Les exilés du Kamchattka: BOIELDIEU
Berceuse, piano, op. 57, D♭ major <- Variantes: CHOPIN
Berceuse d'Ataïcho Enia <- Kolysanka: SZYMANOWSKI
Berceuse élégiaque <- Des Mannes Wiegenlied am Sarge seiner
   Mutter: BUSONI
Berenice <- Le gare d'amore e di politica: A.SCARLATTI
Bergakungen <- Besvärjelse: ALFVÉN
Berggeist, Der / Schicksal und Treue -> Rübezahl: DANZI
Bergsymphonie / Mountain symphony -> Ce qu'on entend sur la
   montagne: LISZT
Bess of Bedlam <- Mad Bess: PURCELL
Bestiaire, Le <- Le cortège d'Orphée: POULENC
Besuch, Der -> Dithyrambe, D. 47: SCHUBERT
Besvärjelse -> Bergakungen: ALFVÉN
Betly <- La capanna svizzera: DONIZETTI
Betrothal in the monastery, The -> The duenna: PROKOFIEV
Betrug durch Aberglauben <- Die Schatzgräber: DITTERSDORF
Between twelve and three -> From dusk till dawn: BAX
Bianca e Faliero <- Il consiglio dei tre: ROSSINI
Bianca rosa, La -> Sei pur bella: HÄNDEL
Biante, Il <- La Laurinda: STRADELLA
Biblical sonata no. 1 -> Biblische Historien (Il combatti-
   mento trà David e Goliath): KUHNAU
Biblical sonata no. 2 / David and Saul -> Biblische Historien
   (Saul malinconico e trastullato per mezzo della musica:KUHNAU
Biblical sonata no. 3 -> Biblische Historien (Il maritaggio
   di Giacomo): KUHNAU
Biblical sonata no. 4 -> Biblische Historien (Hiskia agoniz-
   zante e risanato): KUHNAU
Biblical sonata no. 5 -> Biblische Historien (Gideon salva-
   vatore del populo d'Israel): KUHNAU
Biblical sonata no. 6 -> Biblische Historien (La tomba di
   Giacob): KUHNAU
Biblical sonatas / Mystery sonatas / Rosary sonatas / Rosen-
   kranz-Sonaten -> Sonata, violin & continuo (Bayerische
   Staatsbibliothek: Mus. Ms. 4123) no. 1, D minor; no. 2, A
   major; no. 3, B minor; no. 4, D minor; no. 5, A major:
   no. 6, C minor; no. 7, F major; no. 8, B♭ major; no. 9, A

minor; no. 10, G minor; no. 11, G major; no. 12, C major;
no. 13, D minor; no. 14, D major; no. 15, C major; no. 16,
G minor: BIBER
Biblische Historien (Il combattimento trà David e Goliath)
<- Biblical sonata no. 1: KUHNAU
Biblische Historien (Gideon salvatore del populo d'Israel)
<- Biblical sonata no. 5: KUHNAU
Biblische Historien (Hiskia agonizzante e risanato) <- Bib-
lical sonata no. 4: KUHNAU
Biblische Historien (Il maritaggio di Giacomo) <- Biblical
sonata no. 3: KUHNAU
Biblische Historien (Saul malinconico e trastullato per mezzo
della musica) <- Biblical sonata no. 2 / David and Saul:
KUHNAU
Biblische Historien (La tomba di Giacob) <- Biblical sonata
no. 6: KUHNAU
Bicentennial symphony 1776 -> Symphony, no. 13: HARRIS
Bicinia -> Novae aliquot et ante: LASSUS
Billets chéris / Cifre d'amore -> La corrispondenza amorosa:
DONIZETTI
Biondolina / La giardiniera fortunata -> L'amante combattuto
dalle donne di punto: CIMAROSA
Bird quartet / Vogel-Quartett / Russian quartets / Jungfern-
Quartette / Maiden quartets -> Quartet, strings, no. 40,
op. 33, no. 3, C major: J.HAYDN
Birth of Manaunaun, The / Irewee's shoonthree -> Manaunaun's
birthing: COWELL
Birthday canon for Mrs. Elizabeth Sprague Coolidge -> Canon
a tre: HINDEMITH
Birthday cantata / Geburtstagskantate / Hunting cantata /
Jagdkantate -> Was mir behagt, S. 208: J.S.BACH
Birthday cantata / Lobkowitz cantata -> Es lebe unser teu-
rer Fürst: BEETHOVEN
Birthday divertimento / Der Geburtstag / Man and wife / Mann
und Weib -> Divertimento, H.II,11, C major: J.HAYDN
Birthday offering -> Works (Selections; arr.): GLAZUNOV
Birthday quartet -> Quartet, strings, no. 10: MILHAUD
Bizarre, La -> Suite, string orchestra, G2, G major: TELEMANN
Bjørnenes Jul <- The children's Christmas Eve: GADE
Black keys etude -> Etude, piano, op. 10, no. 5, G♭ major: CHOPIN
Black mass -> Sonata, piano, no. 9, op. 68, F major: SKRIABIN
Blanche de Provençe <- La cour des fées: BOIELDIEU
Blanche de Provençe <- La cor des fées: CHERUBINI
Blanka, D. 631 <- Das Madchen: SCHUBERT
Bleib bei uns, denn es will Abend werden, S. 6 <- Easter
cantata / Osterkantate: J.S.BACH
Blessed are they that consider the poor <- Foundling hospi-
tal anthem: HÄNDEL

Blessed Virgin's expostulation, The -> Tell me, some pity-
   ing angel: PURCELL
Blue and the white, The <- Brandeis University marching
   song: FINE
Blue Danube waltz / Donauwalzer -> An der schönen blauen
   Donau: JOHANN STRAUSS
Blue Monday <- 135th Street: GERSHWIN
Bluebeard's castle -> Duke Bluebeard's castle: BARTÓK
Bluebird -> The sleeping beauty (Pas de deux;arr.): TCHAI-
   KOVSKY
Blumenballade -> Vergissmichnicht, D. 792; Viola, D. 786:
   SCHUBERT
Böcklin suite -> Tondichtungen nach Arnold Böcklin: REGER
Bolero -> Feuillets d'album , op. 19 (Zaïde): BERLIOZ
Bolero <- Souvenir d'Andalusie: CHOPIN
Bolero, piano <- Oh, my lovely maiden: GLINKA
Bonduca <- The British heroine: PURCELL
Bontà in trionfo, La -> La cenerentola: ROSSINI
Bontems, La -> Pièces de clavecin, 2. livre, 11. ordre
   (L'etincalante): COUPERIN
Book of the hanging gardins, The -> Gedichte aus das Buch
   der hängenden Gärten: SCHÖNBERG
Boréades, Les -> Abaris: RAMEAU
Borová <- Czech dances, piano / Seven Czech dances, piano:
   MARTINŮ
Boston symphony -> Symphony, no. 1: HONEGGER
Bostoniana -> Symphony, no. 2: IBERT
Bouffes parisiens, Les -> Operettas (Selections: arr.):
   OFFENBACH
Bouffonne, La / Suite, string orchestra, C5, C major ->
   Lustige Suite, string orchestra; TELEMANN
Bourse, La <- Suite, orchestra, B11, B♭ major: TELEMANN
Boy was born, A <- Choral variations, op. 3: BRITTEN
Brandeis University marching song -> The blue and the white:
   FINE
Brandenburg concertos -> Concerto grosso, no. 1, F major;
   no. 2, F major; no. 3, G major; no. 4, G major; no. 5, D
   major; no. 6, B♭ major: J.S.BACH
Brasileira, A / The Brazilian -> Sinfonietta, string orch-
   estra: KRENEK
Bravour-Walzer -> Caprice-valse, piano, no. 1: LISZT
Brazilian, The / A Brasileira -> Sinfonietta, string orch-
   estra: KRENEK
Brazilian quartet no. 1 -> Quartet, strings, no. 5: VILLA-
   LOBOS
Brazilian quartet no. 2 -> Quartet, strings, no. 6: VILLA-
   LOBOS
Brettlieder <- Cabaret songs: SCHÖNBERG

Bride's complaint, The / La nouvelle mariée -> Songs, op. 47 (Was I not a little blade of grass?): TCHAIKOVSKY

Brief and Danzi -> Komisches musikalisches sendschreiben: WEBER

Brigg fair <- An English rhapsody: DELIUS

Briséis <- Les amants de Corinthe: CHABRIER

Britannia <- Love and glory: ARNE

Biritish heroine, The -> Bonduca: PURCELL

British worthy, The -> King Arthur: ARNE

Brockes Passion / The passion of Christ -> Passion [ca.1716]: HÄNDEL

Browning <- The leaves be green: BYRD

Bruckenthal symphony -> Symphony, M. 27, G major: J.HAYDN

Bucolic sonata -> Sonata, harpsichord, K. 8 (L. 488) G minor: D.SCARLATTI

Bulgarian rhapsody, op. 16 -> Vardar: VLADIGEROV

Bull quintet -> Quintet, 2 violins, viola & 2 violoncellos, G.275, E major: BOCCHERINI

Bullfinch concerto / Il gardellino -> Concerto, flute, R. 90, D major; Concerto, flute, R. 428, D major: VIVALDI

Buona figliuola, La <- La cecchina: PICCINNI

Buondelmonte -> Maria Stuarda: DONIZETTI

Burla felice, La -> Il fanatico burlato: CIMAROSA

Burlesca -> Sonata, harpsichord, K. 450 (L. 338) G minor: D. SCARLATTI

Burlesque -> Scherzo, piano & orchestra, op. 2: BARTÓK

Burlesque de Quixotte <- Don Qichotte / Suite, string orchestra, G10, G major: TELEMANN

Butterfly etude -> Etude, piano, op. 25, no. 9, G♭ major: CHOPIN

By my sighs <- Vauxhall songs: J.C.BACH

Cabaret songs -> Brettlieder: SCHÖNBERG

Caccia, La -> Sonata, harpsichord, K. 159 (L. 104) C major; Sonata, harpsichord, K. 96 (L. 465) D major: D.SCARLATTI

Caccia, La / Concerto, op. 8, no. 10, B major -> Il cimento dell' armonia e dell' inventione (No. 10): VIVALDI

Caduta di Baldassare, La -> Ciro in Babilonia: ROSSINI

Caduta de' Tarquini, La -> Giunio Bruto: CALDARA

Caduta de' Tarquini, La -> Giunio Bruto: A.SCARLATTI

Cäcilienmesse / Missa Sanctae Caeciliae / St. Caecilia mass / Cantata mass -> Mass, H.XXII,5, C major: J.HAYDN

Cain <- Il primo omicidio: A.SCARLATTI

Cain and Abel -> Sönerna: ROSENBERG

Caixinha de boas festas <- Vitrina encantada / The surprise box: VILLA-LOBOS

Califfo di Bagdad, Il -> Adina: ROSSINI

Caligola delirante -> La pazzia in trono: CAVALLI

Callias <- Nature et patrie: GRÉTRY
Calvary -> Des Heilands letzte Stunden: SPOHR
Camberwell Green / Frühlingslied/ Spring song -> Lieder oh-
    ne Worte, op. 62 (No. 6): MENDELSSOHN
Cambia della valigia, Il -> L'occasione fa il ladro: ROSSINI
Camilla und Eugen <- Der Gartenschlüssel: DANZI
Camp meeting, The -> Symphony, no. 3: IVES
Campanella, La / La clochette -> Concerto, violin, no. 2,
    op. 7, B minor (Rondeau à la clochette): PAGANINI
Campanello di notte, Il <- Il campanello speziale: DONI-
    ZETTI
Campanello speziale, Il -> Il campanello di notte: DONI-
    ZETTI
Canary, The / Der Kanarienvogel -> Deutsche Tänze, orches-
    tra, K. 600 (No. 5): MOZART
Canary cantata / Kanarienvogel-Kantate -> Cantate oder
    Trauer-Music eines kunsterfahrenen Canarienvogels: TELE-
    MANN
Canciones populares españolas <- Suite populaire espagnole:
    FALLA
Candace, La <- Li veri amici: VIVALDI
Cannabich sonata -> Sonata, piano, K. 284b (309) C major:
    MOZART
Canon, piano, Ab major <- Canon für Alexis: SCHUMANN
Canon a tre <- Birthday canon for Mrs. Elizabeth Sprague
    Coolidge: HINDEMITH
Canon for 3 <- In memoriam Igor Stravinsky: CARTER
Canon für Alexis -> Canon, piano, Ab major: SCHUMANN
Canon italien -> Evviva, evviva Bacco: CHERUBINI
Canonic choruses, mixed voices, unacc. <- Chorale canons:
    SCHUMAN
Canonic etudes, op. 56 -> Studien, pedal-piano, op. 56:
    SCHUMANN
Canonic sonatas -> Sonata, 2 flutes, op. 5, no. 1, G major;
    no. 2, D major; no. 3, A minor; no. 4, D minor; no. 5, A
    major; no. 6, A minor
Canonic suite -> Suite, 4 saxophones: CARTER
Cantari alla madrigalesca -> Quartet, strings, no. 3: MALI-
    PIERO
Cantata comica -> Der Schulmeister mit seinen 2 Scholaren:
    PAISIELLO
Cantata mass / Missa Sanctae Caeciliae /Cäcilienmesse / St.
    Caecilia mass -> Mass, H. XXII,5, C major: J.HAYDN
Cantata pastorale eroica <- Nigella e clori: CALDARA
Cantata pastorale per la nacità di nostro Signore <-
    Christmas cantata: A.SCARLATTI
Cantata per il SS. Natale <- Christmas cantata: STRADELLA
Cantata profana <- The giant stags /The nine enchanted

stags: BARTÓK
Cantata spagnuola -> No se emenderá jamas: HÄNDEL
Cantate oder Trauer-Music eines Kunsterfahrenen Canarien-
  Vogels <- Canary cantata / Kanarienvogel-Kantate: TELEMANN
Canterbury guests, The <- A bargain broken: PURCELL
Canticle I / My beloved is mine -> Canticle in the memory of
  Dick Sheppard: BRITTEN
Canticle II -> Abraham and Isaac: BRITTEN
Canticle III -> Still falls the rain: BRITTEN
Canticle IV -> Journey of the magi: BRITTEN
Canticle V -> The death of Narcissus: BRITTEN
Canticle for orchestra -> In praise of Shahn: SCHUMAN
Canticle in the memory of Dick Sheppard <- Canticle I / My
  beloved is mine: BRITTEN
Cantilena pro Adventu, A major <- Ein' Magd, ein' Dienerin:
  J.HAYDN
Cantique -> Adagio solenne, organ (arr.): ELGAR
Cantique de Jean Racine <- A song of praise: FAURÉ
Canzona / Liebestraum -> O Lieb', so lang du lieben kannst:
  LISZT
Canzonets, 1st set <- English canzonettas: J.HAYDN
Canzonets, 2d set <- English canzonettas: J.HAYDN
Canzoni 'e copp' 'o tammurro -> Neapolitanische Lieder:
  HENZE
Capanna svizzera, La -> Betly: DONIZETTI
Capricci and Intermezzi, op. 76 -> Klavierstücke, op. 76:
  BRAHMS
Capriccio -> Sonata, harpsichord, K. 20 (L 375) E major: D.
  SCARLATTI
Capriccio brillante / Spanish overture no. 1 -> Jota aragon-
  esa, orchestra: GLINKA
Capriccio diabolico, guitar <- Homage to Paganini: CASTEL-
  NUOVO-TEDESCO
Caprice, violin, op. 1, no. 1, E major <- Arpeggio caprice:
  PAGANINI
Caprice, violin, op. 1, no. 6, G major <- Tremolo caprice:
  PAGANINI
Caprice, violin, op. 1, no. 9, E major <- La chasse: PAGA-
  NINI
Caprice, violin, op. 1, no. 13, B♭ major <- Le rire du di-
  able / The devil's chuckle: PAGANINI
Caprice, violin, op. 1, no. 14, E♭ major <- Caprice milit-
  aire: PAGANINI
Caprice espagnol -> La jota aragonesa: GOTTSCHALK
Caprice militaire -> Caprice, violin, op.1, no. 14, E♭ maj-
  or: PAGANINI
Caprices poetiques -> Études de concert, piano: LISZT
Caprice-valse, piano, no. 1 <- Bravour-Walzer: LISZT

Caprice-valse, piano, no. 2 <- Melancholischer Walzer: LISZT
Captive, La <- Rêverie: BERLIOZ
Captive queen, The <- The liberated queen: SIBELIUS
Carbonelli, Il -> Concerto, violin, R. 366, B♭ major: VI-
    VALDI
Carignane -> Arabesque, bassoon & piano: IBERT
Carlo cantata -> Io languisco: HÄNDEL
Carmen gallicum Ludovici XI -> Guillaume se va chaufer:
    DEPRÈS
Carnaval, Le <- Mascerade royale / Le Grand Porte-diadème:
    LULLY
Carnaval symphony -> Symphony, K. 94, D major: DITTERSDORF
Carneval de Pesth / Pesther carneval -> Rhapsodie hongroise,
    piano, no. 9: LISZT
Caroline Te Deum -> Te Deum, D major: HÄNDEL
Carte blanche waltz -> Champagne: ALBÉNIZ
Cartoons -> Take-offs, orchestra: IVES
Cartwheel etude -> Etude, piano, op. 25, no. 3, F major:
    CHOPIN
Casa del diavolo, La -> Symphony, G. 506, D minor: BOCCHE-
    RINI
Casey at the bat / Baseball cantata -> The mighty Casey
    [Cantata]: SCHUMAN
Cassation, K. 63, G major <- Finalmusik: MOZART
Cassation, 2 horns, strings & toy instruments, C major
    (Selections): LEOPOLD MOZART <- Kindersinfonie / Sinfonia
    Berchtolsgadensis / Toy symphony: J.HAYDN
Castello di Kenilworth, Il -> Elisabetta: DONIZETTI
Cat and mouse, The -> Scherzo humoristique, piano: COPLAND
Cat waltz -> Waltz, piano, op. 34, no. 3, F major: CHOPIN
Catfish row -> Porgy and Bess (Selections; arr.): GERSHWIN
Cat's fugue, The -> Sonata, harpsichord, K. 30 (L. 499) G
    minor: D.SCARLATTI
Cats on the roof -> Singular pieces, piano, op. 44 (Noct-
    urne): DOHNÁNYI
Cave of the heart, The -> Medea: BARBER
Ce qu'on entend sur la montagne <- Bergsymphonie / Mountain
    symphony: LISZT
Cease awhile, ye winds <- Vauxhall songs: J.C.BACH
Cebell / The cibell -> Trumpet tune, harpsichord, Z. 678, C
    major: PURCELL
Cecchina, La <- La buona figliula: PICCINNI
Cécile et Ermancé <- Les deux couvents: GRÉTRY
Celebrate this festival <- Ode for Queen Mary's birthday
    [1693]: PURCELL
Celebratiòn sinfonica -> Iubilum: GINASTERA
Celeste, La -> Symphony, op. 9, no. 2, E♭ major (Andante):
    J.C.BACH

Celestial gate -> Symphony, no. 6, op. 173: HOVANESS
Celestial music <- Ode for Mr. Louis Maidwell's school:
  PURCELL
Cello quartet / Preussische Quartette / Prussian quartets /
  King of Prussia quartets -> Quartet, strings, K. 575, D
  major: MOZART
Cenerentola, La <- La bontà in trionfo: ROSSINI
Central Park in the dark <- Contemplations / Two contemp-
  lations: IVES
Céphale et Procris <- L'amour conjugal: GRÉTRY
Ceremonial <- Hommage a Varèse: JOLIVET
Cetra, La <- Concerto, op. 9, no. 1, C major; no. 2, A major;
  no. 3, G minor; no. 4, E major; no. 5, A minor; no. 6, A
  major; no. 7, Bb major; no. 8, D minor; no. 9, Bb major;
  no. 10, G major; no. 11, C minor; no. 12, B minor: VIVALDI
Chaconne, strings, G minor <- London chaconne: PURCELL
Chaconne with 21 variations -> Suite, harpsichord, 2d collec-
  tion, no. 2, G major: HÄNDEL
Chamber fantasy on Carmen / Kammerfantasie über Carmen /
  Sonatina super Carmen -> Sonatina, piano, no. 6: BUSONI
Chamber music -> Songs, op. 10: BARBER
Chamber symphony, op. 110 -> Quartet, strings, no. 8, op.
  110 [arr.]: SHOSTAKOVICH
Chamisso-Lieder -> Lieder, op. 40: SCHUMANN
Champagne <- Carte blanche waltz: ALBÉNIZ
Chandos jubilate -> O be joyful in the Lord: HÄNDEL
Chandos Te Deum -> Te Deum, Bb major: HÄNDEL
Changeante, La -> Suite, string orchestra, g2, G minor:
  TELEMANN
Chanson de matelot -> Marine: BIZET
Chanson de rouet -> Le rouet: RAVEL
Chanson géorgienne / Song of Gruzia -> Songs, op. 4 (Oh never
  sing to me again): RACHMANINOFF
Chanson nègre -> Le bananier: GOTTSCHALK
Chansons d'Ariel <- Pièces tirées de la Temple de Shakes-
  peare: MARTIN
Chansons naives <- Pièces enfantines: JOLIVET
Chant de nuit, Le / Song of the night -> Symphony, no. 3, op.
  27: SZYMANOWSKI
Chant héroïque -> L'apothéose: BERLIOZ
Chant national -> Les trois exilés: FRANCK
Chant sur la mort de l'Empereur Napoléon -> Le cinq mai:
  BERLIOZ
Chants hébraïques -> Mélodies hébraïques: RAVEL
Chants sans paroles -> Schumanniana: INDY
Chapel chimes -> The bells of Yale: IVES
Chapultepec -> Obertura republicana: CHAVEZ
Characteristic impressions -> Pieces, piano, op. 103: SIBE-

LIUS
Charakteristisches Allegro -> Lebensstürme: SCHUBERT
Charles de France <- Amour et gloire: BOIELDIEU
Charmer, The -> Songs, op. 65 (Rondel): TCHAIKOVSKY
Charmes de la vie, Les <- Hommage à Watteau: MILHAUD
Chasse,La -> Sonata, piano, op. 16, D major; Trio, piano &
  strings, op. 22, no. 3, C major; Trio, piano & strings,
  op. 29, no. 2, Eb major; Trio, piano & strings, op. 35a,
  no. 3, D major: CLEMENTI
Chasse, La / Hunt quartet -> Quartet, strings, no. 1, op. 1,
  no. 1, Bb major: J.HAYDN
Chasse, La -> Symphony, M. 73, D major: J.HAYDN
Chasse, La -> Caprice, violin, op. 1, no. 9, E major: PAGA-
  NINI
Chateau de Kenilworth, Le -> Leicester: AUBER
Chateau des papes (Suite; arr), Le -> Suite, ondes Martenot
  & piano: MILHAUD
Cherry tree, The -> Songs, op. 26 (Before my window): RACH-
  MANINOFF
Chi dell' altrui si veste presto si spoglia <- Nina e Mar-
  tuffo: CIMAROSA
Chiara e Serafina <- I pirati: DONIZETTI
Childhood memories of ocean moods <- Ocean moods: HARRIS
Children's Christmas Eve, The -> Bjørnenes Jul: GADE
Children's day at the camp meeting -> Sonata, violin & pi-
  ano, no. 4: IVES
Children's march / Kindermarsch -> March, piano, 4 hands, D.
  928, G major: SCHUBERT
Children's pieces, piano, op. 43, book 3 <- Simple variat-
  ions, piano: MIASKOVSKY
Children's suite / Winter holiday -> Winter bonfire, op.
  122: PROKOFIEV
Chinese overture / Overture chinesa, op. 37 -> Turandot
  (Overture): WEBER
Choisy, Le -> Concertos comiques (No. 14): CORRETTE
Chopin variations -> Variationen und Fuge, piano, op. 22, C
  minor: BUSONI
Chopin variations -> Variations sur un nocturne de Chopin,
  piano: SCHUMANN
Chopstick variations -> Paraphrases, piano: BORODIN
Chopstick variations -> Paraphrases, piano: RIMSKY-KORSAKOV
Chor der Engel -> Christ ist erstanden, D. 440: SCHUBERT
Choral fantasy / Chorfantasie -> Fantasia, piano, mixed
  voices & orchestra, op. 80, C minor: BEETHOVEN
Choral settings of poems by John Keats <- Keats settings:
  CASTELNUOVO-TEDESCO
Choral symphony -> Symphony, no. 9, op. 125, D minor: BEETH-
  OVEN

Choral symphony -> Symphony, no. 8: COWELL
Choral symphony -> Symphony, no. 12, op. 188: HOVANESS
Choral variations, op. 3 -> A boy was born: BRITTEN
Chorale, string orchestra <- Quartertone chorale: IVES
Chorale canons -> Canonic choruses, mixed voices, unacc.:
    SCHUMAN
Chorale mass -> Mass, E♭ major: BRUCKNER
Chorale prelude, S. 645 <- Wachet auf, ruft uns die Stimme /
    Schübler chorales: J.S.BACH
Chorale prelude, S. 646 <- Wo soll ich fliehen hin / Schüb-
    ler chorales: J.S.BACH
Chorale prelude, S. 647 <- Wer nur den lieben Gott lasst
    walten / Schübler chorales: J.S.BACH
Chorale prelude, S. 648 <- Meine Seele erhebet den Herrn /
    Schübler chorales: J.S.BACH
Chorale prelude, S. 649 <- Ach bleib bei uns, Herr Jesu
    Christ / Schübler chorales: J.S.BACH
Chorale prelude, S. 650 <- Kommst du nun, Jesu / Schübler
    chorales: J.S.BACH
Chorale prelude, S. 651 <- Komm heiliger Geist, Herre Gott /
    Leipzig chorales: J.S.BACH
Chorale prelude, S. 652 <- Komm heiliger Geist, Herre Gott /
    Leipzig chorales: J.S.BACH
Chorale prelude, S. 653 <- Am Wasserflüssen Babylon / Leip-
    zig chorales: J.S.BACH
Chorale prelude, S. 654 <- Schmücke dich, o liebe Seele /
    Leipzig chorales: J.S.BACH
Chorale prelude, S. 655 <- Herr Jesu Christ, dich zu uns
    wend / Leipzig chorales: J.S.BACH
Chorale prelude, S. 656 <- O Lamm Gottes, unschuldig / Leip-
    zig chorales: J.S.BACH
Chorale prelude, S. 657 <- Nun danket alle Gott / Leipzig
    chorales: J.S.BACH
Chorale prelude, S. 658 <- Von Gott will ich nicht lassen /
    Leipzig chorales: J.S.BACH
Chorale prelude, S. 659 <- Nun komm der Heiden Heiland /
    Leipzig chorales: J.S.BACH
Chorale prelude, S. 660 <- Nun komm der Heiden Heiland /
    Leipzig chorales: J.S.BACH
Chorale prelude, S. 661 <- Nun komm der Heiden Heiland /
    Leipzig chorales: J.S.BACH
Chorale prelude, S. 662 <- Allein Gott in der Höh sei Ehr /
    Leipzig chorales: J.S.BACH
Chorale prelude, S. 663 <- Allein Gott in der Höh sei Ehr /
    Leipzig chorales: J.S.BACH
Chorale prelude, S. 664 <- Allein Gott in der Höh sei Ehr /
    Leipzig chorales: J.S.BACH
Chorale prelude, S. 665 <- Jesus Christus, unser Heiland /

Leipzig chorales: J.S.BACH
Chorale prelude, S. 666 <- Jesus Christus, unser Heiland /
   Leipzig chorales: J.S.BACH
Chorale prelude, S. 667 <- Komm, Gott Schöpfer, heiliger
   Geist / Leipzig chorales: J.S.BACH
Chorale prelude, S. 668 <- Vor deinen Thron tret ich / Wenn
   wir in höchsten Nöten sein / Leipzig chorales: J.S.BACH
Chorale prelude, S. 680 <- Giant fugue: J.S.BACH
Chorale prelude, S. 733 <- Fuga sopra il magnificat: J.S.BACH
Chorale preludes for Christmas, op. 37 -> Die natali: BARBER
Choreographic episodes -> Undertow (Selections): SCHUMAN
Choreographic symphony -> Symphony, no. 1: SCHUMAN
Chorfantasie / Choral fantasy -> Fantasia, piano, mixed
   voices & orchestra, op. 80, C minor: BEETHOVEN
Choros, no. 3 <- Pica-pao / Nozani-na orekna: VILLA-LOBOS
Choros, no. 5 <- Alma brasileira: VILLA-LOBOS
Choses visibles et invisibles, Les -> Messe de la Pentecôte
   (Offertoire): MESSIAEN
Christ in his garden -> Songs, op. 54 (A legend): TCHAIKOVSKY
Christ ist erstanden, D. 440 <- Chor der Engel: SCHUBERT
Christ lag in Todesbanden, S. 4 <- Easter cantata / Oster-
   kantate: J.S.BACH
Christe, qui lux <- Precamur, sancte Domine: BYRD
Christen, ätzet diesen Tag, S. 63 <- Christmas cantata /
   Weihnachts-Kantate: J.S.BACH
Christmas anthem -> Behold, I bring you glad tidings: PURCELL
Christmas cantata / Weihnachts-Kantate -> Christen, ätzet
   diesen Tag, S. 63: J.S.BACH
Christmas cantata -> Vaticini di pace: CALDARA
Christmas cantata -> Cantata pastorale per la nacità di nos-
   tro Signore: A.SCARLATTI
Christmas cantata -> Cantata per il SS. Natale: STRADELLA
Christmas cantata / Weihnachtskantate -> Ehre sei Gott in der
   Höhe: TELEMANN
Christmas cantata -> This day: VAUGHAN WILLIAMS
Christmas carol -> New Year's greetings: KODÁLY
Christmas carols -> Old English carols: HOLST
Christmas concerto -> Concerto grosso, op. 6, no. 8, G mi-
   nor: CORELLI
Christmas concerto -> Concerto grosso, op. 1, no. 8, F mi-
   nor: LOCATELLI
Christmas concerto -> Pastorale per il Sanctissimo Natale,
   op. 3, no. 12: MANFREDINI
Christmas concerto / Pastoral concerto for the Nativity ->
   Concerto grosso, op. 8, no. 6, G minor: TORELLI
Christmas motets -> Angelus ad pastores; Audite principes:
   G.GABRIELI
Christmas oratorio -> Isaiah's prophecy: CRESTON

Christmas oratorio / The Christmas story / Weihnachtshistorie
/ The Nativity -> Historia von der Geburt Jesu Christi: SCHÜTZ
Christmas sonata -> Trio-sonata, flutes & continuo, op. 5,
no. 5, D minor: LOCATELLI
Christmas story, The / Weihnachtshistorie / Christmas oratorio
/ The Nativity -> Historia von der Geburt Jesu Christi: SCHÜTZ
Christmas symphony / Weihnachtssymphonie / Lamentatione ->
Symphony, M. 26, D minor: J.HAYDN
Christoph Columbus <- Columbus overture: WAGNER
Christopher Columbus -> Operas (Selections): OFFENBACH
Chromatic fantasy / Fantasia chromatica -> Fantasia, key-
board instrument, L. 1: SWELINCK
Chromatische Sonate -> Sonata, violin & piano, no. 4, op. 129,
G minor: RAFF
Chrysanthemum-Walzer -> Wilde Rosen: LEHÁR
Church sonatas / Kirchensonaten / Epistle sonatas / Festival so-
natas -> Sonata, organ & orchestra, K. 263, C major; K. 271e
(278) C major; K. 317a (329) C major; Sonata, organ & string
orchestra, K. 41h (67) Eb major; K. 41i (68) Bb major; K. 41k
(69) D major; K. 124a (144) D major; K. 124b (145) F major; K.
212, Bb major; K. 241, G major; K. 241a (224) F major; K. 241b
(225) A major; K. 244, F major; K. 245, D major; K. 271d (274) G
major; K. 317c (328) C major; K. 336d (336) C major: MOZART
Chute de phaéton, La / Metamorphosen-Sinfonien / Ovid symphonies -> Symphony, K. 74: DITTERSDORF
Cibell, The / Cebell -> Trumpet tune, harpsichord, Z. 678, C
major: PURCELL
Cidli -> Der Rosenband, D. 280: SCHUBERT
Ciel sans nuages -> Piezas caracteristicás, piano (Barcarolle): ALBÉNIZ
Cifre d'amore / Billets chéris -> La corrispondenza amorosa:
DONIZETTI
Cimento dell' armonia e dell' inventione, Il <- Concerto, op. 8,
no. 1, E major; no. 2, Bb major; no. 3, F major; no. 4, F minor;
no. 5, Eb major; no. 6, C minor; no. 7, D minor; no. 8, G minor;
no. 9, D minor; no. 10, Bb major; no. 11, D major; no. 12, C major: VIVALDI
Cimento dell' armonia e dell' inventione, Il (No. 1) <- La
primavera / Spring / Concerto, op. 8, no. 1, E major: VIVALDI
Cimento dell' armonia e dell' inventione, Il (No. 2) <- L'estate / Summer / Concerto, op. 8, no. 2, Bb major: VIVALDI
Cimento dell' armonia e dell' inventione, Il (No. 3) <- L'autunno / Autumn / Concerto, op. 8, no. 3, F major: VIVALDI
Cimento dell' armonia e dell' inventione, Il (No. 4) <- L'inverno / Winter / Concerto, op. 8, no. 4, F minor: VIVALDI
Cimento dell' armonia e dell' invention, Il (No. 1-4) <- The
four seasons / Le quattro stagioni: VIVALDI
Cimento dell' armonia e dell' inventione, Il (No. 5) <- Il temp-

esta di mare / Concerto, op. 8, no. 5, E♭ major: VIVALDI
Cimento dell' armonia e dell' inventione, Il (No. 6) <- Il
    piacere / Concerto, op. 8, no. 6, C minor: VIVALDI
Cimento dell' armonia e dell' inventione, Il (No. 10) <- La
    caccia / Concerto, op. 8, no. 10, B♭ major: VIVALDI
Cinq mai, Le <- Chant sur la mort de l'Empereur Napoléon:
    BERLIOZ
Cioè, Il / La finta frascatana -> Amor vuol sofferenze: LEO
Circe <- Amor di Circe con Ulisse: CIMAROSA
Circe -> Symphony, no. 18, op. 204: HOVANESS
Circus overture <- Side show: SCHUMAN
Ciro in Babilonia <- La caduta di Baldassare: ROSSINI
City of light -> Symphony, no. 22, op. 236: HOVANESS
Clair de lune -> Nuits d'été (Au cimetière): BERLIOZ
Classical symphony <- Symphony, no. 1, op. 25, D major: PRO-
    KOFIEV
Clavier-Büchlein vor Wilhelm Friedemann Bach <- Notebook for
    Wilhelm Friedemann Bach: J.S.BACH
Clavierbüchlein der Anna Magdalena Bach -> Notenbuch der Anna
    Magdalena Bach [1725]: J.S.BACH
Clemenza di Tito, La <- Titus: MOZART
Cleonice -> Demetrio: GLUCK
Cloches, Les / The bells -> Sonata, harpsichord, K. 328 (L.
    s. 27) G major: D.SCARLATTI
Clochette, La / La campanella -> Concerto, violin, no. 2, op.
    7, B minor (Rondeau à clochette): PAGANINI
Clock symphony / Die Uhr -> Symphony, M. 101, D major: J.
    HAYDN
Club anthem -> I will always give thanks: BLOW
Cockaigne <- In London town: ELGAR
Cockcrow sonata -> Sonata, violin & piano, no. 10, op. 96, G
    major: BEETHOVEN
Coffee cantata / Kaffee-Kantate -> Schweiget stille, plau-
    dert nicht, S. 211: J.S.BACH
Colas Breugnon -> The master of Clamecy: KABALEVSKY
Colinette à la cour -> La double épreuve: GRÉTRY
Collective farm symphony -> Symphony, no. 12, op. 35, G mi-
    nor: MIASKOVSKY
Colloredo serenade -> Serenade, K. 189b (203) D major: MOZART
Columbine Cameron -> Harlequin incendiary: ARNE
Columbus overture -> Christoph Columbus: WAGNER
Come, Colin <- Vauxhall songs: J.C.BACH
Come, ye sons of art <- Ode for Queen Mary's birthday [1694]:
    PURCELL
Comedy overture -> Scapino: WALTON
Coming of light, The / Lousadzak -> Concerto, piano & string
    orchestra, no. 1, op. 48: HOVANESS
Complainte <- Dumka: BALAKIREV

Compliment quartet / Komplimentierungsquartett -> Quartet,
   strings, no. 2, op. 18, no. 2, G major: BEETHOVEN
Concentus musico-instrumentalis (No. 7) <- Nürnberger part-
   ita: FUX
Concert à la cour, Le <- La débutante: AUBER
Concert allegro / Concert solo -> Allegro, piano, op. 46:
   ELGAR
Concert dramatique -> Concerto, violin, no. 1, op. 21, A
   minor: HUBAY
Concert piece, viola & piano <- Fantasy, viola & piano: BAX
Concert polonaise -> Polonaise, violin & orchestra, op. 4,
   D major: WIENIAWSKI
Concert royal -> Concerto, violin, no. 3: MILHAUD
Concert sans orchestre -> Sonata, piano, no. 2, op. 14, F
   minor: SCHUMANN
Concert solo / Concert allegro -> Allegro, piano, op. 46:
   ELGAR
Concert-Allegro mit Introduction, piano & orchestra, op. 134
   <- Introduction and Allegro, piano & orchestra: SCHUMANN
Concert-march passacaglia -> The quest: HARRIS
Concerto, op. 3, no. 1, D major -> L'estro armonico (No. 1):
   VIVALDI
Concerto, op. 3, no. 2, G minor -> L'estro armonico (No. 2):
   VIVALDI
Concerto, op. 3, no. 3, G major -> L'estro armonico (No. 3):
   VIVALDI
Concerto, op. 3, no. 4, E minor -> L'estro armonico (No. 4):
   VIVALDI
Concerto, op. 3, no. 5, A major -> L'estro armonico (No. 5):
   VIVALDI
Concerto, op. 3, no. 6, A minor -> L'estro armonico (No. 6):
   VIVALDI
Concerto, op. 3, no. 7, F major -> L'estro armonico (No. 7):
   VIVALDI
Concerto, op. 3, no. 8, A minor -> L'estro armonico (No. 8):
   VIVALDI
Concerto, op. 3, no. 9, D major -> L'estro armonico (No. 9):
   VIVALDI
Concerto, op. 3, no. 10, B minor -> L'estro armonico (No.
   10): VIVALDI
Concerto, op. 3, no. 11, D minor -> L'estro armonico (No.
   11): VIVALDI
Concerto, op. 3, no. 12, E major -> L'estro armonico (No.
   12): VIVALDI
Concerto, op. 4, no. 1, Bb major -> La stravaganza (No. 1):
   VIVALDI
Concerto, op. 4, no. 2, E minor -> La stravaganza (No. 2):
   VIVALDI

Concerto, op. 4, no. 3, G major -> La stravaganza (No. 3):
    VIVALDI
Concerto, op. 4, no. 4, A minor -> La stravaganza (No. 4):
    VIVALDI
Concerto, op. 4, no. 5, A major -> La stravaganza (No. 5):
    VIVALDI
Concerto, op. 4, no. 6, G minor -> La stravaganza (No. 6):
    VIVALDI
Concerto, op. 4, no. 7, C major -> La stravaganza (No. 7):
    VIVALDI
Concerto, op. 4, no. 8, D minor -> La stravaganza (No. 8):
    VIVALDI
Concerto, op. 4, no. 9, F major -> La stravaganza (No. 9):
    VIVALDI
Concerto, op. 4, no. 10, C minor -> La stravaganza (No. 10):
    VIVALDI
Concerto, op. 4, no. 11, D major -> La stravaganza (No. 11):
    VIVALDI
Concerto, op. 4, no. 12, G major -> La stravaganza (No. 12):
    VIVALDI
Concerto, op. 8, no. 1, E major / La primavera / Spring / Le
    quattro stagioni / The four seasons -> Il cimento dell'
    armonia e dell' inventione (No. 1): VIVALDI
Concerto, op. 8, no. 2, B♭ major / L'estate / Summer / Le
    quattro stagione / The four seasons -> Il cimento dell'
    armonia e dell' inventione (No. 2): VIVALDI
Concerto, op. 8, no. 3, F major / L'autunno / Autumn / Le
    quattro stagioni / The four seasons -> Il cimento dell'
    armonia e dell' inventione (No. 3): VIVALDI
Concerto, op. 8, no. 4, F minor / L'inverno / Winter / Le
    quattro stagioni / The four seasons -> Il cimento dell'
    armonia e dell' inventione (No. 4): VIVALDI
Concerto, op. 8, no. 5, E♭ major / Il tempesta di mare ->
    Il cimento dell' armonia e dell' inventione (No. 5): VIV-
    ALDI
Concerto, op. 8, no. 6, C minor / Il piacere -> Il cimento
    dell' armonia e dell' inventione (No. 6): VIVALDI
Concerto, op. 8, no. 7, D minor -> Il cimento dell' armonia
    e dell' inventione (No. 7): VIVALDI
Concerto, op. 8, no. 8, G minor -> Il cimento dell' armonia
    e dell' inventione (No. 8): VIVALDI
Concerto, op. 8, no. 9, D minor -> Il cimento dell' armonia
    e dell' inventione (No. 9): VIVALDI
Concerto, op. 8, no. 10, B♭ major / La caccia -> Il cimento
    dell' armonia e dell' inventione (No. 10): VIVALDI
Concerto, op. 8, no. 11, D major -> Il cimento dell' armonia
    e dell' inventione (No. 11): VIVALDI
Concerto, op. 8, no. 12, C major -> Il cimento dell' armonia

e dell' inventione (No. 12): VIVALDI
Concerto, op. 9, no. 1, C major -> La cetra (No. 1): VIVALDI
Concerto, op. 9, no. 2, A major -> La cetra (No. 2): VIVALDI
Concerto, op. 9, no. 3, G minor -> La cetra (No. 3): VIVALDI
Concerto, op. 9, no. 4, E major -> La cetra (No. 4): VIVALDI
Concerto, op. 9, no. 5, A minor -> La cetra (No. 5): VIVALDI
Concerto, op. 9, no. 6, A major -> La cetra (No. 6): VIVALDI
Concerto, op. 9, no. 7, B♭ major -> La cetra (No. 7): VIV-
    ALDI
Concerto, op. 9, no. 8, D minor -> La cetra (No. 8): VIVALDI
Concerto, op. 9, no. 9, B♭ major -> La cetra (No. 9): VIV-
    ALDI
Concerto, op. 9, no. 10, G major -> La cetra (No. 10): VIV-
    ALDI
Concerto, op. 9, no. 11, C minor -> La cetra (No. 11): VIV-
    ALDI
Concerto, op. 9, no. 12, B minor -> La cetra (No. 12): VIV-
    ALDI
Concerto, accordion -> Theme and variations, accordion &
    orchestra: HARRIS
Concerto, bassoon & string orchestra, R. 501, B♭ major <-
    La notte: VIVALDI
Concerto, 3 bassoons & continuo -> Phénix: CORRETTE
Concerto, clarinet, no. 2, op. 74, E♭ major (Alla polacca)
    <- Polonaise, op. 74: WEBER
Concerto, clarinet & jazz ensemble -> Ebony concerto, clar-
    inet & jazz ensemble: STRAVINSKY
Concerto, flute, R. 428, D major <- Bullfinch concerto / Il
    gardellino: VIVALDI
Concerto, flute, R. 433, F major <- Il tempesta di mare:
    VIVALDI
Concerto, flute, R. 439, G minor <- La notte: VIVALDI
Concerto, flute & string orchestra, op. 50 / Dawn, god of
    Urardu -> Elibris: HOVANESS
Concerto, flute, violin, harpsichord & string orchestra, S.
    1044, A minor <- Triple concerto: J.S.BACH
Concerto, horn & string orchestra, op. 78a -> Artik: HOVA-
    NESS
Concerto, horn & string orchestra, op. 94 -> Diran the re-
    ligious singer: HOVANESS
Concerto, 2 hurdy-gurdies, H. VIIh, 1, C major <- Lira con-
    certi / Lirenkonzerte: J.HAYDN
Concerto, 2 hurdy-gurdies, H. VIIh, 2, G major <- Lira con-
    certi / Lirenkonzerte: J.HAYDN
Concerto, 2 hurdy-gurdies, H. VIIh, 3, G major <- Lira con-
    certi / Lirenkonzerte: J.HAYDN
Concerto, 2 hurdy-gurdies, H. VIIh, 4, F major <- Lira con-
    certi / Lirenkonzerte: J.HAYDN

Concerto, 2 hurdy-gurdies, H. VIIh, 5, F major <- Lira con-
certi / Lirenkonzerte: J.HAYDN
Concerto, orchestra, E♭ <- Dumbarton Oaks concerto: STRAVIN-
SKY
Concerto, orchestra, no. 1, op. 88 <- Arevakal: HOVANESS
Concerto, orchestra, R. 28, G minor <- La notte: VIVALDI
Concerto, orchestra, R. 29, B♭ major <- Concerto funèbre:
VIVALDI
Concerto, orchestra, R. 556, C major <- Concerto per la
solennità di S. Lorenzo: VIVALDI
Concerto, orchestra, R. 562, D major <- Concerto per la
solennità di S. Lorenzo: VIVALDI
Concerto, orchestra, R. 570, F major <- Il tempesta di mare:
VIVALDI
Concerto, orchestra, R. 577, G minor <- Concerto per l'orch-
estra di Dresda: VIVALDI
Concerto, organ, F major [1739] <- The cuckoo and the night-
ingale: HÄNDEL
Concerto, organ, op. 7, no. 3, B♭ major <- Hallelujah con-
certo: HÄNDEL
Concerto, piano, K. 246, C major <- Lützow concerto: MOZART
Concerto, piano, K. 271, E♭ major <- Jeunehomme concerto:
MOZART
Concerto, piano, K. 456, B♭ major <- Kinder concerto: MOZART
Concerto, piano, K. 467, C major <- Elvira Madigan concerto:
MOZART
Concerto, piano, K. 537, C major <- Coronation concerto /
Krönungskonzert: MOZART
Concerto, piano, no. 1, E♭ major <- Triangle concerto: LISZT
Concerto piano, no. 2 -> Atlantische dansen, piano & orch-
estra: BADINGS
Concerto, piano, no. 3, op. 50 <- Youth concerto: KABALEVSKY
Concerto, piano, no. 4 <- Incantation: MARTINŮ
Concerto, piano, no. 5, op. 73, E♭ major <- Emperor concerto:
BEETHOVEN
Concerto, piano, no. 5, op. 103, F major <- Egyptian con-
certo: SAINT-SAËNS
Concerto, piano, op. 15, E♭ major (Rondo) <- The ploughboy:
DUSSEK
Concerto, piano, op. 40, B♭ major <- Military concerto:
DUSSEK
Concerto, piano, op. 77 -> Zartik Parkim: HOVANESS
Concerto, piano, op. 78, A minor <- Concerto fantastique:
ALBÉNIZ
Concerto, piano, op. 110, E major <- Les adieux: HUMMEL
Concerto, piano & string orchestra, no. 1, op. 48 <- The
coming of light / Lousadzak: HOVANESS
Concerto, piano, 4 trumpets & percussion -> Khaldis: HOVANESS

Concerto, 3 pianos, K. 242, F major <- Lodron concerto:
  MOZART
Concerto, recorder, oboe & continuo, C major <- Zampogna:
  BOISMORTIER
Concerto, string orchestra, D <- Basler concerto: STRAVINSKY
Concerto, string orchestra, D major <- Dance suite: TELEMANN
Concerto, string orchestra, R. 117, C major <- Concerto alla
  francese: VIVALDI
Concerto, string orchestra, R. 129, D minor <- Concerto mad-
  rigalesco: VIVALDI
Concerto, string orchestra, R. 151, G major <- Concerto alla
  rustica / Pastoral concerto: VIVALDI
Concerto, string orchestra, R. 169, B minor <- Sinfonia al
  Santo Sepolcro: VIVALDI
Concerto, trumpet & string orchestra, D major <- Concerto di
  melante: TELEMANN
Concerto, viola -> Der Schwanendreher: HINDEMITH
Concerto, viola & string orchestra, op. 93 -> Talin: HOVA-
  NESS
Concerto, violin, H. VIIa,3, A major <- Melk concerto: J.
  HAYDN
Concerto, violin, K. 218, D major <- Strassburg concerto:
  MOZART
Concerto, violin, K. 219, A major <- Turkish concerto: MOZ-
  ART
Concerto, violin, no. 1 <- Concerto italiano / Italian con-
  certo: CASTELNUOVO-TEDESCO
Concerto, violin, no. 1, op. 21, A minor <- Concert drama-
  tique: HUBAY
Concerto, violin, no. 2 <- The prophet: CASTELNUOVO-TEDESCO
Concerto, violin, no. 2, op. 7, B minor (Rondeau à la cloch-
  ette) <- La campanella / La clochette: PAGANINI
Concerto, violin, no. 3 <- Concert royal: MILHAUD
Concerto, violin, no. 4, op. 101, C major <- Concerto all'
  antica: HUBAY
Concerto, violin, no. 5, op. 37, A minor <- Grêtry concerto:
  VIEUXTEMPS
Concerto, violin, no. 8, op. 47, A minor <- Gesangszene: SPOHR
Concerto, violin, op. 29, G minor <- Concerto russe: LALO
Concerto, violin, R. 208, D major <- Grosso mogul: VIVALDI
Concerto, violin, R. 256, Eb major <- Il ritiro: VIVALDI
Concerto, violin, R. 366, Bb major <- Il carbonelli: VIVALDI
Concerto, violin & string orchestra, A minor -> Emma und
  Eginhard (Overture): TELEMANN
Concerto, violin & string orchestra, Bb major, no. 3 <- Pi-
  sendel concerto: TELEMANN
Concerto, violin & string orchestra, op. 7, no. 1, D minor
  <- A l'infant: LECLAIR

Concerto, violin & string orchestra, R. 199, C minor <- Il
  sospetto: VIVALDI
Concerto, violin & string orchestra, R. 234, D major <- L'
  inquietudine: VIVALDI
Concerto, violin & string orchestra, R. 270, E major <- Il
  riposo: VIVALDI
Concerto, violin & string orchestra, R. 271, E major <- L'
  amoroso: VIVALDI
Concerto, violin & string orchestra, R. 286, F major <- Concerto per la solennità di S. Lorenzo: VIVALDI
Concerto, violin & string orchestra, R. 335, A major <- Il
  cucù / Cuckoo concerto: VIVALDI
Concerto, violin & string orchestra, R. 340, A major <- Pi-
  sendel concerto: VIVALDI
Concerto, violin & string orchestra, R. 363, B♭ major <- Il
  corneto da posta / Posthorn concerto: VIVALDI
Concerto, violin & string orchestra, R. 552, A major <- Con-
  certo per eco / Echo concerto: VIVALDI
Concerto, violin & string orchestra, R. 582, D minor <- Con-
  certo per la SS. Assunzione di Maria Vergine: VIVALDI
Concerto, violin, violoncello & piano, op. 56, C major <-
  Triple concerto: BEETHOVEN
Concerto, violin, violoncello & string orchestra, R. 546, A
  major <- Concerto all' inglese: VIVALDI
Concerto, 2 violins & string orchestra, R. 556, C major <-
  Concerto San Lorenzo: VIVALDI
Concerto, 3 violins & string orchestra, R. 256, F major <-
  Il ritiro: VIVALDI
Concerto, 3 violins & string orchestra, R. 277, E minor <-
  Il favorito: VIVALDI
Concerto, violoncello & string orchestra, R. 544, F major <-
  Il Proteo: VIVALDI
Concerto a quattro, string orchestra, op. 7, no. 6, E♭ major
  <- Ariadne's lament / Il pianto d'Arianna: LOCATELLI
Concerto all' antica -> Concerto, violin, no. 4, op. 101, C
  major: HUBAY
Concerto all' inglese -> Concerto, violin, violoncello &
  string orchestra, R. 546, A major: VIVALDI
Concerto alla francese -> Concerto, string orchestra, R.117,
  C major: VIVALDI
Concerto alla rustica / Pastoral concerto -> Concerto,
  string orchestra, R. 151, G major: VIVALDI
Concerto d'après deux poèmes -> Divertimento, violin & orch-
  estra, op. 24, A major: YSAŸE
Concerto di melante -> Concerto, trumpet & string orchestra,
  D major: TELEMANN
Concerto fantastique -> Concerto, piano, op. 78, A minor:
  ALBÉNIZ

Concerto funèbre -> Concerto, orchestra, R. 29, B♭ major:
    VIVALDI
Concerto grosso, C major <- Alexander's feast concerto:
    HÄNDEL
Concerto grosso [1736] no. 12, D minor <- La follia: GEMINI-
    ANI
Concerto grosso, no. 1, F major <- Brandenburg concertos:
    J.S.BACH
Concerto grosso, no. 2, F major <- Brandenburg concertos:
    J.S.BACH
Concerto grosso, no. 3, G major <- Brandenburg concertos:
    J.S.BACH
Concerto grosso, no. 4, G major <- Brandenburg concertos:
    J.S.BACH
Concerto grosso, no. 5, D major <- Brandenburg concertos:
    J.S.BACH
Concerto grosso, no. 6, B♭ major <- Brandenburg concertos:
    J.S.BACH
Concerto grosso, op. 1, no. 8, F minor <- Christmas con-
    certo: LOCATELLI
Concerto grosso, op. 6, no. 7, B♭ major <- Hornpipe con-
    certo: HÄNDEL
Concerto grosso, op. 6, no. 8, G minor <- Christmas con-
    certo: CORELLI
Concerto grosso, op. 8, no. 6, G minor <- Christmas con-
    certo / Pastoral concerto for the Nativity: TORELLI
Concerto italiano / Italian concerto -> Concerto, violin,
    no. 1: CASTELNUOVO-TEDESCO
Concerto madrigalesco -> Concerto, string orchestra, R.
    129, D minor: VIVALDI
Concerto nach italienischen Gusto, harpsichord unacc., F
    major <- Italian concerto / Italienisches Konzert: J.S.
    BACH
Concerto pathétique -> Konzertsolo: LISZT
Concerto per eco / Echo concerto -> Concerto, violin &
    string orchestra, R. 552, A major: VIVALDI
Concerto per la solennità di San Lorenzo -> Concerto, orch-
    estra, R. 556, C major; Concerto, orchestra, R. 562, D
    major; Concerto, violin & string orchestra, R. 286, F
    major: VIVALDI
Concerto per la SS. Assunzione di Maria Vergine -> Concerto,
    violin & string orchestra, R. 582, D major: VIVALDI
Concerto per l'orchestra di Dresda -> Concerto, orchestra,
    R. 577, G minor: VIVALDI
Concerto russe -> Concerto, violin, op. 29, G minor: LALO
Concerto San Lorenzo -> Concerto 2 violins & string orch-
    estra, R. 556, C major: VIVALDI
Concerto-rhapsody, violoncello & orchestra <- Rhapsody con-

certo: KHACHATURIAN
Concertos comiques (No. 1) <- Le mirliton: CORRETTE
Concertos comiques (No. 3) <- Margoton: CORRETTE
Concertos comiques (No. 4) <- Le quadrille en quator: CORR-
    ETTE
Concertos comiques (No. 6) <- Le plaisir des dames: CORRETTE
Concertos comiques (No. 7) <- La servante au bon tabac:
    CORRETTE
Concertos comiques (No. 10) <- Ma mie Margot: CORRETTE
Concertos comiques (No. 11) <- La tante Tourelourette:
    CORRETTE
Concertos comiques (No. 12) <- La découpure: CORRETTE
Concertos comiques (No. 14) <- Le choisy: CORRETTE
Concertos comiques (No. 16) <- V'la c'que c'est qu'd'aller
    aux bois: CORRETTE
Concertos comiques (No. 17) <- Les pantins: CORRETTE
Concertos comiques (No. 18) <- La touriere: CORRETTE
Concertos comiques (No. 20) <- Nous vous marirons dimanche:
    CORRETTE
Concertos comiques (No. 25) <- Les sauvages el la Fürstem-
    berg: CORRETTE
Concertos de Noël (No. 5) <- Noel allemande: CORRETTE
Concertstück, violin & orchestra, op. 84, F minor <- Allegro
    appassionato und Adagio: BRUCH
Confidenza, La -> Symphony, no. 51, B♭ major: M.HAYDN
Concord sonata -> Sonata, piano, no. 2: IVES
Conquête du Mexique, La -> Fernand Cortez: SPONTINI
Consiglio dei tre, Il -> Bianca e Faliero: ROSSINI
Consiglio dell' ombra, Il -> L'emireno: A.SCARLATTI
Constitutionslied / Am Namensfeste des Kaisers / Geburts-
    tags-Hymne -> Am Geburtstage des Kaisers, D. 748: SCHUBERT
Consueño -> Danzas fantásticas, orchestra (Ensueño): TURINA
Contadina astuta, La -> Livietta e Tracollo: PERGOLESI
Conte di Chalais, Il -> Maria di Rohan: DONIZETTI
Conte di Essex, Il -> Roberto Devereux: DONIZETTI
Contemplation -> Lieder ohne Worte, op. 30 (No. 3): MENDELS-
    SOHN
Contemplations / Two contemplations -> Central Park in the
    dark; The unanswered question: IVES
Contesa delle stagioni <- Le quattro stagioni: D.SCARLATTI
Contest between Phoebus and Pan, The / Phoebus und Pan / Der
    Streit zwischen Phoebus und Pan -> Geschwinde, geschwinde,
    ihr wirbelnde Winde, S. 201: J.S.BACH
Conti, La -> Pièces de clavecin, 3. livre, 16. ordre (Les
    graces incomparables): COUPERIN
Contrabandista, El -> Rondo fantastique sur un thème espagn-
    ol, piano: LISZT
Contredanse serenade -> Serenade, K. 250a (101) F major:

MOZART

Contretanz, K. 535 <- La bataille / Die Belagerung Belgrads / The siege of Belgrad: MOZART

Contretanz, K. 587 <- Der Sieg vom Helden Coburg / The victory of the hero of Coburg: MOZART

Convenienze e le inconvenienze teatrali, Le <- Viva la mamma: DONIZETTI

Conversation sonata -> Trio-sonata, violins & continuo, W. 161, no. 1, C minor: C.P.E.BACH

Conversione di Maddalena, La -> Il trionfo della gratia: A. SCARLATTI

Conversione di S. Guglielmo d'Aquitania, La -> Guglielmo d' Aquitania: PERGOLESI

Convitato di pietra, Il -> Don Juan: GLUCK

Coppélia <- La fille aux yeux d'émail: DELIBES

Coranto, keyboard instrument, H. 40 <- Adieu coranto / A toy: GIBBONS

Corbeille d'oranges, La -> Zerline: AUBER

Corde du pendu, La -> Murillo: MEYERBEER

Corelli fugue -> Fugue, organ, S. 579, B minor: J.S.BACH

Corneto da posta, Il / Posthorn concerto -> Concerto, violin & string orchestra, R. 363, B♭ major: VIVALDI

Corona disprezzata, La -> Tolomeo e Alessandro: A.SCARLATTI

Coronach, D. 836 <- Totengesang der Frauen und Mädchen / Funeral song: SCHUBERT

Coronation anthem -> My heart is inditing of a good matter: PURCELL

Coronation anthems (The King shall rejoice) <- Dettingen anthem: HÄNDEL

Coronation concerto / Krönungskonzert -> Concerto, piano, K. 537, C major: MOZART

Coronation march / Solemn march for the coronation of Alexander III -> Festival coronation march: TCHAIKOVSKY

Coronation march [1937] -> Crown imperial: WALTON

Coronation march [1953] -> Orb and sceptre: WALTON

Coronation mass -> Mass, no. 11, A major: CHERUBINI

Coronation mass / Imperial mass / Nelson mass / Missa in augustiis -> Mass, H.XXII,11, D minor: J.HAYDN

Coronation mass / Krönungsmesse -> Mass, K. 317, C major: MOZART

Corrispondenza amorosa, La <- Cifre d'amore / Billets chéris: DONIZETTI

Cortège -> Sonata, harpsichord, K. 380 (L. 23) E major: D. SCARLATTI

Cortège d'Orphée, Le -> Le bestiaire: POULENC

Cost, The <- Songs of a great war: IRELAND

Costantino overture -> Overture, K. 333, C major: FUX

Coulée -> Étude, organ, no. 2: LIGETI

Counterpoint mass -> Missa brevis, K. 186h (194) D major:
  MOZART
Cour des fées, La -> Blanche de Provence: BOIELDIEU
Cour des fées, La -> Blanche de Provence: CHERUBINI
Courtisane amoureuse, La / The maid of Cashmere -> Le dieu
  et la bayadère: AUBER
Covent Garden-Walzer / Festival valse comique -> Erinnerung
  an Covent Garden: JOHANN STRAUSS
Covetous knight, The -> The miserly knight: RACHMANINOFF
Cracow mazurka -> Mazurka, piano, op. 59, no. 1, A minor:
  CHOPIN
Cradle song <- A peasant's lullaby / Sleep, son of peasants:
  MUSORGSKY
Creation mass / Schöpfungsmesse / Missa solemnis -> Mass, H.
  XXII,13, B♭ major: J.HAYDN
Creation's hymn -> Lieder, op. 48 (Die Ehre Gottes aus der
  Natur): BEETHOVEN
Credendum <- Article of faith: SCHUMAN
Credo mass -> Mass, K. 257, C major: MOZART
Crème de menthe variation -> Rapsodie sur un thème de Paga-
  nini, piano & orchestra (Variation, no. 24): RACHMANINOFF
Cri de délivrance -> Battle cry of freedom: GOTTSCHALK
Criminels dramatiques, Les -> Tromb-al-Cazar: OFFENBACH
Croquefer <- Le dernier des paladins: OFFENBACH
Crown imperial <- Coronation march [1937]: WALTON
Cruel Stephon <- Vauxhall songs: J.C.BACH
Crusader's return -> Romanze des Richard Löwenherz, D. 907:
  SCHUBERT
Crux <- Hymne des marins: LISZT
Cuban country scenes -> Escenas campestres: GOTTSCHALK
Cuban overture <- Rhumba: GERSHWIN
Cuckold in conceit, The -> The picture: ARNE
Cuckolds make themselves -> The wives excuse: PURCELL
Cuckoo and the nightingale, The -> Concerto, organ, F major
  [1739]: HANDEL
Cuckoo concerto / Il cucù -> Concerto, violin & string orch-
  estra, R. 335, A major: VIVALDI
Cuckoo sonata -> Sonata, piano, no. 25, op. 79, G major:
  BEETHOVEN
Cucù, Il / Cuckoo concerto -> Concerto, violin & string orch-
  estra, R. 335, A major: VIVALDI
Cuentos de España <- Impressions of Spain: TURINA
Cunning little vixen, The -> The sly little fox: JANÁČEK
Cupid and Psyche <- Farnesina: HINDEMITH
Cupido e onestà <- Il trionfo dell' onestà: A.SCARLATTI
Cupid's game is deceitful -> Quando amor vuol ferirmi: A.
  SCARLATTI
Curious impertinent, The -> The married beau: PURCELL

Czech dances, piano / Seven Czech dances -> Borová: MARTINŮ
Czech madrigals -> Madrigals, mixed voices, unacc. [1939]:
  MARTINŮ
Czech suite -> Suite, orchestra, op. 39, D minor: DVOŘÁK

Da quel giorno fatale -> Delirio amoroso: HÄNDEL
Daila / L'ange de Niside / Elda / Leonora -> La favorite:
  DONIZETTI
Dal male il bene -> Tutto il mal non vien per nocere: A.
  SCARLATTI
Dalarapsodi / Dalecartian rhapsody -> Swedish rhapsody,
  orchestra, no. 3, op. 48: ALFVÉN
Dalecartian rhapsody / Dalarapsodi -> Swedish rhapsody,
  orchestra, no. 3, op. 48: ALFVÉN
Dalli sdegni d'amore <- L'Orismene: LEO
Dames de St. Pétersbourgh, Les -> Wiener Frauen-Walzer,
  orchestra: JOHANN STRAUSS
Dance suite -> Concerto, string orchestra, D major: TELE-
MANN
Dance symphony -> Symphony, no. 7, op. 92, A major: BEETHO-
VEN
Dance symphony -> Symphony, op. 118, no. 4: HOVANESS
Dance variations / Tanzvariationen -> Variationen über das
  Lied Zeg kwezelke wilde gij dansen, orchestra: BADINGS
Danger d'écouter aux portes, Le -> Le trésor supposé: MÉHUL
Danger des richesses, Le -> Euloge: CAMPRA
Danish songs, op. 5 -> Hjertets melodier: GRIEG
Dans le goût théatral -> Les goûts réunis (Concert, no. 8):
  COUPERIN
Dans l'Isle de Cythère <- Les solitaires: COUPERIN
Danse andalouse / Andalusian dance -> Las mollares: GLINKA
Danse cubaine -> Ojos criollos; Réponds moi; La gallina:
  GOTTSCHALK
Danse de le foire -> Petroushka (Fête populaire de la sem-
aine grasse): STRAVINSKY
Danse des adolescents -> Le sacre du printemps (Les augures
printaniers): STRAVINSKY
Danse pensée, piano <- Rosemary: ELGAR
Danse triste -> Danzas españolas, piano, op. 37 (No. 10):
  GRANADOS
Danses, harp & string orchestra <- Danses sacrée et profane
/ Sacred and profane dances: DEBUSSY
Danses des nègres -> Bamboula: GOTTSCHALK
Danses espagnoles, piano, op. 164 (Tango) <- Tango español,
  piano, A minor: ALBÉNIZ
Danses sacrée et profane / Sacred and profane dances ->
  Danses, harp & string orchestra: DEBUSSY
Dante sonata -> Années de pèlerinage, 2. année (Après une

lecture de Dante): LISZT
Dante symphony -> Symphony, no. 3, op. 118: HUBAY
Dante symphony -> Eine Symphonie zu Dantes Divina commedia:
  LISZT
Danza delle libellule, La <- Die drei Grazien: LEHÁR
Danzas españolas, piano, op. 37 (No. 5) <- Playera: GRANADOS
Danzas españolas, piano, op. 37 (No. 10) <- Danse triste:
  GRANADOS
Danzas fantasticas, orchestra (Ensueño) <- Consueño: TURINA
Daphnis et Pandrose <- La vengeance de l'amour: MÉHUL
Dark meadow -> La hija de Colquide: CHAVEZ
Darmstädter-Trio -> Trio-sonata, violin, viola da gamba &
  continuo, F major: TELEMANN
David and Saul / Biblical sonata no. 2 -> Biblische Histo-
  rien (Saul malinconico e trastullato per mezzo della mus-
  ica): KUHNAU
Davidsbündlertänze, piano <- Eighteen characteristic pieces,
  op. 6: SCHUMANN
Dawn god of Urardu / Concerto, flute & string orchestra, op.
  50 -> Elibris: HOVANESS
De la musique avant toute chose -> Pièces enfantines:
  FRANÇAIX
Death and the maiden / Der Tod und das Mädchen -> Quartet,
  strings, D. 810, D minor: SCHUBERT
Death of Alexander the Great, THe -> The rival queens: ARNE
Death of machines -> Sonata, piano, no. 3: ANTHEIL
Death of St. Narcissus, The <- Canticle V: BRITTEN
Débutante, La -> Le concert à la cour: AUBER
Deceit outwitted -> L'infedeltà delusa: J.HAYDN
Découpure, La -> Concertos comiques (No. 12): CORRETTE
Delroye pavan -U Pavan, 5 viols, A minor: GIBBONS
Deliciae Basilienses -> Symphony, no. 4: HONEGGER
Delirio amoroso <- Da quel giorno fatale: HÄNDEL
Dem Gerechten muss das Licht, S. 195 <- Hochzeits-Kantate /
  Wedding cantata: J.S.BACH
Demetrio <- Cleonice: GLUCK
Dentelle s'abolit, Une -> Pli selon pli (Improvisation sur
  Mallarmé, no. 2): BOULEZ
Departure, The -> Lieder ohne Worte, op. 62 (No. 2): MEN-
  DELSSOHN
Déploration de Jehan Ockeghem, La -> Nymphes des bois,
  déesses des fontaines: DEPRÈS
Der Fürstin Abendlied-> Abendlied der Fürstin, D. 495: SCHU-
  BERT
Der lebt ein Leben wonniglich / Das Glück der Freundschaft
  -> Vita felice: BEETHOVEN
Derbyshire marches -> Marches, wood-winds & brasses, H.VIII,
  1-2: J.HAYDN

Dernier des paladins, Le -> Croquefer: OFFENBACH
Des Frauleins Liebesläuschen -> Liebesläuschen, D. 698: SCHU-
    BERT
Des Heilands letzte Stunden <- Calvary: SPOHR
Des Mannes Wiegenlied am Sarge seiner Mutter -> Berceuse élé-
    giaque: BUSONI
Désespérance -> Sonate-fantaisie, violin & piano, no. 1:
    VILLA-LOBOS
Desperation -> Prelude, piano, op. 28, no. 8, F# minor: CHO-
    PIN
Dettingen anthem -> Coronation anthems (The King shall re-
    joice): HÄNDEL
Dettingen Te Deum (Vouchsafe, O Lord; arr.) <- Prayer: HÄN-
    DEL
Deutsche Eiche, Die -> Tantum ergo, D. 730: SCHUBERT
Deutsche Kirchenlieder und liturgische Gesänge (Jesu Chris-
    te) <- Die fünf Wunden: LISZT
Deutsche Messe / German mass -> Mass, D. 872, B♭ major: SCHU-
    BERT
Deutsche Tänze, orchestra, K. 600 (No. 5) <- Der Kanarienvo-
    gel / The canary: MOZART
Deutsche Tänze, orchestra, K. 602 (No. 4) <- Der Leiermann /
    The organ grinder: MOZART
Deutsche Tänze, orchestra, K. 605 (No. 3) <- Die Schlitten-
    fahrt / The sleigh ride: MOZART
Deutsche Tänze und Ecossaisen, piano, D. 783 <- Tyrolean
    dances: SCHUBERT
Deutsche Trauermesse, D. 621 <- Deutsches Requiem: SCHUBERT
Deutscher Siegesmarsch -> Vom Fels zu Meer: LISZT
Deutsches Hochamt -> Hier liegt vor Deiner Majestät: M.HAYDN
Deutsches Kriegslied, Ein / A German war song -> Ich möchte
    wohl der Kaiser sein: MOZART
Deutsches Requiem, Ein <- Requiem: BRAHMS
Deutsches Requiem -> Deutsche Trauermesse, D. 621: SCHUBERT
Deutsches Salve regina, D. 379, F major <- Hymne an die Hei-
    lige Mutter / Salve regina: SCHUBERT
Deutsches Stabat mater -> Stabat mater, D. 383: SCHUBERT
Deutsches Te Deum / German Te Deum -> Herr, grosser Gott,
    dich loben wir: M.HAYDN
Deux couvents, Les -> Cécile et Ermancé: GRETRY
Deux journées, Les <- Der Wassertrager / The water carrier:
    CHERUBINI
Deux paravents, Les -> Rien de trop: BOIELDIEU
Deux sous de charbon <- Le suicide de bigorneau: DELIBES
Devil's chuckle, The / Le rire du diable -> Caprice, violin,
    op. 1, no. 13, B major: PAGANINI
Devil's trill sonata / Trillo del diavolo -> Sonata, violin
    & continuo, G minor: TARTINI

Di tre re -> Symphony, no. 5: HONEGGER
Diabelli variations -> Veränderungen über einen Walzer von
  A. Diabelli, piano, op. 120: BEETHOVEN
Diabelli variations -> Veränderungen uber einen Walzer, pi-
  ano, D. 718, C minor: SCHUBERT
Diabolin-Polka, orchestra <- Neue Satanella-Polka: JOHANN
  STRAUSS
Dialogue between two shepherds, A -> Songs of sundrie nat-
  ures (Who made thee, Hob): BYRD
Dialogue of a nymph and a shepherd -> Madrigals, book 9 (Bel
  pastor): MONTEVERDI
Dialogus inter Deus et hominem -> Accedo ad te mi Jesus:
  COUPERIN
Dialogus zwischen Furcht und Hoffnung -> O Ewigkeit, O Don-
  nerwort, S. 60: J.S.BACH
Diana vendicata -> Orione: J.C.BACH
Didone abbandonata -> Sonata, piano, op. 50, no. 3, G minor:
  CLEMENTI
Didone abbandonata -> Sonata, violin & continuo, G minor
  (Didone abbandonata): TARTINI
Die natali <- Chorale preludes for Christmas, op. 37: BARBER
Dies irae <- Auschwitz oratorio: PENDERECKI
Dietro l'orme fugaci -> Armida abbandonata: HÄNDEL
Dieu et la bayadère, Le <- La courtisane amoureuse / The
  maid of Cashmere: AUBER
Dieux de l'Egypte, Les -> Les festes de l'Himen et de l'Am-
  our: RAMEAU
Dieux rivaux, Les <- Les fêtes de Cythère: SPONTINI
Digte, op. 4 <- German songs, op. 4: GRIEG
Dinorah -> Le pardon de Ploërmel: MEYERBEER
Dioclesian <- The prophetess: PURCELL
Diran, the religious singer <- Concerto, horn & string orch-
  estra, op. 74: HOVANESS
Dirges, op. 9a -> Nénies: BARTÓK
Dissonanzen-Quartett / Haydn quartets -> Quartet, strings,
  K. 465, C major: MOZART
Distratto, Il -> Symphony, M. 60, C major: J.HAYDN
Distressed innocence <- The princess of Persia: PURCELL
Dithyrambe, D. 47 <- Der Besuch: SCHUBERT
Diva de l'Empire, La <- American intermezzo: SATIE
Divertimenti, H.XI <- Baryton trios: J.HAYDN
Divertimento, H.II,11, C major <- Der Geburtstag / Birthday
  divertimento / Mann und Weib / Man and wife: J.HAYDN
Divertimento, H.II,33, F major <- Weinzierler trios: J.HAYDN
Divertimento, H.II,38, A major <- Weinzierler trios: J.HAYDN
Divertimento, H.II,39, Eb major <- Echo divertimento: J.
  HAYDN
Divertimento, H.IV,1, C major <- London trios: J.HAYDN

Divertimento, H.IV,2, C major <- London trios: J.HAYDN
Divertimento, H.IV,3, G major <- London trios: J.HAYDN
Divertimento, H.IV,4, G major <- London trios: J.HAYDN
Divertimento, K. 125a (136) D major <- Salzburg symphonies:
  MOZART
Divertimento, K. 125b (137) B♭ major <- Salzburg symphonies:
  MOZART
Divertimento, K. 125c (138) F major <- Salzburg symphonies:
  MOZART
Divertimento, K. 287, B♭ major <- Lodronische Nachtmusik:
  MOZART
Divertimento, K. 563, E♭ major <- Puchberg divertimento:
  MOZART
Divertimento, no. 1 -> Sextet, piano & woodwinds (Scherzo):
  MARTINŮ
Divertimento, no. 2 -> Sextet, piano & woodwinds (Blues):
  MARTINŮ
Divertimento, no. 3, op. 25 <- Impressioni ungheresi: WEINER
Divertimento, string orchestra, no. 2, op. 24 <- Hungarian
  folk melodies: WEINER
Divertimento, violin & orchestra, op. 24, A major <- Concer-
  to d'après deux poèmes: YSAŸE
Divertissement, orchestra, op. 43 [arr.] <- Trapeze: PROKOF-
  IEV
Divertissement à l'hongroise, piano, 4 hands, D. 818, G min-
  or <- Ungarische Melodien / Hungarian melodies: SCHUBERT
Divertissement de Chambord, Le -> Monsieur de Pourceaugnac:
  LULLY
Divertissement royal -> Les amants magnifiques: LULLY
Divertissement sur 20 airs de Kentucky -> Kentuckiana: MIL-
  HAUD
Divine poem -> Symphony, no. 3, op. 43, C major-minor:
  SKRIABIN
Djamileh <- L'esclave amoureuse: BIZET
Do not speak, beloved / A summer love -> Songs, op. 6 (Not a
  word, O my friend): TCHAIKOVSKY
Doctor Syntax -> Pedagogic overture: WALTON
Dog waltz / Minute waltz -> Waltz, piano, op. 64, no. 1, D♭
  major: CHOPIN
Doll, The / La poupée -> Jeux d'enfants (Berceuse): BIZET
Dolorès <- Le miracle de la femme laide: JOLIVET
Domine, ne in furore tuo <- Penitential psalms: LASSUS
Dominicus mass / Missa Dominica -> Mass, K. 66, C major:
  MOZART
Dominos, Les -> Pièces de clavecin, 3. livre, 13. ordre (Les
  folies françoises): COUPERIN
Don Alvaro -> La forza del destino: VERDI
Don Coribaldi <- L'usurpato prepotenza: DITTERSDORF

Don de sagesse, Le -> Messe de la Pentecôte (Consécration):
  MESSIAEN
Don Gayseros, D. 93 <- Der Mohrenkönig: SCHUBERT
Don Gregorio -> L'ajo nell' imbarazzo: DONIZETTI
Don Juan <- Il convitato di pietra: GLUCK
Don Juan fantasy -> Reminiscences of Don Juan: LISZT
Don Quichotte <- Burlesque de Don Quixotte / Suite, string
  orchestra, G10, G major: TELEMANN
Donauwalzer / Blue Danube waltz -> An der schönen blauen Do-
  nau: JOHANN STRAUSS
Donna che in ciel -> Anniversario della liberatione di Roma
  dal terremoto: HÄNDEL
Donner und Blitz-Polka -> Unter Donner und Blitz: JOHANN
  STRAUSS
Donnerode / Ode to thunder -> Wie ist dein Name so gross:
  TELEMANN
Donnerwetter, Das / The thunderstorm -> Kontretanz, K. 534:
  MOZART
Dorfjahrmarkt, Der <- Der Jahrmarkt: BENDA
Dorfmusikanten-Sextett / Bauernsinfonie -> Ein musikalischer
  Spass, K. 522: MOZART
Doria <- La tyrannie détruite: MÉHUL
Dorian toccata -> Prelude and fugue, organ, S. 538, D minor:
  J.S.BACH
Doric quartet -> Quartet, strings, no. 2, D major: RESPIGHI
Dorisbe -> L'amor volubile e tiranno: A.SCARLATTI
Double discovery, The -> The Spanish friar: PURCELL
Double épreuve, Le <- Colinette à la cour: GRÉTRY
Double notes etude -> Etude, piano, op. 25, no. 6, G# minor:
  CHOPIN
Double sixths etude -> Etude, piano, op. 25, no. 8, Db ma-
  jor: CHOPIN
Double symphony / Irdisches und Göttliches im Menschenleben
  -> Symphony, no. 7, op. 121, C major: SPOHR
Dove descending breaks the air, The <- Anthem: STRAVINSKY
Dowolno <- Genug-Polka: JOHANN STRAUSS
Dramatic overture / Tragic overture -> Alfred (Overture):
  DVOŘÁK
Dramatic symphony / Symphonie dramatique -> Symphony, no. 4,
  op. 95, D minor: RUBINSTEIN
Dream, The -> Beneath a shady willow: HÄNDEL
Dream quartet / Traum-Quartett / Preussische Quartette /
  Prussian quartets -> Quartet, strings, no. 48, op. 50, no.
  5, F major: J.HAYDN
Drei Grazien, Die -> La danza delle libellule: LEHÁR
Drei Wünsche, Die -> Der Holzhauer: BENDA
Dreigroschenoper, Die (Suite) <- Kleine Dreigroschenmusik:
  WEILL

Dresden trio sonatas -> Trio-sonata, op. 2, no. 3, F major;
no. 8, G minor; no. 9, E major: HANDEL
Dress rehearsal The / Die Generalprobe -> Il maestro di cappella: CIMAROSA
Dried flowers variations / Trockne Blumen-Variationen -> Introduction et variations sur un thème original, flute &
piano, D. 802, E minor: SCHUBERT
Drum quartet / Haydn quartets -> Quartet, strings, K. 464, A
major: MOZART
Drum roll symphony / Paukenwirbel-Symphonie / London sym-
phonies / Salomon symphonies -> Symphony, M. 103, E♭ ma-
jor: J.HAYDN
Du aber Daniel, gehe hin <- Trauer-Kantate / Funeral canta-
ta: TELEMANN
Due baroni di Rocca Azzurra, I <- La sposa in contrasto / Il
barone deluso: CIMAROSA
Due supposti conti, I <- Lo sposo senza moglie: CIMAROSA
Duello per complimento, Il -> I nemici generosi: CIMAROSA
Duenna, The <- The betrothal in the monastery: PROKOFIEV
Duenna, The (Suite) <- Summer night: PROKOFIEV
Dürnitz sonata -> Sonata, piano, K. 205b (284) D major: MO-
ZART
Duet, viola & violoncello, K. 32, E major <- Eyeglass duet:
BEETHOVEN
Duet, 1 violin, C major <- Duo merveille / Sonata, violin,
op. 20, C major: PAGANINI
Duets, violin & guitar, op. 60 <- Duetti fiorentini / Flo-
rentine duets: PAGANINI
Duets, violin (Selections;arr.) <- Little suite, piano: BAR-
TÓK
Duetti fiorentini / Florentine duets -> Duets, violin & gui-
tar: PAGANINI
Duke Bluebeard's castle <- Bluebeard's castle: BARTÓK
Dukes of Dunstable, The -> The fool's preferment: PURCELL
Dum essent in unum -> Motets, 6 part (Dum complerentur):
PALESTRINA
Dumbarton Oaks concerto -> Concerto, orchestra, E♭: STRAVIN-
SKY
Dumka -> Complainte: BALAKIREV
Dumky trio -> Trio, piano & strings, no. 4, op. 90, E minor:
DVOŘÁK
Duo merveille / Sonata, violin, op. 20, C major -> Duet, 1
violin, C major: PAGANINI
Duport variations -> Variationen über ein Menuett von Du-
port, piano, K. 573: MOZART
Dying Christian to his soul -> Verklärung, D. 59: SCHUBERT
Dynamiden <- Geheime Anziehungskräfte: JOSEPH STRAUSS

Earl of Oxford march, The / My Lord of Oxenford's maske ->
The battell (The march before the battle: BYRD
Earl of Ross march, The -> Marche écossaise sur un thème po-
pulaire, piano, 4 hands: DEBUSSY
Earl Stafford's galliard -> Galliard, keyboard instrument,
T. 42; Galliard, keyboard instrument, T. 44: TOMKINS
Earl Stafford's pavan -> Pavan, keyboard instrument, T. 41;
Pavan, keyboard instrument, T. 43: TOMKINS
Earth's call <- Sylvan rhapsody: IRELAND
Easter cantata / Osterkantate -> Christ lag in Todesbanden,
S. 4; Bleib bei uns, denn es will Abend werden, S. 6; Der
Himmel lacht, die Erde jubiliert, S. 31; Erfreut euch, ihr
Herzen, S. 66; Ein Herz, das seinen Jesum lebend weiss, S.
134; Wir müssen durch viel Trübsal in das Reich Gottes
eingehen, S. 146: J.S.BACH
Easter cantata / Die Feier der Auferstehung -> Lazarus, D.
689: SCHUBERT
Easter story, The / The resurrection -> Historia von der
Auferstehung Jesu Christi: SCHÜTZ
Easy sonatas / Essay sonatas / Probesonaten -> Sonata, harp-
sichord, W. 63, no. 1, C major; no. 2, D minor; no. 3, A
major; no. 4, B minor; no. 5, Eb major; no. 6, F minor: C.
P.E.BACH
Ebony concerto, clarinet & jazz ensemble <- Concerto, clar-
inet & jazz ensemble: STRAVINSKY
Ecce veniet dies illa -> Motets, 8 part (Fili, non te fran-
gant labores): PALESTRINA
Echo concerto / Concerto per eco -> Concerto, violin &
string orchestra, R. 552, A major: VIVALDI
Echo divertimento -> Divertimento, H.II,39, Eb major: J.
HAYDN
Echo fantasia -> Fantasia, keyboard instrument, L. 12: SWE-
LINCK
Echo psalm -> Psalmen Davids [1619] (Jauchzet dem Herren,
alle Welt): SCHÜTZ
Echo song -> O la, o che bon eccho: LASSUS
Echo symphony -> Symphony, M. 38, C major: J.HAYDN
Ecossaisen, piano <- Kontertänze: WEBER
Eden <- Adam and Eve: ROSENBERG
Educational music -> Schulwerk: HINDEMITH
Edward ballad -> Ballade, piano, op. 10, no. 1, D minor:
BRAHMS
Effuderunt sanguinem sanctorum <- Graduale in festo SS. In-
nocentium extra Dominicam: M.HAYDN
Eglogue <- Hirtengedicht: FRANCK
Egmont (Freudvoll und Leidvoll) <- Klärchen-Lieder: BEETHO-
VEN

Egmont (Die Trommel) <- Klärchen-Lieder: BEETHOVEN
Egual impegno d'amore e di fede, L' -> Tigrane: A.SCARLATTI
Egyptian concerto -> Concerto, piano, no. 5, op. 103, F major: SAINT-SAËNS
Ehre der Nation, Die -> Schwergewicht: KŘENEK
Ehre sei Gott in der Höhe <- Christmas cantata / Weihnachtskantate: TELEMANN
Eichendorff-Lieder -> Lieder, op. 9: PFITZNER
Eighteen characteristic pieces, piano, op. 6 -> Davidsbündlertänze, piano: SCHUMANN
1848 symphony -> Symphony, no. 4: MILHAUD
Einige kanonische Veränderungen, organ, S. 769 <- Vom Himmel hoch, da komm ich her, S. 769: J.S.BACH
Einsiedelei, Die, D. 337 <- Lob der Einsamkeit: SCHUBERT
Elda / Daila / L'ange de Niside / Leonora -> La favorite: DONIZETTI
Election day is action day -> Remember November: HARRIS
Elections songs -> Vote for names; William Will: IVES
Elegiac song -> Sanft wie du lebtest, op. 118: BEETHOVEN
Elegiac song, An -> Ode, orchestra: STRAVINSKY
Elegiac symphony -> Sinfonia funebre, F minor: LOCATELLI
Elegiac trio -> Trio, flute, viola & harp: BAX
Elegie / Klagendes Lied -> Lieder ohne Worte, op. 85 (No. 4): MENDELSSOHN
Élégie harmonique sur la mort de Son Altesse Royale le Prince Louis Ferdinand de Prusse -> Sonata, piano, op. 61, F# minor: DUSSEK
Elegy, horn & organ, op. 5 <- Notturno elegiaco: ALFVÉN
Elegy in memory of M.P. Belyaev -> Elegy, string quartet, op. 105: GLAZUNOV
Elegy on the death of John Playford / A pastoral elegy on the death of John Playford -> Gentle shepherds, you that know: PURCELL
Elegy on the death of Queen Mary -> Incassum, Lesbia, rogas: PURCELL
Elegy on the death of Thomas Farmer -> Young Thirsis' fate ye hills and groves deplore: PURCELL
Eleonoren-Sonate -> Sonata, piano, K. 51, C minor: BEETHOVEN
Elevation motet -> Tu lumen, tu splendor patris: DEPRÈS
Elfenkönigin, Die -> Sylphen, D. 341: SCHUBERT
Elibris <- Concerto, flute & string orchestra, op. 50 / Dawn god of Urardu: HOVANESS
Élisa <- Le voyage au Mont-Bernard: CHERUBINI
Elisabethsklänge -> Myrthen-Kränze-Walzer, orchestra: JOHANN STRAUSS
Elisabetta <- Il castello di Kenilworth: DONIZETTI
Ellens Gesang, D. 839 <- Ave Maria / Hymn to the Virgin: SCHUBERT

Elvira Madigan concerto -> Concerto, piano, K. 467, C major:
MOZART

Embarquement pour Cythère <- Valse-musette, 2 pianos: POUL-
ENC

Emireno, L' <- Il consiglio dell' ombra: A.SCARLATTI

Emma <- La promesse imprudente: AUBER

Emma -> An Emma, D. 113: SCHUBERT

Emma und Eginhard (Overture) <- Concerto, violin & string
orchestra, A minor: TELEMANN

Emperor concerto -> Concerto, piano, no. 5, op. 73, E♭ major:
BEETHOVEN

Emperor quartet / Kaiser-Quartett / Erdödy quartets -> Quartet, strings, no. 78, op. 76, no. 3, C major: J.HAYDN

Emperor variations -> Quartet, strings, no. 78, op. 76, no.
3, C major (Poco cantabile): J.HAYDN

Emporté, L' -> L'irato: MÉHUL

Empress and the necromancer, The -> The poisoned kiss:
VAUGHAN WILLIAMS

En avril -> Petite Marguerite: BIZET

Enchanted bird, The -> Uirapuru: VILLA-LOBOS

Enfantines -> The nursery: MUSORGSKY

England of Elizabeth, The (Selections;arr.) <- Shakespeare
sketches: VAUGHAN WILLIAMS

English canzonettes -> Canzonets, 1st set; Canzonets, 2d
set: J.HAYDN

English rhapsody, An -> Brigg fair: DELIUS

English suites -> Suite, harpsichord, S. 806, A major; S.
807, A minor; S. 808, G minor; S. 809, F major; S. 810, E
minor; S. 811, D minor: J.S.BACH

English symphony -> Symphony, no. 8, op. 88, G major: DVOŘÁK

Enigma variations -> Variations on an original theme, orchestra: ELGAR

Entfernte Geliebte, Die -> Als ich sie erröten sah, D. 153:
SCHUBERT

Entführung aus dem Serail, Die <- Il seraglio: MOZART

Entzückung an Laura, Die, D. 390 <- Die seligen Augenblicke:
SCHUBERT

Entzückung an Laura, Die, D. 577 <- Die seligen Augenblicke:
SCHUBERT

Epiphany cantata -> In fest trium regium: BIBER

Episoden aus Lenaus Faust (Der Tanz in der Dorfschenke) <-
Mephisto waltz, no. 1: LISZT

Epistel / Sendschreiben -> Herrn Josef Spaun, D. 749: SCHU-
BERT

Epistle sonatas / Church sonatas / Kirchensonaten / Festival
sonatas -> Sonata, organ & orchestra, K. 271e (278) C major; K. 317a (329) C major; K. 263, C major; Sonata, organ
& string orchestra, K. 41h (67) E♭ major; K. 41i (68) B♭

major; K. 41k (69) D major; K. 124a (144) D major; K. 124b
(145) F major; K. 212, B♭ major; K. 241, G major; K. 241a
(224) F major; K. 241b (225) A major; K. 244, F major; K.
245, D major; K. 271d (274) G major; K. 317c (328) C major; K. 336d (336) C major: MOZART

Epitaphe d'un paresseux -> Jean s'en alla comme il étoit venu: COUPERIN

Equivoci in amore, Gli <- La rosaura: A.SCARLATTI

Equivoci nel sembiante, Gli <- L'errore innocente / Amor non
vuole inganni: A.SCARLATTI

Era l'ora -> Il pescatore: DONIZETTI

Eraste et Lucinde -> Silvain: GRÉTRY

Erde und Frühling, Die / Genesungs-Kantate -> Kantate zur
Feier der Genesung des Fräulein Irene von Kiesewetter, D.
936: SCHUBERT

Erdödy quartets -> Quartet, strings, no. 76, op. 76, no. 1,
G major; no. 77, op. 76, no. 2, D minor; no. 78, op. 76,
no. 3, C major; no. 79, op. 76, no. 4, B♭ major; no. 80,
op. 76, no. 5, D major; no. 81, op. 76, no. 6, E♭ major:
J.HAYDN

Erede riconosciuta, L' -> La pescatrice: PICCINNI

Erfreut euch, ihr Herzen, S. 66 <- Easter cantata /Osterkan-
tate: J.S.BACH

Erinnerung -> Die Erscheinung, D. 229: SCHUBERT

Erinnerung an Covent Garden <- Covent Garden-Walzer / Festival valse comique: JOHANN STRAUSS

Erinnerungen an Riga -> Souvenir de Nizza: JOHANN STRAUSS

Erlafsee, D. 586 <- Am Erlafsee: SCHUBERT

Eroica sonata -> Sonata, violin & piano, no. 7, op. 30, no.
2, C minor: BEETHOVEN

Eroica symphony / Heroic symphony -> Symphony, no. 3, op.
55, E♭ major: BEETHOVEN

Eroica variations -> Variations, piano, op. 35, E♭ major:
BEETHOVEN

Errore innocente, L' / Amor non vuole inganni -> Gli equivoci nel sembiante: A.SCARLATTI

Erscheinung, Die, D. 229 <- Erinnerung: SCHUBERT

Erste Walpurgisnacht, Die <- Walpurgisnacht: MENDELSSOHN

Erste Walzer / First waltzes -> Originaltänze, piano, D. 365:
SCHUBERT

Erzherzog-Trio / Archduke trio -> Trio, piano & strings, no.
6, op. 97, B major: BEETHOVEN

Es lebe unser teurer Fürst <- Birthday cantata / Lobkowitz
cantata: BEETHOVEN

Escenas campestres <- Cuban country scenes: GOTTSCHALK

Esclave amoureuse, L' -> Djamileh: BIZET

Esiliati in Siberia, Gli -> Otto mesi in due ore: DONIZETTI

Esop in the shades -> Lethe: ARNE

Espagne <- Souvenirs: ALBÉNIZ

Esportes -> Prole do bebê, no. 3: VILLA-LOBOS

Esquisses japonaises / Japanese sketches -> Haikai: MESSIAEN

Essay sonatas / Easy sonatas / Probesonaten -> Sonata, harpsichord, W. 63, no. 1, C major; no. 2, D minor; no. 3, A
major; no. 4, B minor; no. 5, E♭ major; no. 6, F minor: C.
P.E.BACH

Estate, L' / Summer / Concerto, op. 8, no. 2, B♭ major -> Il
cimento dell' armonia e dell' inventione (No. 2): VIVALDI

Esterhazy sonatas -> Sonata, piano, no. 21, C major; no. 22,
E major; no. 23, F major; no. 24, D major; no. 25, E♭ major; no. 26, A major: J.HAYDN

Esther <- Queen Esther: HÄNDEL

Estrella de Soria (Overture) <- Tragic overture: BERWALD

Estro armonico, L' <- Concerto, op. 3, no. 1, D major; no.
2, G minor; no. 3, G major; no. 4, E minor; no. 5, A major; no. 6, A minor; no. 7, F major; no. 8, A minor; no. 9,
D major; no. 10, B minor; no. 11, D minor; no. 12, E major: VIVALDI

Esule di Roma, L' <- Il proscritto / Settimio: DONIZETTI

États d'ame -> Sonata, piano, no. 3, op. 23, F# minor:
SKRIABIN

Etchmiadzin symphony -> Symphony, no. 21, op. 234: HOVANESS

Étendard de Grenade, L' -> Les Abencérages: CHERUBINI

Etude, organ, no. 1 <- Harmonies: LIGETI

Etude, organ, no. 2 <- Coulée: LIGETI

Etude, piano, op. 8, no. 10, D major <- Study in thirds:
SKRIABIN

Etude, piano, op. 10, no. 1, C major <- Arpeggio etude: CHO-
PIN

Etude, piano, op. 10, no. 3, E major <- Grief / L'intimité /
Tristesse: CHOPIN

Etude, piano, op. 10, no. 4, C# minor <- Torrent: CHOPIN

Etude, piano, op. 10, no. 5, G♭ major <- Black keys etude:
CHOPIN

Etude, piano, op. 10, no. 11, E♭ major <- Extended chords
etude: CHOPIN

Etude, piano, op. 10, no. 12, C minor <- Revolutionary e-
tude: CHOPIN

Etude, piano, op. 25, no. 1, A♭ major <- Aeolian harp etude
/ Shepherd boy etude / Harp etude: CHOPIN

Etude, piano, op. 25, no. 3, F major <- Cartwheel etude:
CHOPIN

Etude, piano, op. 25, no. 4, A minor <- Syncopations etude:
CHOPIN

Etude, piano, op. 25, no. 6, G# minor <- Double notes etude:
CHOPIN

Etude, piano, op. 25, no. 8, D♭ major<- Double sixths etude:

CHOPIN
Etude, piano, op. 25, no. 9, Gb major <- Butterfly etude:
  CHOPIN
Etude, piano, op. 25, no. 10, B minor <- Octaves etude:
  CHOPIN
Etude, piano, op. 25, no. 11, A minor <- Winter wind etude:
  CHOPIN
Etude, piano, op. 25, no. 12, C minor <- Ocean etude: CHOPIN
Etude, piano, op. 31, no. 3, E major <- Night / La nuit:
  GLAZUNOV
Etude, piano, op. 52, no. 6, Db major <- Étude en forme de
  valse: SAINT-SAËNS
Etude en forme de valse -> Etude, piano, op. 52, no. 6, Db
  major: SAINT-SAËNS
Études basées sur un thème de Beethoven, piano <- Beethoven
  variations: SCHUMANN
Études de concert, piano <- Caprices poétiques: LISZT
Études de concert, piano (No. 1) <- Il lamento: LISZT
Études de concert, piano (No. 2) <- La leggierezza: LISZT
Études de concert, piano (No. 3) <- Un sospiro: LISZT
Études d'exécution transcendante, piano <- Transcendental
  etudes: LISZT
Études en forme de variations, piano, op. 13 <- Etudes sym-
  phoniques / Symphonic studies: SCHUMANN
Études symphoniques / Symphonic studies -> Études en forme
  de variations, piano, op. 13: SCHUMANN
Euloge <- Le danger des richesses: CAMPRA
Euphrosine <- Le tyran corrigé: MÉHUL
European anthem, The / L'hymne européen -> Symphony, no. 9,
  op. 125, D minor (Presto; arr.): BEETHOVEN
Eva <- Das Fabriksmädel: LEHÁR
Evening hymn -> Now that the sun hath veiled his light: PUR-
  CELL
Evening service, op. 37 / The vigil -> Vesper mass: RACHMA-
  NINOFF
Evening song -> Tzaikerk: HOVANESS
Evening star, The -> Lieder ohne Worte, op. 38 (No. 1): MEN-
  DELSSOHN
Evening voices -> Songs from the Norwegian (Twilight fan-
  cies): DELIUS
Eventail de Jeanne, L' -> Pastourelle: POULENC
Eventyr <- Once upon a time: DELIUS
Evesham andante -> Harmony music, winds (Andante con varia-
  zioni): ELGAR
Evocations (Houang Ti) <- God of war: BLOCH
Evviva, evviva Bacco <- Canon italien: CHERUBINI
Exilées du Kamchattka, Les -> Béniowski: BOIELDIEU
Extended chords etude -> Etude, piano, op. 10, no. 11, Eb

major: CHOPIN
Extremum Dei judicium <- Judicium extremum: CARISSIMI
Exile symphony -> Symphony, no. 1, op. 17, no. 2: HOVANESS
Eyeglass duet -> Duet, viola & violoncello, K. 32, E♭ major:
    BEETHOVEN

Fabriksmädel, Das -> Eva: LEHÁR
Faction of Carthage, The -> Regulus: PURCELL
Fair maid of the inn, The -> Molly Mog: HÄNDEL
Faisons du temps <- Vaudeville: COUPERIN
Faith / Belief -> Lieder ohne Worte, op. 102 (No. 6): MEN-
    DELSSOHN
Faithful maid, The -> The melancholy nymph: HÄNDEL
Faithless, ungrateful <- The forsaken maid's complaint:
    HÄNDEL
Falegname di Livonia, Il <- Pietro il Grande, czar delle
    Russie: DONIZETTI
Falstaff <- Le tre burle: SALIERI
Falstaff opera -> Sir John in love: VAUGHAN WILLIAMS
Famiglia in scompiglio, Il -> Gli amanti comici: CIMAROSA
Fanatico burlato, Il <- La burla felice: CIMAROSA
Fanatico in Berlina, Il -> La locanda: PAISIELLO
Fancies, piano, op. 25 / Whimsies -> Bizarreries: MIASKOVSKY
Fancy -> Tell me, where is fancy bred: KODÁLY
Fanfare de chasse <- Rendez-vous de chasse: ROSSINI
Fanfare for France -> Portraits (Portrait of Max Kahn):
    THOMSON
Fanfare fugue -> Fugue, harpsichord, S. Anh. 90, C major: J.
    S.BACH
Fantaisie, piano & orchestra, op. 89, G minor -> Africa:
    SAINT-SAËNS
Fantaisie brillante sur des motifs de l'opéra Faust, violin
    & orchestra <- Faust fantasy: WIENIAWSKI
Fantaisie de concert sur des thèmes russes, violin & orch-
    estra, op. 33 <- Russian fantasy: RIMSKY-KORSAKOV
Fantaisie orientale / Oriental fantasy -> Islamey: BALAKIREV
Fantaisie polonaise -> Polonaise-fantaisie, piano, op. 61,
    A♭ major: CHOPIN
Fantaisie sur des motifs favoris de l'opéra La sonnambula de
    Bellini, piano <- Sonnambula fantasy: LISZT
Fantaisie-tableaux -> Fantasia, 2 pianos, op. 5: RACHMANI-
    NOFF
Fantaisies symphoniques -> Symphony, no. 6: MARTINŮ
Fantasia, keyboard instrument, L. 1 <- Chromatic fantasy /
    Fantasia chromatica: SWELINCK
Fantasia, keyboard instrument, L. 5 <- Hexachord fantasia:
    SWELINCK
Fantasia, keyboard instrument, L. 12 <- Echo fantasia: SWE-

LINCK
Fantasia, piano, D. 605A, C major <- Grazer-Fantasie: SCHU-
    BERT
Fantasia, piano, D. 760, C major <- Wanderer fantasy: SCHU-
    BERT
Fantasia, piano, op. 28, F# minor <- Sonate écossaise: MEN-
    DELSSOHN
Fantasia, piano, 4 hands, D. 1, G major <- Leichenfantasie:
    SCHUBERT
Fantasia, piano, mixed voices & orchestra, op. 80, C minor
    <- Choral fantasy / Chorfantasie: BEETHOVEN
Fantasia, 2 pianos, op. 5 <- Fantaisie-tableaux: RACHMANI-
    NOFF
Fantasia chromatica / Chromatic fantasy -> Fantasia, key-
    board instrument, L. 1: SWELINCK
Fantasia on Polish airs / Polish fantasy -> Grande fantaisie
    sur des airs polonais, piano & orchestra, op. 13: CHOPIN
Fantasia on the G-string / Moses fantasy -> Sonata a preg-
    hiera con variazioni, violin & orchestra: PAGANINI
Fantasia upon one note -> Fantasias, 3-7 viols (No. 15):
    PURCELL
Fantasias, 3-7 viols (No. 15) <- Fantasia upon one note:
    PURCELL
Fantasie über ungarische Volksmelodien, piano & orchestra <-
    Hungarian fantasia: LISZT
Fantasie und Fuge über den Choral Ad nos ad salutarem undam,
    organ <- Ad nos ad salutarem undam: LISZT
Fantasie unter freier Benutzung schottischer Volksmelodien,
    violin & orchestra, op. 46 <- Scottish fantasy: BRUCH
Fantasiebilder -> Faschingsschwank aus Wien: SCHUMANN
Fantasie-Sonate -> Sonata, organ, no. 2, op. 65, A♭ major;
    no. 17, op. 181, B major: RHEINBERGER
Fantasiestücke, piano, op. 12 <- Pièces romantiques / Fan-
    tastic pieces: SCHUMANN
Fantasirejse til Farøerne, En -> Rhapsodisk overture: NIEL-
    SEN
Fantastic pieces / Pièces romantiques -> Fantasiestücke, pi-
    ano, op. 12: SCHUMANN
Fantastico, Il <- Il nuovo Don Chisciotte: LEO
Fantasy, piano, op. 15 <- The last rose of summer: MENDELS-
    SOHN
Fantasy, viola & piano -> Concert piece, viola & piano: BAX
Fantasy and fugue on B.A.C.H. -> Präludium und Fuge über den
    Namen Bach, organ: LISZT
Fantasy on a Bulgarian dance theme, op. 18 -> Khoro, violin
    & piano: VLADIGEROV
Fantasy on the G-string / Moses fantasy -> Sonata a preg-
    hiera con variazioni, violin & orchestra: PAGANINI

Fantasy quartet -> Phantasy, oboe & strings, op. 2: BRITTEN
Fantasy sonata -> Sonata, piano, no. 1: TIPPETT
Farewell, The / Les adieux -> Sonata, piano, op. 44, E♭ major: DUSSEK
Farewell symphony / Abschiedssymphonie -> Symphony, M. 45, F# minor: J.HAYDN
Farewell to pioneers <- A symphonic elegy: HARRIS
Farewell waltz / Valse de l'adieu -> Waltz, piano, op. 69, no. 1, A major: CHOPIN
Farewell, ye soft scenes <- Vauxhall songs: J.C.BACH
Farnesina -> Cupid and Psyche: HINDEMITH
Farruca -> El sombrero del tres picos (Danza del molinaro): FALLA
Faschingsschwank aus Wien <- Fantasiebilder: SCHUMANN
Fatal marriage, The -> Isabella: ARNE
Fatal marriage, The <- The innocent adultery: PURCELL
Fate symphony / Schicksalssinfonie -> Symphony, no. 5, op. 67, C minor: BEETHOVEN
Father Marquette -> Symphony, no. 12: HARRIS
Fausses apparences, Les <- L'amant jaloux: GRÉTRY
Faust <- Margarethe: GOUNOD
Faust fantasy -> Fantaisie brillante sur des motifs de l' opéra Faust, violin & orchestra: WIENIAWSKI
Faust overture -> Scenen aus Goethes Faust (Overture): SCHUMANN
Faust quartets -> Grosse Fuge, string quartet, op. 133, B♭ major; Quartet, strings, no. 15, op. 132, A minor; no. 16, op. 135, F major: BEETHOVEN
Faust sonata -> Sonata, piano, no. 1, op. 28, D major: RACHMANINOFF
Faux prodigue, Le -> La robe de dissention: RAMEAU
Faux-monnayeurs, Les -> Le serment: AUBER
Favore per favore -> Aldimiro: A.SCARLATTI
Favorite, La <- L'ange de Niside / Daila / Elda / Leonora: DONIZETTI
Favorito, Il -> Concerto, 3 violins & string orchestra, R. 277, E minor: VIVALDI
Fear not, o land <- Harvest anthem: ELGAR
Feast of Apollo, The -> Sonata, harpsichord, C major [c. 1789]: J.C.BACH
Fedra -> Ippolito: GLUCK
Feier der Auferstehung, Der / Easter cantata -> Lazarus: SCHUBERT
Feiger Gedanken -> Goethe-Lieder (Beherzigung): WOLF
Feldlager in Schlesien, Ein <- Vielka: MEYERBEER
Feldpartiten, H.II,46 <- St. Anthony chorale: J.HAYDN
Felszállott a páva / Peacock variations -> Variations on a Hungarian folksong: KODÁLY

Fenice sul rogo, La -> La morta di S. Giuseppe: PERGOLESI
Fenster, Die -> Arlecchino: BUSONI
Fernand Cortez <- La conquète du Mexique: SPONTINI
Festa degli indolenti, La -> Quattro invenzioni: MALIPIERO
Feste Burg ist unser Gott, Ein', S. 80 <- Reformation can-
tata: J.S.BACH
Festes de l'Himen et de l'Amour, Les <- Les dieux de l'Ég-
ypte: RAMEAU
Festes de l'Hymen, Les <- La roze: RAMEAU
Festes de Versailles, Les -> Grande divertissement royal:
LULLY
Festino cverture -> Symphony, M. 53, D major (1st movement):
J.HAYDN
Festiva laetis cantibus <- Motet de St. Anne: COUPERIN
Festival cantata, op. 30 -> Rejoice in the lamb: BRITTEN
Festival coronation march <- Solemn march for the coronation
of Alexander III / Coronation march: TCHAIKOVSKY
Festival mass / Slavonic mass -> Glagolitic mass: JANÁČEK
Festival mass / Graner Messe -> Missa solennis: LISZT
Festival sonatas / Church sonatas / Kirchensonaten / Epistle
sonata -> Sonata, organ & orchestra, K. 263, C major: K.
271e (278) C major; K. 317a (329) C major; Sonata, organ &
string orchestra, 41h (67) E♭ major; K. 41i (68) B♭ major;
K. 41k (69) D major; K. 124a (144) D major; K. 124b (145)
F major; K. 212, B♭ major; K. 241, G major; K. 241a (224)
F major; K. 241b (225) A major; K. 244, F major; K. 245, D
major; K. 271d (274) G major; K. 317c (328) C major; K.
336d (336) C major: MOZART
Festival valse comique / Covent Garden-Walzer -> Erinnerung
an Covent Garden: JOHANN STRAUSS
Festival-Quadrille <- Londoner-Quadrille: JOHANN STRAUSS
Festive cantata / Festkantate -> Preiset den Herrn: BRUCKNER
Festive march suite -> Suite, piano, op. 21, G major: SUK
Festive suite / Festliche Suite -> Suite, string orchestra,
A5, A major: TELEMANN
Festive symphony <- Triumphal symphony: SMETANA
Festkantate / Festive cantata -> Preiset den Herrn: BRUCKNER
Festliche Suite / Festive suite -> Suite, string orchestra,
A5, A major: TELEMANN
Fest-Polonaise, orchestra <- Kaiser-Wilhelm-Polonaise: JO-
HANN STRAUSS
Fête de la vertu, La -> La rosière républicaine: GRÉTRY
Fête pamilie, La -> La naissance d'Osiris: RAMEAU
Fêtes de Cythère, Les -> Les dieux rivaux: SPONTINI
Fêtes d'Hébé, Les <- Les talens lyriques: RAMEAU
Feuersbrunst, Die <- Das abgebrannte Haus: J.HAYDN
Feuersymphonie / Fire symphony -> Symphony, M. 59, A major:
J.HAYDN

Feuillets d'album -> Pièces brèves, piano: FAURÉ
Feuillets d'album, op. 19 (Les champs) <- Aubade: BERLIOZ
Feuillets d'album, op. 19 (Zaïde) <- Boléro: BERLIOZ
Fiddle fugue -> Prelude and fugue, organ, S. 539, D minor:
    J.S.BACH
Fidelio <- Leonore: BEETHOVEN
Fiery angel / Flaming angel -> Symphony, no. 3, op. 44, C
    minor: PROKOFIEV
Figaro quartet -> Quartet, strings, op. 6, no. 2, B♭ major:
    DANZI
Fighting for the people's new free world / A war son march
    -> They are there: IVES
Figlia dell' arciere, La -> Adelia: DONIZETTI
Figlio per azzardo, Il -> Il signor Bruschino: ROSSINI
Fille aux yeux d'émail, La -> Coppélia: DELIBES
Fille du bandit, La -> Marco Spada: AUBER
Filosofo di campagna, Il -> La pastorella, D. 513: SCHUBERT
Finalmusik -> Cassation, K. 63, G major; Serenade, K. 62a
    (100) D major; K. 167a (185) D major: MOZART
Findelkind, Das <- Unverhofft kommt oft: BENDA
Fingal's cave overture -> Die Hebriden: MENDELSSOHN
Finta frascatana, La -> La frascatana nobile: CIMAROSA
Finta frascatana, La / Il cioè -> Amor vuol sofferenze: LEO
Finte nontesse, Le <- Il matrimonio inaspettato / Le marquis
    de Tulipano: PAISIELLO
Finto pazzo, Il -> Lo pazzo apposto: LEO
Finto Stanislao, Il -> Il giorno di regno: VERDI
Fire symphony / Feuersymphonie -> Symphony, M. 59, A major:
    J.HAYDN
Fireman's parade on Main Street -> The gong on the hook and
    ladder: IVES
Fireworks music <- Music for the Royal fireworks / The Royal
    fireworks: HÄNDEL
First of May / May Day symphony -> Symphony, no. 3, op. 20:
    SHOSTAKOVICH
First of the few, The (Prelude and fugue) <- Spitfire pre-
    lude: WALTON
First waltzes, op. 9 / Erste Walzer -> Originaltänze, piano,
    D. 365: SCHUBERT
Fischer variations -> Variationen über ein Menuett von J.C.
    Fischer, piano, K. 189a (179): MOZART
Fitzwilliam sonatas -> Sonata, recorder & continuo, B. 156,
    1, B♭ major; B. 156, 2, D minor; B. 156, 3, D minor: HAN-
    DEL
Flaming angel / Fiery angel -> Symphony, no. 3, op. 44, C
    minor: PROKOFIEV
Fleecy clouds / Night vision -> Lieder ohne Worte, op. 53
    (No. 2): MENDELSSOHN

Fleurette <- Näherin und Trompeter: OFFENBACH
Fleurs enchantées, Les -> La guirlande: RAMEAU
Fliederrequiem / American requiem / A requiem for those we
love -> When lilacs last in the door-yard bloom'd: HINDE-
MITH
Flight, The -> Lieder ohne Worte, op. 53 (No. 6): MENDELS-
SOHN
Florentine duets / Duetti fiorentini -> Duets, violin & gui-
tar, op. 60: PAGANINI
Florentine song -> Songs, op. 38 (Pimpinella): TCHAIKOVSKY
Floridoro <- Moro per amore / Rodrigo: STRADELLA
Florizel and Perdita -> The sheep-shearing: ARNE
Flüchtling, Der, D. 67 <- Morgenfantasie: SCHUBERT
Flüchtling, Der, D. 402 <- Morgenfantasie: SCHUBERT
Folies d'Espagne, Les -> Variations on La folie d'Espagne,
harpsichord: C.P.E.BACH
Folk song / Volkslied / Triumphal chant -> Lieder ohne Wor-
te, op. 53 (No. 5): MENDELSSOHN
Folksong symphony -> Symphony, no. 4: HARRIS
Follia, La -> Sonata, violin & continuo, op. 12, no. 5, D
minor: CORELLI
Follia, La -> Concerto grosso [1736] no. 12, D minor: GEMINI-
ANI
Follia, La -> Sonata, violin & continuo, R. 63, D minor: VI-
VALDI
Fondation de Thèbes, Le -> Les amazones: MÉHUL
Fool's preferment, The <- The three Dukes of Dunstable: PUR-
CELL
Force of love, The -U Theodosius: ARNE
Force of love, The -> Theodosius: PURCELL
Forefathers' Day -> Holidays (Thanksgiving Day): IVES
Forellen-Quintett / Trout quintet -> Quintet, piano &
strings, D. 667, A major: SCHUBERT
Forest of prophetic sound, The -> Sosi: HOVANESS
Forest of the Amazon -> Green mansions (Selections): VILLA-
LOBOS
Forêt enchantée, La <- Harald: INDY
Forget-me-not polka -> Polka pomenka, piano, C major: DVOŘÁK
Forgotten <- After the battle / Left alone / Ballade: MUSORG-
SKY
Forqueray, La -> Pièces de clavecin, 3. livre, 17. ordre (La
superbe): COUPERIN
Forsaken maid's complaint, The -> Faithless, ungrateful:
HÄNDEL
Forsaken nymph, The <- Leander: HÄNDEL
Forza dell' amicizia, La <- Pilade ed Oreste: CALDARA
Forza del destino, La <- Don Alvaro: VERDI
Forza della fedeltà, La -> Pirro e Demetrio: A.SCARLATTI

Fosse Ardeatine, Le / The Ardeatine caves -> Symphony, no.
  9: SCHUMAN
Foundling hospital anthem -> Blessed are they that consider
  the poor: HÄNDEL
Four ages of man, The / De fyra tidsåldarna -> Symphony, no.
  3: ROSENBERG
Four seasons, The / Le quattro stagioni -> Il cimento dell'
  armonia e dell' inventione (No. 1-4): VIVALDI
Four temperaments, The <- Theme and variations, piano &
  string orchestra: HINDEMITH
Four temperaments, The -> Symphony, no. 2, op. 16: NIELSEN
Fra Diavolo <- L'hotellerie de Terracine: AUBER
Fräulein im Turme, Das <- Rosalia von Montanver: SCHUBERT
Fragments des modernes -> Télémaque: CAMPRA
Från havsbandet -> Symphony, no. 4, op. 39, C minor: ALFVÉN
Frascatana mobile, La <- La finta frascatana: CIMAROSA
Frei aber einsam -> Sonata, violin & piano [1853]: SCHUMANN
Freie Sonate -> Sonata, violoncello & piano, no. 4, op. 102,
  no. 1, C major: BEETHOVEN
Freigeisterei der Leidenschaft -> Der Kampf, D. 594: SCHU-
  BERT
Freiheits-Lieder-Walzer, orchestra <- Barrikaden-Lieder: JO-
  HANN STRAUSS
Freischützmesse -> Mass, no. 1, op. 75a, Eb major: WEBER
Fremdling, Der / Der Unglückliche -> Der Wanderer, D. 489:
  SCHUBERT
French suites -> Suite, harpsichord, S. 812, D minor; S.
  813, C minor; S. 814, B minor; S. 815, Eb major; S. 816, G
  major; S. 817, E major: J.S.BACH
Freunde von Salamanka, Die <- Die beiden Freunde von Sala-
  manka: SCHUBERT
Freundschaft und Wein -> Trinklied, D. 183: SCHUBERT
Freysinger sonata -> Sonata, piano, K. 284c (311) D major:
  MOZART
Fröhliche Werkstatt / Merry workshop -> Sonatina, wood-winds
  & brasses, no. 2, Eb major: R.STRAUSS
Frog he went a-courting, A <- Variations on an old English
  nursery song: HINDEMITH
Frog quartet / Froschquartett / Preussische Quartette /
  Prussian quartets -> Quartet, strings, no. 50, op. 50, no.
  6, D major: J.HAYDN
From an invalid's workshop / Aus dem Werkstatt eines Invali-
  den -> Sonatina, wood-winds & brasses, no. 1, F major: R.
  STRAUSS
From dusk till dawn <- Between twelve and three: BAX
From my life -> Quartet, strings, no. 1, E minor: SMETANA
From old note books -> Sonata, piano, no. 4, op. 29, C mi-
  nor: PROKOFIEV

From the Bavarian highlands (Selections; arr.) <- Bavarian
    dances: ELGAR
From the New World / New World symphony -> Symphony, no. 9,
    op. 95, E minor: DVOŘÁK
From the Salvation Army / A revival service -> Quartet,
    strings, no. 1: IVES
From the street / Z ulice / Sonata l.X.1905 -> Sonata, pi-
    ano, Eb minor: JANÁČEK
Froschquartett / Frog quartet / Preussische Quartette /
    Prussian quartets -> Quartet, strings, no. 50, op. 50, no.
    6, D major: J.HAYDN
Frühlingsgesang, D. 740 <- Frühlingslied: SCHUBERT
Frühlingskanate / Spring cantata -> Alles tönet, schallt und
    singt: TELEMANN
Frühlingsklänge -> Symphony, no. 8, op. 205, A major: RAFF
Frühlingslied / Spring song / Camberwell Green -> Lieder oh-
    ne Worte, op. 62 (No. 6): MENDELSSOHN
Frühlingslied -> Frühlingsgesang, D. 740; Mailied, D. 503:
    SCHUBERT
Frühlingsmorgen, Der -> Kantate zum Geburtstag des Sängers
    J.M. Vogl, D. 666: SCHUBERT
Frühlingsquartett / Spring quartet / Haydn quartets ->
    Quartet, strings, K. 387, G major: MOZART
Frühlings-Quintett / Spring quintet -> Quintet, strings, op.
    88, F major: BRAHMS
Frühlingssonate / Spring sonata -> Sonata, violin & piano,
    no. 5, op. 24, F major: BEETHOVEN
Frühlingssymphonie / Spring symphony -> Symphony, no. 4, op.
    60, Bb major: BEETHOVEN
Frühlingssymphonie / Spring symphony -> Symphony, no. 1, op.
    38, Bb major: SCHUMANN
Frühlingssymphonie / Spring symphony -> Symphony, A major,
    no. 4: STAMITZ
Fünf Wunden, Die -> Deutsche Kirchenlieder und liturgische
    Gesänge (Jesu Christe): LISZT
Für Elise -> Bagatelle, piano, K. 59, A minor: BEETHOVEN
Für kommende Zeiten <- Texten intuitiver Musik für kommende
    Zeiten: STOCKHAUSEN
Fuga del gatto, Il / The cat's fugue -> Sonata, harpsichord,
    K. 30 (L. 499) G minor: D.SCARLATTI
Fuga sopra il Magnificat -> Chorale prelude, S. 733: J.S.
    BACH
Fugue, organ, S. 577, G major <- Jig fugue: J.S.BACH
Fugue, organ, S. 579, B minor <- Corelli fugue: J.S.BACH
Fugue, organ, S. Anh. 90, C major <- Fanfare fugue: J.S.BACH
Funérailles de Phocion, Les <- Hommage à Poussin: MILHAUD
Funeral anthem -> The souls of the righteous: BOYCE
Funeral anthem <- Ode on the death of Queen Caroline: HÄNDEL

Funeral cantata / Trauer-Kantate -> Du aber, Daniel, gehe
hin: TELEMANN

Funeral march / Queen's funeral march, The -> March and canzona, Z. 860, F minor: PURCELL

Funeral march / Trauermarsch, op. 40 -> Grande marche, piano, 4 hands, D. 819, no. 5: SCHUBERT

Funeral march prelude -> Prelude, piano, op. 28, no. 20, C
minor: CHOPIN

Funeral march sonata / Trauermarsch-Sonate -> Sonata, piano,
no. 12, op. 26, A♭ major: BEETHOVEN

Funeral march sonata -> Sonata, piano, no. 2, op. 35, B♭ minor: CHOPIN

Funeral ode / Trauer-Ode -> Lass Fürstin, lass noch einen
Strahl, S. 198: J.S.BACH

Funeral song / Totengesang der Frauen und Mädchen -> Coronach, D. 836: SCHUBERT

Funeral symphony / Trauer-Symphonie -> Symphony, M. 44, E
minor: J.HAYDN

Furcht der Geliebten, D. 285 <- An Cidli: SCHUBERT

Fyra tidsåldarna, De / The four ages of man -> Symphony, no.
3: ROSENBERG

Gabrielle d'Estrées <- Les amours d'Henri IV: MÉHUL

Gaelic symphony -> Symphony, no. 3: COWELL

Gagaku / Impressions of court music -> Ongaku: COWELL

Gaillarde, La -> Suite, string orchestra, D13, D major: TELEMANN

Gaité, La -> Polonaise, violoncello & piano, op. 3, C major: CHOPIN

Gaité, La -> Rondo brillante, piano, op. 62, E♭ major: WEBER

Gaité parisienne -> Operas (Selections; arr.): OFFENBACH

Galante, La -> Introduction and Rondo, piano, op. 120: HUMMEL

Galante, La -> Suite, string orchestra, D5, D major: TELEMANN

Galilee -> Silhouette: BERNSTEIN

Galitzin quartets -> Quartet, strings, no. 12, op. 127, E♭
major; no. 13, op. 130, B♭ major; no. 15, op. 132, A minor: BEETHOVEN

Galliard, keyboard instrument, H. 19 <- Lord Salisbury's
galliard: GIBBONS

Galliard, keyboard instrument, H. 20 <- Lady Hatton's galliard: GIBBONS

Galliard, keyboard instrument, T. 42 <- Earl Stafford's
galliard: TOMKINS

Galliard, keyboard instrument, T. 44 <- Earl Stafford's
galliard: TOMKINS

Galliarda bray -> Pavan and galliard, virginal, MB 59: BYRD

Gallina, La <- Danse cubaine: GOTTSCHALK
Gamacho -> Die Hochzeit des Gamach: MENDELSSOHN
Game of chance -> Mora: HOVANESS
Gardellino, Il / Bullfinch concerto -> Concerto, flute, R.
    90, D major; Concerto, flute, R. 428, D major: VIVALDI
Gare d'amore e di politica, Le -> Berenice: A.SCARLATTI
Gare dell' amor paterno, Le <- L'oratio: STRADELLA
Gare generose, La <- Gli schiavi per amore: PAISIELLO
Gartenschlüssel, Der -> Camilla und Eugen: DANZI
Gassenhauer-Trio -> Trio, piano, clarinet & violoncello,
    op. 11, B♭ major: BEETHOVEN
Gastein symphony / Great C major symphony -> Symphony, D.
    944, C major: SCHUBERT
Gaukelspiel, Der -> Hokus-Pokus: DITTERSDORF
Geburtstag, Der / Birthday divertimento / Mann und Weib /
    Man and wife -> Divertimento, H.II,11, C major: J.HAYDN
Geburtshymne / Genesungs-Hymne / Des Tages Weihe -> Hymne
    zur Genesung des Herrn Ritter, D. 763: SCHUBERT
Geburtstags-Hymne / Am Namensfeste des Kaisers / Constitu-
    tionslied -> Am Geburtstage des Kaisers, D. 748: SCHUBERT
Geburtstagskantate /Birthday cantata / Jagdkantate / Hunt-
    ing cantata -> Was mir behagt, S. 208: J.S.BACH
Geburtstagslied -> Der Wintertag, D. 984: SCHUBERT
Gedankenflüchtling -> Gedankenflug-Walzer, orchestra: JO-
    HANN STRAUSS
Gedankenflug-Walzer, orchestra <- Gedankenflüchtling: JO-
    HANN STRAUSS
Gedemütigte Stolz, Der -> Der Fernengewinnst: DITTERSDORF
Gedenkblätter <- Memento: JOSEPH STRAUSS
Gedichte, op. 35 <- Kerner-Lieder: SCHUMANN
Gedichte, op. 35 (Wanderlust) <- Wanderlied: SCHUMANN
Gedichte, op. 90 <- Lenau-Lieder: SCHUMANN
Gedichte aus dem Buch der hängenden Gärten <- The book of
    the hanging gardens: SCHÖNBERG
Gedichte von Mathilde Wesendonk <- Wesendonk songs: WAGNER
Geharnischte Suite -> Suite, orchestra, no. 2, op. 34a:
    BUSONI
Geheime Anziehungskräfte -> Dynamiden: JOSEPH STRAUSS
Geheimnis, Das <- Liebe und Wahrheit: BEETHOVEN
Geheimnis, D. 491 <- An Franz Schubert: SCHUBERT
Gehen wir in Prater, K. 558 <- Prater canons: MOZART
Gehorsam / Gretchen gehorsam -> Refrainlieder (Die Unter-
    scheidung): SCHUBERT
Geistertrio / Ghost trio -> Trio, piano & strings, no. 4,
    op. 70, no. 1, D major: BEETHOVEN
Geistervariationen / Mit Gott -> Andante, piano, G major:
    SCHUMANN
Geistliche Concerte -> Kleine geistliche Concerte: SCHÜTZ

Geistliche Gesänge aus G.C. Schemellis Musikalischem Gesangbuch <- Geistliche Lieder: J.S.BACH

Geistliche Lieder -> Geistliche Gesänge aus G.C. Schemellis
Musikalischem Gesangbuch: J.S.BACH

Geistliche Vermählungsmusik / Sposalizio-Trauung -> Ave Maria, no. 3: LISZT

Gelebt, gestrebt, gelitten -> Symphony, no. 6, op. 189, D
minor: RAFF

Gelehrte Hufschmied, Der -> Il maniscalco: DITTERSDORF

Gellert-Lieder -> Lieder, op. 48: BEETHOVEN

Gelosa pazzia, La -> Orlando: A.SCARLATTI

Geloso andace, Il -> Gli amanti in cimento: SPONTINI

Generalprobe, Die / The dress rehearsal -> Il maestro di
cappella: CIMAROSA

Genesis -> In the beginning: COPLAND

Genesungs-Hymne / Geburtshymne / Des Tages Weihe -> Hymne
zur Genesung des Herrn Ritter, D. 763: SCHUBERT

Genesungs-Kantate / Die Erde und der Frühling -> Kantate zur
Feier der Genesung des Fräulein Irene von Kiesewetter:
SCHUBERT

Gensericus -> Sieg der Schönheit: TELEMANN

Gentle shepherds, you that know <- Elegy on the death of
John Playford / Pastoral elegy on the death of John Playford: PURCELL

Genug-Polka -> Dowolno: JOHANN STRAUSS

Genzinger sonata -> Sonata, piano, no. 49, Eb major: J.HAYDN

Georges Dandin -> Le grand divertissement royal de Versailles: LULLY

Géorgiennes, Les <- Die schönen Weiber von Georgien: OFFEN-
BACH

German mass / Deutsche Messe, D. 872, Bb major -> Mass, D.
872, Bb major: SCHUBERT

German requiem -> Musicalische Exequien: SCHÜTZ

German songs, op. 2 -> Lieder, op. 2: GRIEG

German songs, op. 4 -> Digte, op. 4: GRIEG

German suites -> Partita, harpsichord, S. 825, Bb major; S.
826, C minor; S. 827, A minor; S. 828, D major; S. 829, G
major; S. 830, E minor: J.S.BACH

German Te Deum / Deutsches Te Deum -> Herr, grosser Gott,
dich loben wir: M.HAYDN

German war song / Ein deutsches Kriegslied -> Ich möchte
wohl der Kaiser sein: MOZART

Gerusalemme / Jerusalem -> I Lombardi alla prima crociata:
VERDI

Gesänge, op. 83 <- Goethe-Lieder: BEETHOVEN

Gesänge aus Wilhelm Meister, D. 877, no. 2-4 <- Lied der
Mignon: SCHUBERT

Gesang an die Harmonie, D. 394 <- An die Harmonie: SCHUBERT

Gesang der Mönche -> Rasch tritt der Tod: BEETHOVEN
Gesang vom Reigen der Geister -> Indianisches Tagebuch, 2.
  Buch: BUSONI
Gesangszene -> Concerto, violin, no. 8, op. 47, A minor:
  SPOHR
Geschöpfe des Prometheus, Die <- Prometheus: BEETHOVEN
Geschwinde, geschwinde, ihr wirbelnden Winde, S. 201 <- Der
  Streit zwischen Phoebus und Pan / Phoebus und Pan / The
  contest between Phoebus and Pan: J.S.BACH
Geschwindmarsch -> Symphonia serena (Rather fast): HINDEMITH
Gesellenreise -> Die ihr einem neuen Grade: MOZART
Geselligkeit, Die, D. 609 <- Im traulichen Kreise / Lebens-
  lust: SCHUBERT
Gesellschaftsmenüette -> Minuets, orchestra, K. 10: BEETHO-
  VEN
Gettysburg symphony -> Symphony, no. 6: HARRIS
Ghost trio / Geistertrio -> Trio, piano & strings, no. 4,
  op. 70, no. 1, D major: BEETHOVEN
Gianni Schicchi <- Il trittico: PUCCINI
Giant, The -> Symphony, no. 5, C# minor: MAHLER
Giant fugue -> Chorale prelude, S. 680: J.S.BACH
Giant stags, The / The nine enchanted stags -> Cantata pro-
  fana: BARTÓK
Giardiniera fortunata, La / Biondolina -> L'amante comattuto
  dalle donne di punto: CIMAROSA
Giardino di amore, Il <- Venere e Adone: A.SCARLATTI
Gigue, piano, K. 574, G major <- Leipzig gigue: MOZART
Gijsbrecht van Aemstel (Overture) <- Heroic overture: BAD-
  INGS
Giorno di regno, Il <- Il finto Stanislao: VERDI
Giovane scaltra, La -> L'amor ingegnoso: PAISIELLO
Giovanna de Guzman -> Les vêpres siciliennes: VERDI
Giovedi Grasso, Il <- Il nuovo Pourceaugnac: DONIZETTI
Giuglielmo Wellingrode -> Stiffelio: VERDI
Giulietta ed Armidoro -> La stravaganze d'amore: CIMAROSA
Giunio Bruto <- La caduta de' Tarquini: CALDARA
Giunio Bruto <- La caduta de' Tarquini: A.SCARLATTI
Glagolitic mass <- Festival mass / Slavonic mass: JANÁČEK
Glinka variations / Variations on a theme by Glinka -> Va-
  riations, piano, op. 35: LIADOV
Glinka variations / Variations on a romance by Glinka -> Va-
  riations, oboe & band: RIMSKY-KORSAKOV
Gloria concertata -> Selva morale e spirituale (Gloria):
  MONTEVERDI
Glorreiche Augenblick, Der <- Preis der Tonkunst: BEETHOVEN
Glück der Freundschaft, Das <- Lebensglück / Vita felice:
  BEETHOVEN
Glückliches geheimnis / Ostwind -> Suleika, D. 720: SCHUBERT

Glückwunschkantate -> Vereinigte Zwietracht der wechselnden
    Saiten, S. 207; Lasst uns sorgen, lasst uns wachen, S.
    213: J.S.BACH
God of war -> Evocations (Houang Ti): BLOCH
Goethe-Lieder -> Gesänge, op. 83: BEETHOVEN
Goethe-Lieder (An die Türen) <- Harfenspieler-Lieder: WOLF
Goethe-Lieder (Beherzigung) <- Feiger Gedanken: WOLF
Goethe-Lieder (Wer nie sein Brot mit Tränen ass) <- Harfen-
    spieler-Lieder: WOLF
Goethe-Lieder (Wer sich der Einsamkeit ergibt) <- Harfen-
    spieler-Lieder: WOLF
Götter Griechenlands, Die, D. 677 <- Strophe von Schiller:
    SCHUBERT
Goldberg variations -> Aria mit 30 Veränderungen, harpsi-
    chord, S. 998: J.S.BACH
Golden age, The <- The age of gold: SHOSTAKOVICH
Golden journey to Samarkand, The -> Hassan: DELIUS
Golden rain, The / Goldregen / Pluie d'or -> Pluie de dia-
    mants: WALDTEUFEL
Golden sonata -> Sonatas of four parts (No. 9): PURCELL
Goldregen / The golden rain / Pluie d'or -> Pluie de dia-
    mants: WALDTEUFEL
Gong on the hook and ladder, The <- Fireman's parade on Main
    Street: IVES
Good luck at last -> The virtuous wife: PURCELL
Gortschakoff-Impromptu -> Impromptu, piano, F major: LISZT
Gothic symphony / Symphonie gothique -> Symphony, organ, no.
    9, op. 70: WIDOR
Gott, der Herr, ist Sonn' und Schild, S. 79 <- Reformation
    cantata: J.S.BACH
Gott erhalte Franz den Kaiser <- Kaiserhymne: J.HAYDN
Gott Mars <- Der Hauptmann von Bärenzahn: DITTERSDORF
Gott und die Bajadere, Der, D. 254 <- Indische Legende:
    SCHUBERT
Goûts réunis, Les (Concert, no. 8) <- Dans le goût théat-
    rale: COUPERIN
Goûts réunis, Les (Concert, no. 9) <- Ritratto dell' amore:
    COUPERIN
Goyescas [Piano work] <- Los majos enamorados: GRANADOS
Grab, Das, D. 569 <- Das stille Land: SCHUBERT
Grabgesang· -> Am Grabe: BRUCKNER
Grablied auf einen Soldaten, D. 454 <- Totenmarsch: SCHUBERT
Grabmusik, K. 35a (42) <- Passionskantate: MOZART
Gracieuse, La -> Ballade, piano, no. 2, op. 38, F major:
    CHOPIN
Graduale in festo SS. Innocentium die Dominica -> Laudate
    pueri Dominum: M.HAYDN
Graduale in festo SS. Innocentium extra Dominicam -> Effun-

derunt sanguinem sanctorum: M.HAYDN

Gradualia, book 1 (Turbarum voces in Passione Domini) <- St. John Passion / The Passion according to St. John: BYRD

Graduation ball -> Works (Selections; arr.): JOHANN STRAUSS

Gran partita -> Serenade, K. 361, B♭ major: MOZART

Granatbäume -> Les grenadiers: WALDTEUFEL

Grand divertissement royal de Versailles, Le <- Georges Dandin: LULLY

Grand duo, op. 140 -> Sonata, piano, 4 hands, D. 812, C major: SCHUBERT

Grand military septet / Military septet -> Septet, piano, winds & strings, op. 114, C major: HUMMEL

Grande Porte-diadème, Le -> Le carnaval: LULLY

Grand sonata -> Sonata, piano, op. 37, G major: TCHAIKOVSKY

Grand trio -> Trio, piano & strings, no. 3, C major: MARTINŮ

Gran trompeur de dames, Le -> Le prince troubadour: MÉHUL

Grande divertissement royale <- Les festes de Versailles: LULLY

Grande fantaisie sur des airs polonais, piano & orchestra, op. 13 <- Polish fantasy / Fantasy on Polish airs: CHOPIN

Grande marche, piano, 4 hands, D. 819, no. 5 <- Funeral march / Trauermarsch: SCHUBERT

Grande messe des morts -> Requiem: BERLIOZ

Grande ouverture -> Sonata, piano, 4 hands, C major: DUSSEK

Grande valse brillante / Invitation to the waltz -> Waltz, piano, op. 18, E♭ major: CHOPIN

Grandes études de Paganini, piano <- Paganini etudes: LISZT

Grandes études de Paganini, piano (No. 1) <- Tremolo etude: LISZT

Grandes études de Paganini, piano (No. 2) <- Octave etude: LISZT

Grandes études de Paganini, piano (No. 4) <- Arpeggio etude: LISZT

Graner Messe / Festival mass -> Missa solennis: LISZT

Grass grows green, The -> Songs, op. 54 (Spring): TCHAIKOVSKY

Gratulations-Kantate -> Die Zeit, die Tag und Jahre macht, S. 134a: J.S.BACH

Gratulations-Kantate -> Namensfeier für Franz Michael Vierthaler, D. 294: SCHUBERT

Gratulations-Menüett -> Minuet, orchestra, K. 3, E♭ major: BEETHOVEN

Grazer-Fantasie -> Fantasia, piano, D. 605A, C major: SCHUBERT

Great C major symphony / Gastein symphony -> Symphony, D. 944, C major: SCHUBERT

Great E minor prelude / Wedge fugue -> Prelude and fugue, organ, S. 548, E minor: J.S.BACH

Great elopement, The -> Operas (Selections; arr.): HÄNDEL

Great G minor symphony -> Symphony, K. 550, G minor: MOZART

Great mass / Grosse Messe -> Mass, no. 3, F minor: BRUCKNER

Great national symphony -> Symphony, no. 3, G major: CLEMEN-
TI

Great organ mass / Grosse Orgelmesse -> Mass, H.XXII,4, E♭
major: J.HAYDN

Great Russian Easter overture -> Russian Easter overture:
RIMSKY-KORSAKOV

Green mansions (Selections) <- Forest of the Amazon: VILLA-
LOBOS

Greenwich Village potpourri / Impressions of bohemian life
-> Potpourri, orchestra: SCHUMAN

Greetings overture <- Salutatory overture: MIASKOVSKY

Greisengesang, D. 778 <- Vom künftigen Alter: SCHUBERT

Grenadiermarsch -> March, wood-winds & horns, K. 29, B♭ major: BEETHOVEN

Grenadiers, Les <- Granatbäume: WALDTEUFEL

Gretchen gehorsam / Gehorsam -> Refrainlieder (Die Unterscheidung): SCHUBERT

Gretchen im Zwinger / Gretchen vor der Mater Dolorosa ->
Gretchens Bitte, D. 564: SCHUBERT

Gretchen vor der Mater Dolorosa / Gretchen im Zwinger ->
Gretchens Bitte, D. 564: SCHUBERT

Gretchens Bitte, D. 564 <- Gretchen im Zwinger / Gretchen
vor der Mater Dolorosa: SCHUBERT

Grétry concerto -> Concerto, violin, no. 5, op. 37, A minor:
VIEUXTEMPS

Grief / L'intimité / Tristesse -> Prelude, piano, op. 10,
no. 3, E major: CHOPIN

Grobschmied-Variationen / The harmonious blacksmith ->
Suite, harpsichord, 1st collection, no. 5, E major (Air):
HÄNDEL

Grönland -> Johann von Finland: HUMMEL

Grosse Fuge, string quartet, op. 133, B♭ major <- Faust
quartets: BEETHOVEN

Grosse Jugendmesse -> Mass, E♭ major: WEBER

Grosse Messe / Great mass -> Mass, no. 3, F minor: BRUCKNER

Grosse Orgelmesse / Great organ mass -> Mass, H.XXII,4, E♭
major: J.HAYDN

Grosser Festmarsch, orchestra <- American centennial march /
American festival march: WAGNER

Grosses deutsches Volk sind wir, Ein <- Kriegslied der Österreicher: BEETHOVEN

Grosso mogul -> Concerto, violin, R. 208, D major: VIVALDI

Grotesque fantasie <- The banjo: GOTTSCHALK

Guerra, A -> Symphony, no. 3: VILLA-LOBOS

Guggenheim sonata -> Sonata, piano, no. 2: THOMSON

Guglielmo d'Aquitania <- La conversione di S. Guglielmo d'

Aquitania: PERGOLESI
Guillaume se va chaufer <- Carmen gallicum Ludovici XI: DE-
  PRÈS
Guirlande, La <- Les fleurs enchantées: RAMEAU
Gustave III <- La bal masqué: AUBER
Gustav Vasa <- Minnesång: ALFVÉN
Gutsherr, Der <- Hannchen und Gürge: DITTERSDORF
Gypsy andante -> Ruralia hungarica (No. 2): DOHNÁNYI
Gypsy fantasy -> The stone flower (Suite): PROKOFIEV
Gypsy song -> Kosa: GLINKA
Gypsy trio / Zigeunertrio -> Trio, piano & strings, H.XV,25,
  G major: J.HAYDN

Habanera / Pièce en forme de habanera / Vocalise -> Voca-
  lise en forme de habanera: RAVEL
Händel variations -> Variationen über ein Thema von Händel,
  piano, op. 24: BRAHMS
Häusliche Krieg, Der -> Die Verschworenen: SCHUBERT
Haffner march -> March, orchestra, K. 249, D major: MOZART
Haffner serenade -> Serenade, K. 248b (250) D major: MOZART
Haffner symphony -> Symphony, K. 385, D major: MOZART
Haïkaï <- Japanese sketches / Esquisses japonaises: MESSIAEN
Hail to Stalin -> Toast to Stalin: PROKOFIEV
Halle sonatas -> Sonata, flute & continuo, B.8,1, A minor;
  B.8,2, B minor; B.8,3, B minor: HÄNDEL
Hallelujah concerto -> Concerto, organ, op. 7, no. 3, B♭ ma-
  jor: HÄNDEL
Hamburg symphonies -> Symphony, string orchestra, W. 182,
  no. 2, B♭ major; W. 182, no. 3, C major; W. 182, no. 4, A
  major; W. 182, no. 5, B minor: C.P.E.BACH
Hamburger Ebb und Fluht / Water music -> Suite, orchestra, C
  major: TELEMANN
Hammerklavier sonata -> Sonata, piano, no. 29, op. 106, B♭
  major: BEETHOVEN
Hannchen und Gürge -> Der Gutsherr: DITTERSDORF
Hannibal's overthrow -> Sophonisba: PURCELL
Hannover-Sinfonie -> Symphony, no. 8: BADINGS
Harald -> La forêt enchantée: INDY
Hardanger <- Homage to Grieg: BAX
Harfenquartett / Harp quartet -> Quartet, strings, no. 10,
  op. 74, E♭ major: BEETHOVEN
Harfenspieler-Lieder -> Goethe-Lieder (An die Türen); Goethe-
  Lieder (Wer sich der Einsamkeit ergibt); Goethe-Lieder (Wer
  nie sein Brot mit Tränen ass): WOLF
Hark how the trumpet <- The soldier's call to the war: HÄN-
  DEL
Harlekins Reigen -> Rondo arlecchino, orchestra: BUSONI
Harlequin incendiary <- Columbine Cameron: ARNE

Harmoniemesse / Wind-band mass -> Mass, H.XXII,14, B♭ major:
   J.HAYDN
Harmonies -> Étude, organ, no. 1: LIGETI
Harmonious blacksmith, The / Grobschmied-Variationen ->
   Suite, harpsichord, 1st collection, no. 5, E major (Air):
   HÄNDEL
Harmony music, winds (Andante con variazioni) <- Evesham
   andante: ELGAR
Harp etude / Aeolian harp etude / Shepherd boy etude -> E-
   tude, piano, op. 25, no. 1, A♭ major: CHOPIN
Harp of the poet, The -> Lieder ohne Worte, op. 38 (No. 3):
   MENDELSSOHN
Harp quartet / Harfenquartett -> Quartet, strings, no. 10,
   op. 74, E♭ major: BEETHOVEN
Harper's song, The / Song of the old man -> Old man's song:
   MUSORGSKY
Harvest anthem -> Fear not, O land: ELGAR
Harvest of sorrow -> Songs, op. 4 (The drooping corn): RACH-
   MANINOFF
Hassan <- The golden journey to Samarkand: DELIUS
Haugtussa <- The mountain maid: GRIEG
Hauptmann von Bärenzahn, Der -> Gott Mars: DITTERSDORF
Hauserl-Offertorium -> Inter natos mulierum, K. 74f (72):
   MOZART
Hausmusik / Vortragsstücke -> Suite, violin & piano, op.
   103a, A minor: REGER
Haute-Savoie -> In the mountains: BLOCH
Havana hornpipe <- Piper's dance: COWELL
Haydée <- Le secrèt: AUBER
Haydn quartets -> Quartet, strings, K. 387, G major; K. 417b,
   (421) D minor; K. 421b (428) E♭ major; K. 458, B♭ major;
   K. 464, A major; K. 465, C major: MOZART
Haydn variations -> Variationen über ein Thema von Haydn,
   orchestra: BRAHMS
Hears not my Phyllis <- Knotting son: PURCELL
Hebräische Melodien -> Lieder, op. 15: BUSONI
Hebrew overture -> Overture on Hebrew themes, piano, clari-
   net & string quartet: PROKOFIEV
Hebrew rhapsody -> Schelomo: BLOCH
Hebrew song <- Song of Solomon: MUSORGSKY
Hebriden, Die <- Fingal's cave overture: MENDELSSOHN
Heiligmesse / Missa Sancti Bernardi de Offida -> Mass, H.
   XXII,10, B♭ major: J.HAYDN
Heimatskinder -> Wiener Kinder-Walzer, orchestra: JOSEPH
   STRAUSS
Heimkehr aus die Fremde <- Son and stranger: MENDELSSOHN
Heimliches Lieben, D. 922 <- An Myrtill: SCHUBERT
Heimweh, no. 1 -> Lieder und Gesänge, op. 63 (Wie traulich

war): BRAHMS

Heimweh, no. 2 -> Lieder und Gesänge, op. 63 (O wüsst ich doch den Weg zurück): BRAHMS

Heimweh, no. 3 -> Lieder und Gesänge, op. 63 (Ich sah als Knabe): BRAHMS

Heine-Lieder -> Lieder, op. 4: PFITZNER

Heine-Lieder, 3. Heft <- Sternen-Lieder: CASTELNUOVO-TEDESCO

Hejre Kati -> Scènes de la csárda, no. 4, op. 32: HUBAY

Heldenquartett / Rasumovsky quartets -> Quartet, strings, no. 9, op. 59, no. 3, C major: BEETHOVEN

Helen of Troy -> La belle Hélène: OFFENBACH

Heliopolis -> Aus Heliopolis, D. 753; Aus Heliopolis, D. 754: SCHUBERT

Hen, The / La poule -> Symphony, M. 83, G minor: J.HAYDN

Henriette, L' -> Sonata, flute & continuo, op. 2, no. 1, G major: BLAVET

Henri IV en voyage -> Les béarnais: BOIELDIEU

Henry and Emma <- The nutbrown maid: ARNE

Herbstnacht -> Die Wehmut, D. 404: SCHUBERT

Herbstweisen -> Pomone: WALDTEUFEL

Hercule changé en dieu / Ovid symphonies / Metamorphosen-Sinfonien -> Symphony, K. 81: DITTERSDORF

Hercules auf dem Scheidewege / Glückwunschkantate -> Lasst uns sagen, lasst uns wachen, S. 213: J.S.BACH

Here beauty dwells -> Songs, op. 21 (How fair this spot): RACHMANINOFF

Here's that will challenge <- Bartholomew fair: PURCELL

Heroic lament -> Héroïde funèbre: LISZT

Heroic marches / Marches héroïques -> Musique héroïque: TE-LEMANN

Heroic overture -> Gijsbrecht van Aemstel (Overture): BAD-INGS

Heroic polonaise / Polonaise héroique -> Polonaise, piano, op. 53, A♭ major: CHOPIN

Heroic symphony / Eroica symphony -> Symphony, no. 3, op. 55, E♭ major: BEETHOVEN

Héroïde-elégiaque -> Rhapsodie hongroise, piano, no. 5: LISZT

Héroïde funèbre <- Heroic lament: LISZT

Herr denket an uns, Der, S. 196 <- Hochzeits-Kantate / Wedding cantata / Trauungskantate: J.S.BACH

Herr, grosser Gott, dich loben wir <- Deutsches Te Deum / German Te Deum: M.HAYDN

Herr Jesu Christ, dich zu uns wend / Leipzig chorales -> Chorale prelude, S. 655: J.S.BACH

Herrn Josef Spaun, D. 749 <- Sendschreiben / Epistel: SCHUBERT

Herz, das seinen Jesum lebend weiss, Ein, S. 134 <- Easter cantata / Osterkantate: J.S.BACH

Hesperusbahnen-Walzer, orchestra <- In Bauernkleidern: JOS-
EPH STRAUSS
Hexachord fantasia -> Fantasia, keyboard instrument, L. 5:
SWELINCK
Hexachord fantasias -> Ut mi re; Ut re mi: BYRD
Hexachord mass -> Missa, Ut, re, mi, fa sol, la: PALESTRINA
Hexameron variation -> Variation, piano, op. posth., E ma-
jor: CHOPIN
Hexenmenüett / Witches' minuet -> Quartet, strings, no. 77,
op. 76, no. 2, D minor (Minuet): J.HAYDN
Hier liegt vor Deiner Majestät <- Deutsches Hochamt: M.HAYDN
High on a throne of glittering ore <- Ode to Queen Mary:
PURCELL
Hija de Colquide, La <- Dark meadow: CHAVEZ
Hiketides -> Suppliantes d'Eschyle: XENAKIS
Hilarité -> Polacca brillante, piano, op. 72, E major: WEBER
Hilft's nicht so schadt's nicht -> Das rote Käppchen: DITTER-
SDORF
Hiller variations -> Variationen und Fuge über ein lustiges
Thema von J.A. Hiller, orchestra, op. 100: REGER
Himmel lacht, die Erde jubiliert, Der, S. 31 <- Osterkanta-
te / Easter cantata: J.S.BACH
Himmelfahrts-Oratorium / Ascension oratorio -> Lobet Gott in
seinen Reichen, S. 11: J.S.BACH
Hindemith variations -> Variations on a theme by Hindemith,
orchestra: WALTON
Hino academico -> Hino ao estudo: VILLA-LOBOS
Hino ao estudo <- Hino academico: VILLA-LOBOS
Hirtengedicht -> Eglogue: FRANCK
Histoire de Babar, le petit elephant <- Babar, the elephant:
POULENC
Historia des Leidens und Sterbens unsers Herrn Jesu Christi
nach dem Evangelisten St. Johannem / St. John Passion ->
Passion [St. John]: SCHÜTZ
Historia des Leidens und Sterbens unsers Herrn Jesu Christi
nach dem Evangelisten St. Mattheus / St. Matthew Passion
-> Passion [St. Matthew]: SCHÜTZ
Historia von der Auferstehung Jesu Christi <- The Easter sto-
ry / The resurrection: SCHÜTZ
Historia von der Geburt Jesu Christi <- The nativity /
Christmas oratorio / The Christmas story / Weihnachtshis-
torie: SCHÜTZ
Historische Sinfonie -> Symphony, no. 6, op. 116, G major:
SPOHR
History of Dioclesian, The -> The prophetess: ARNE
History of King Richard II, The <- The Sicilian usurper:
PURCELL
Hjertets melodier <- Danish songs, op. 5: GRIEG

Hochzeit des Gamacho, Die <- Gamacho: MENDELSSOHN
Hochzeits-Kantate / Wedding cantata -> Der Herr denket an uns,
    S. 196; Dem Gerechten muss das Licht, S. 195; Weichet nur,
    betrübte Schatten, S. 202; O holder Tag, S. 210; Vergnügte
    Pleissen Stadt, S. 216: J.S.BACH
Hoffmeister quartet -> Quartet, strings, K. 499, D major:
    MOZART
Hoffnung -> Arietten, op. 82 (Dimmi, ben mio): BEETHOVEN
Hoffnung des Wiedersehens, Die -> Süsse Hoffnung, wenn ich
    frage: TELEMANN
Hokus-Pokus <- Der Gaukelspiel: DITTERSDORF
Holberg suite -> Aus Holbergs Zeit: GRIEG
Holding your own -> Scherzo, string quartet: IVES
Holidays (Thanksgiving Day) <- Forefathers' Day: IVES
Holland Festival overture -> Overture [1954]: BADINGS
Holy sonnets of John Donne, The <- John Donne sonnets:
    BRITTEN
Holzhauer, Der <- Die drei Wünsche: BENDA
Homage to Grieg -> Hardanger: BAX
Homage to Ives -> Night thoughts: COPLAND
Homage to Paderewski -> Mazurka, piano: MARTINŮ
Homage to Paganini -> Capriccio diabolico, guitar: CASTEL-
    NUOVO-TEDESCO
Homenajes (A C.Debussy) <- In memory of Debussy / Le tom-
    beau de Claude Debussy: FALLA
Hommage à Chopin -> Stimmungen (Studie): GRIEG
Hommage à Jenny Lind -> Impromptu-caprice, piano, op. 7:
    RUBINSTEIN
Hommage à Paul Sacher -> Puneña, no. 2: GINASTERA
Hommage à Poussin -> Les funerailles de Phocion: MILHAUD
Hommage à Varèse -> Ceremonial: JOLIVET
Hommage à Watteau -> Les charmes de la vie: MILHAUD
Hommage au passé -> Quartet, strings, no. 7, op. 107, C ma-
    jor: GLAZUNOV
Hope -> Lieder ohne Worte, op. 38 (No. 4): MENDELSSOHN
Hornpipe concerto -> Concerto grosso, op. 6, no. 7, Bb ma-
    jor: HÄNDEL
Hornpipe quartet / Lark quartet / Lerchenquartett / Tost
    quartets -> Quartet, strings, no. 68, op. 64, no. 5, D ma-
    jor: J.HAYDN
Hornsignal-Sinfonie / Auf dem Anstand -> Symphony, M. 31, D
    major: J.HAYDN
Horrible festin, L' -> Vent du soir: OFFENBACH
Horseman quartet / Reiterquartett / Apponyi quartets ->
    Quartet, string, no. 75, op. 74, no. 3, G minor: J.HAYDN
Hortulanus / Örtagårsmästaren / The keeper of the garden ->
    Symphony, no. 5: ROSENBERG
Hos drottning Margareta <- Junker Nils sjunger till lutan:

ALFVÉN
Hotellerie de Terracine, L' -> Fra Diavolo: AUBER
Household music-> Preludes, orchestra: VAUGHAN WILLIAMS
Household suite -> La muse ménagère: MILHAUD
How to get your way with men without them finding out / The
    ladies' game -> Le astuzie femminili: CIMAROSA
Hugh Aston's ground <- Tregian's ground: BYRD
Hugh the drover <- Love in the stocks: VAUGHAN WILLIAMS
Huldigung, D. 240 <- Minnesang: SCHUBERT
Huldigungsmarsch <- March in homage of Ludwig II of Bavaria:
    WAGNER
Humanitã nelle fiere, L' <- Il Lucullo: A.SCARLATTI
Humble complaint of a sinner, The -> Where righteous doth
    say: DOWLAND
Humble sute of a sinner, The -> O Lord of whom I do depend:
    DOWLAND
Humboldt cantata -> Begrüssung: MENDELSSOHN
Hungaria, 1848 -> Ungaria-Kantate: LISZT
Hungarian Christmas song / Ungarisches Weihnachtslied ->
    Pastorale, piano: DOHNÁNYI
Hungarian fantasia -> Fantasie über ungarische Volksmelo-
    dien, piano & orchestra: LISZT
Hungarian folk dances -> Suite, piano, 4 hands, op. 18: WEI-
    NER
Hungarian folk melodies, string orchestra -> Divertimento,
    string orchestra, no. 2, op. 24: WEINER
Hungarian march / Marche hongroise -> Ungarischer Sturm-
    Marsch, piano: LISZT
Hungarian melodies / Ungarische Melodien -> Divertissement à
    l'hongroise, piano, 4 hands, D. 818, G minor: SCHUBERT
Hungarian rondo / Magyar rondo -> Régi magyar katonadalok:
    KODALY
Hunnenschlacht <- The Huns: LISZT
Huns, The -> Hunnenschlacht: LISZT
Hunt quartet / La chasse -> Quartet, strings, no. 1, op. 1,
    no. 1, Bb major: J.HAYDN
Hunt quartet / Jagd-Quartett / Haydn quartets -> Quartet,
    strings, K. 458, Bb major: MOZART
Hunt sonata / Jagd-Sonate -> Sonata, piano, no. 18, o. 31,
    no. 3, Eb major: BEETHOVEN
Hunt sonata / Jagd-Sonate / Trumpet sonata -> Sonata, piano,
    K. 576, D major: MOZART
Hunting cantata / Jagdkantate / Birthday cantata / Geburts-
    tagskantate -> Was mir behagt, S. 208: J.S.BACH
Hunting song -> The morning is charming: HÄNDEL
Hunting song / Jägerlied -> Lieder ohne Worte, op. 19 (No. 3):
    MENDELSSOHN
Hunt's up, The <- Peascod time: BYRD

Hunt's up, The -> Peascod time: GIBBONS
Hussites, Les <- Le siège de Naumbourg: MÉHUL
Huszt -> The ruins: KODÁLY
Hymn to Poland -> Largo, piano, op. post., E♭ major [arr.]:
  CHOPIN
Hymn to the Virgin / Ave Maria -> Ellens Gesang, D. 839:
  SCHUBERT
Hymne an den heiligen Geist -> Hymne an den Unendlichen, D.
  232: SCHUBERT
Hymne an den Unendlichen, D. 232 <- Hymne an den heiligen
  Geist: SCHUBERT
Hymne and die heilige Mutter Gottes / Salve Regina -> Deut-
  sches Salve Regina, D. 379, F major: SCHUBERT
Hymne des marins -> Crux: LISZT
Hymne européen, L' / The European anthem -> Symphony, no. 9,
  op. 125, D minor (Presto; arr.): BEETHOVEN
Hymne zur Genesung des Herrn Ritter, D. 763 <- Genesungs-
  Hymne / Geburtshymne / Des Tages Weihe: SCHUBERT
Hymnus Ambrosianus / Ambrosian hymn -> Symphony, no. 3: MIL-
  HAUD
Hyperboles -> Quartet, strings, no. 4: PEPIN

I got plenty o' nuttin' <- Banjo song: GERSHWIN
I hate music <- Kid songs: BERNSTEIN
I will always give thanks <- Club anthem: BLOW
Icelandic symphony -> Symphony, no. 16: COWELL
Ich bin in mir vegnügt, S. 204 <- Kantate von der Vergnüg-
  samkeit: J.S.BACH
Ich liebe dich -> Zärtliche Liebe: BEETHOVEN
Ich möchte wohl der Kaiser sein <- Ein deutsches Kriegslied
  / A German war song: MOZART
Ich schlief, da träumte mir / As I slept, I dreamt -> Vari-
  ationen uber die Arie Ich schlief, da träumte mir: QUANTZ
Ich will den Kreuzstab gerne tragen, S. 56 <- Kreuzstab-
  Kantate: J.S.BACH
Idalide -> La vergine del sole: CIMAROSA
Ideala -> Nereid: BAX
Idomeneo <- Ilia ed Idamante: MOZART
Idyll -> Once I passed through a populous city: DELIUS
If prayers and tears <- Song for our late Sovereign King
  Charles II: PURCELL
Ihr Auge -> Nimm einen Strahl der Sonne: LISZT
Ihr einem neuen Grade, Die <- Gesellenreise: MOZART
Ihr Tore zu Zion, S. 193 <- Ratswahlkantate: J.S.BACH
Il faut aimer -> La pastorelle: COUPERIN
Ilia ed Idamante -> Idomeneo: MOZART
Illibata Dei virgo nutrix <- Marian motes: DEPRÈS
Ilya Murometz -> Symphony, no. 3, op. 42, B minor: GLIÈRE

Im Dunkeln ist nicht gut munkeln <- Irrung über Irrung:
  DITTERSDORF
Im Hochgebirge / Heliopolis -> Aus Heliopolis, D. 754: SCHU-
  BERT
Im Jänner 1817, D. 876 <- Tiefes Leid: SCHUBERT
Im Kirchhof -> Auf einen Kirchhof, D. 151: SCHUBERT
Im Krapfenwaldl <- Im Pawlowsk-Walde: JOHANN STRAUSS
Im Pawlowsk-Walde -> Im Krapfenwaldl: JOHANN STRAUSS
Im Postzug -> Symphony, K. 48, Eb major: DITTERSDORF
Im Sommer -> Symphony, no. 9, op. 208, E minor: RAFF
Im traulichen Kreise / Lebenslust -> Die Geselligkeit, D.
  609: SCHUBERT
Im Walde -> Symphony, no. 3, op. 153, F major: RAFF
Im Walde, D. 708 <- Waldesnacht: SCHUBERT
Imbroglio scoperto, L' -> La mpeca scoperta: LEO
Imperial mass / Nelson mass / Missa in augustiis / Corona-
  tion mass -> Mass, H.XXII,11, D minor: J.HAYDN
Impériale, L' -> Symphony, M. 53, D major: J.HAYDN
Impressão rapida de todo o Brazil -> Nonet, mixed voices &
  orchestra: VILLA-LOBOS
Impressioni ungheresi -> Divertimento, no. 3, op. 25: WEINER
Impressions of bohemian life / Greenwich Village potpourri
  -> Potpourri, orchestra: SCHUMAN
Impressions of court music / Gagaku -> Ongaku: COWELL
Impressions of Paris / Paris suite -> Suite symphonique:
  IBERT
Impressions of Spain -> Cuentos de España: TURINA
Impromptu, piano, F major <- Gortschakoff-Impromptu: LISZT
Impromptu-caprice, piano, op. 7 <- Hommage à Jenny Lind:
  RUBINSTEIN
Improvisations, orchestra -> Variations, orchestra: BAX
Improvisations, piano, op. 20 <- Improvisations on Hungarian
  peasant songs: BARTÓK
Improvisations on Hungarian peasant songs -> Improvisations,
  piano, op. 20: BARTÓK
In Bauernkleidern -> Hesperusbahnen-Walzer, orchestra: JOSEPH
  STRAUSS
In candidum -> Symphony, no. 8: ROSENBERG
In dem Alpen -> Symphony, no. 7, op. 201, Bb major: RAFF
In festo nativitatis Domini -> Motets [1563] (Dies sanctifi-
  catus): PALESTRINA
In festo trium regium <- Epiphany cantata: BIBER
In fountain court -> Tryst: IRELAND
In London town -> Cockaigne: ELGAR
In Krohnen erlangte Glücks-Wechsel, Der -> Almira: HÄNDEL
In memoriam <- An Irish elegy: BAX
In memoriam Igor Stravinsky -> Canon for 3: CARTER
In memoriam of Gallén-Kallela -> Pieces, organ, op. 14: SI-

BELIUS
In memory of a great artist -> Trio, piano, & strings, op.
  50, A minor: TCHAIKOVSKY
In memory of Debussy / Le tombeau de Claude Debussy -> Home-
  najes (A C.Debussy): FALLA
In memory of Fauré -> Quartet, strings, no. 12: MILHAUD
In memory of Garcia Lorca -> Sonata, violin & piano, D mi-
  nor: POULENC
In memory of I.I. Sollertinsky -> Trio, piano & strings, no.
  2, op. 67, E minor: SHOSTAKOVICH
In praise of Shahn <- Canticle for orchestra: SCHUMAN
In the beginning <- Genesis: COPLAND
In the boat -> Songs, op. 60 (While I wait): GRIEG
In the mountains <- Haute-Savoie: BLOCH
In the south <- Alassio: ELGAR
In this shady blest retreat <- Vauxhall songs: J.C.BACH
In this summer night / O thou moonlit night -> Songs, op. 73
  (In this moonlight): TCHAIKOVSKY
Incantation -> Concerto, piano, no. 4: MARTINŮ
Incassum, Lesbia, rogas <- Elegy on the death of Queen Mary:
  PURCELL
Inconstant, The -> Der Weiberfreund, D. 271: SCHUBERT
Incoronazione di Dario, L' (Sinfonia) <- Symphony, string
  orchestra, C major: VIVALDI
Indian canzonetta / Indian lament -> Sonatina, violin & pi-
  ano, op. 100, G major (Larghetto): DVOŘÁK
Indian lament / Indian canzonetta -> Sonatina, violin & pi-
  ano, op. 100, G major (Larghetto): DVOŘÁK
Indian sketches -> Sketches based on Indian themes, string
  quartet: GRIFFES
Indian suite -> Suite, orchestra, no. 2, op. 48: MACDOWELL
Indianisches Tagebuch, 2. Buch <- Gesang vom Reigen der
  Geister: BUSONI
Indische Legende -> Der Gott und die Bajadere, D. 254: SCHU-
  BERT
Inextinguishable, The -> Symphony, no. 4, op. 29: NIELSEN
Infedeltà delusa, L' <- Deceit outwitted: J.HAYDN
Infedeltà fedele, L' -> Rosmene: A.SCARLATTI
Inganni felici, Gl' <- Agarista: A.SCARLATTI
Innate, The -> Adagio cantabile, string quartet, double bass
  & piano: IVES
Innocent adultery, The -> The fatal marriage: PURCELL
Innocenza difesa dall' inganno, L' -> La santa Genninda: A.
  SCARLATTI
Innocenza giustificata, La <- La vestale / Der Triumph der
  Unschuld: GLUCK
Inquietudine, L' -> Concerto, violin & string orchestra, R.
  234, D major: VIVALDI

Inter natos mulierum, K. 74f (72) <- Hauserl-Offertorium:
  MOZART
Intimate pages -> Quartet, strings, no. 2: JANÁČEK
Intimité, L / Grief / Tristesse -> Etude, piano, op. 10, no.
  3, E major: CHOPIN
Introduction and Allegro, piano & orchestra -> Concert-All-
  egro mit Introduction, piano & orchestra, op. 134: SCHU-
  MANN
Introduction and Rondo, piano, op. 16, E major <- Rondo é-
  légante: CHOPIN
Introduction and Rondo, piano, op. 120 -> La galante: HUM-
  MEL
Introduction et polonaise brillante, violoncello & piano,
  op. 3, C major <- Polonaise brillante: CHOPIN
Introduction et variations sur un thème original, flute &
  piano, D. 802, E minor <- Trockne Blumen-Variationen /
  Dried flowers variations: SCHUBERT
Introduction und Allegro appassionato, piano & orchestra,
  op. 92 <- Konzertstuck, op. 92: SCHUMANN
Introduzione e variazioni sul tema Nel cor più non mi sento
  <- Sonata appassionata con variazioni: PAGANINI
Introitus <- T.S. Eliot in memoriam: STRAVINSKY
Inverno, L' / Winter / Concerto, op. 8, no. 4, F minor / The
  four seasons / Le quattro stagioni -> Il cimento dell'
  armonia e dell' inventione (No. 4): VIVALDI
Invitation to the waltz / Grande valse brillante -> Waltz,
  piano, op. 18, E♭ major: CHOPIN
Invocation, L' -> Sonata, piano, op. 77, F minor: DUSSEK
Invocation -> Songs, op. 27 (To sleep): TCHAIKOVSKY
Io languisco <- Carlo cantata: HÄNDEL
Io ti lascio, e questo addio <- Ombra felice: MOZART
Ippolito <- Fedra: GLUCK
Irato, L' <- L'emporté: MÉHUL
Irdisches und Göttliches im Menschenleben / Double symphony
  -> Symphony, no. 7, op. 121: SPOHR
Irene -> La reine de Shaba: GOUNOD
Irewee's shoonthree / The birth of Manaunaun -> Manaunaun's
  birthing: COWELL
Irish elegy, An -> In memoriam: BAX
Irish legends -> Tales of our countryside: COWELL
Irish tone poem, An / The pleasant plain -> Moy Mell: BAX
Irish waltz -> Three-quarter blues: GERSHWIN
Irlande -> Mélodies, op. 2: BERLIOZ
Irrfahrten der Wahrheit, Die -> Il Re Cervo: HENZE
Irrung über Irrung -> Im Dunkeln ist nicht gut munkeln:
  DITTERSDORF
Isabella <- The fatal marriage: ARNE
Isabelle et Gertrude <- Les sylphes supposées: GRÉTRY

Isaiah's prophecy <- Christmas oratorio: CRESTON
Islamey <- Fantaisie orientale / Oriental fantasy: BALAKIREV
Island sequence, An -> Sarnia: IRELAND
Isle de Merlin, L' <- Le monde renversé: GLUCK
Isola di Circe, L' <- Il Telemacco: GLUCK
Israel -> Mi chomocho: HARRIS
Italian concerto / Italienisches Konzert -> Concerto nach
    italienischen Gusto, harpsichord unacc., S. 971, F major:
    J.S.BACH
Italian concerto / Concerto italiano -> Concerto, violin, no.
    1: CASTELNUOVO-TEDESCO
Italian overture -> Symphony, K. 318, G major: MOZART
Italian overtures -> Overture, D. 590, D major; Overture, D.
    591, C major: SCHUBERT
Italian quartets -> Quartet, strings, K. 73f (80) G major;
    K. 134a (155) D major; K. 134b (156) G major; K. 157, C ma-
    jor; K. 158, F major; K. 159, B♭ major; K. 159a (160) E♭
    major: MOZART
Italian symphony / Symphonie italienne -> Symphony, no. 1:
    INDY
Italian symphony -> Symphony, no. 4, op. 90, A major: MEN-
    DELSSOHN
Italienische Liebeslieder -> Arietten, op. 82: BEETHOVEN
Italienisches Konzert / Italian concerto -> Concerto nach
    italienischen Gusto, harpsichord unacc., S. 971, F major:
    J.S.BACH
Italy -> Années de pèlerinage, 2. année: LISZT
Iubilum <- Celebration sinfonica: GINASTERA
Ivan Susanin -> A life for the czar: GLINKA
Izi <- Amerindian legend: VILLA-LOBOS

Jabuka <- Das Apfelfest: JOHANN STRAUSS
Jägerlied / Hunting song -> Lieder ohne Worte, op. 19 (No. 3):
    MENDELSSOHN
Jagdchor -> Jagdlied, D. 521: SCHUBERT
Jagdkantate / Hunting cantata / Birthday cantata / Geburts-
    tagskantate -> Was mir behagt, S. 208: J.S.BACH
Jagdlied, D. 532 <- Jagdchor: SCHUBERT
Jagd-Quartett / Hunt quartet / Haydn quartets -> Quartet,
    strings, K. 458, B♭ major: MOZART
Jagd-Sonate / Hunt sonata -> Sonata, piano, no. 18, op. 31,
    no. 3, E♭ major: BEETHOVEN
Jagd-Sonate / Hunt sonata / Trumpet sonata -> Sonata, piano,
    K. 576, D major: MOZART
Jahreszeiten, Die / The seasons -> Symphony, no. 9, op. 143:
    SPOHR
Jahrmarkt, Der -> Der Dorfjahrmarkt: BENDA
Japanese sketches / Esquisses japonaises -> Haïkaï: MESSIAEN

Jasbo Brown blues -> Piano playin' Jazzbo Brown: GERSHWIN
Jason qui enlève la toison d'or / Metamorphosen-Sinfonien /
  Ovid symphonies -> Symphony, K. 79: DITTERSDORF
Jazz sonata -> Sonata, piano, no. 4: ANTHEIL
Je suis déshéritée -> Missa sine nomine: PALESTRINA
Je suis povene de leesse -> Qui latuit in virgine: DUFAY
Je te veux <- Valse chantée: SATIE
Jean s'en alla comme il était venu <- Epitaphe d'un paress-
  eux: COUPERIN
Jena symphony: BEETHOVEN -> Symphony, C major [ca. 1822]:
  FRIEDRICH WITT
Jeremiah <- Symphony, no. 1: BERNSTEIN
Jerusalem / Gerusalemme -> I Lombardi alla prima crociata:
  VERDI
Jesus Christus, unser Heiland / Leipzig chorales -> Chorale
  prelude, S. 665; Chorale prelude, S. 666: J.S.BACH
Jesus Christus unser Heiland, D. 168A <- Osterlied: SCHUBERT
Jesus Navin <- Joshua: MUSORGSKY
Jeu de Robin et Marion, Le <- Robin et Marion: ADAM DE LA
  HALLE
Jeunehomme concerto -> Concerto, piano, K. 271, E♭ major:
  MOZART
Jeux <- Poème dansé: DEBUSSY
Jeux d'enfants (Berceuse) <- La poupée / The doll: BIZET
Jeux d'enfants (Galop) <- Le bal / The ball: BIZET
Jeux d'enfants (Impromptu) <- La toupie / The spinning top:
  BIZET
Jeux d'enfants (Marche) <- Trompette et tambour / Trumpet
  and drum: BIZET
Jeux olympiques, Les -> Sonata, violin & harpsichord, op. 25,
  no. 5, D major: CORRETTE
Jig fugue -> Fugue, organ, S. 577, G major: J.S.BACH
Johann von Finnland <- Grönland: HUMMEL
Johannis uppenbarelse / The revelation of St. John -> Sym-
  phony, no. 4: ROSENBERG
John Donne sonnets -> The holy sonnets of John Donne: BRITTEN
Joke, The / Der Scherz / Russian quartets / Jungfern-Quar-
  tette / Maiden quartets -> Quartet, strings, no. 39, op.
  33, no. 2, E♭ major: J.HAYDN
Jolie fille de Perth, La (Selections) <- Scènes bohémiennes:
  BIZET
Josef Kajetán Tyl (Overture) <- My country: DVOŘÁK
Joshua -> Jesus Navin: MUSORGSKY
Jota aragonesa, La <- Caprice espagnol: GOTTSCHALK
Jota aragonesa, orchestra <- Spanish overture, no. 1 / Cap-
  riccio brillante: GLINKA
Jouer avec le feu -> Zanetta: AUBER
Journey of the magi <- Canticle IV: BRITTEN

Joyeuse marche, orchestra <- Marche française: CHABRIER
Joyous peasant, The / Kinderstück -> Lieder ohne Worte, op.
  102 (No. 5): MENDELSSOHN
Joyous symphony -> Symphony, no. 5: ANTHEIL
Jubelmesse -> Mass, no. 2, op. 76, G major: WEBER
Jucunda vox ecclesiae <- Motet de St. Augustin: COUPERIN
Judicium extremum -> Extremum Dei judicium: CARISSIMI
Julie <- Le roi de la paix: SPONTINI
Juliette <- The key to dreams: MARTINŮ
Jumping frog, The -> Take-offs, piano (Rough and ready et
  al): IVES
Junge Lieder, no. 1 -> Lieder und Gesänge, op. 63 (Meine
  Liebe ist grün): BRAHMS
Junge Lieder, no. 2 -> Lieder und Gesänge, op. 63 (Wenn um
  den Hollunder): BRAHMS
Jungfernquartette / Maiden quartets / Russian quartets ->
  Quartet, strings, no. 38, op. 33, no. 1, B minor; no. 39,
  op. 33, no. 2, Eb major; no. 40, op. 33, no. 3, C major;
  no. 41, op. 33, no. 4, Bb major; no. 42, op. 33, no. 5, G
  major; no. 43, op. 33, no. 6, D major: J.HAYDN
Junker Nils sjunger till lutan -> Hos drottning Margareta:
  ALFVÉN
Junon jalouse -> Platée: RAMEAU
Jupiter symphony -> Symphony, M. 13, D major: J.HAYDN
Jupiter symphony -> Symphony, K. 551, C major: MOZART
Jupiters Reise auf die Erde -> Philemon und Baucis: J.HAYDN
Juvenile quartet -> Quartet, strings, D minor: SUK

K. Darcies galliard -> Queene Elizabeth, her galliard:
  DOWLAND
Kaddish <- Symphony, no. 3: BERNSTEIN
Kären <- Little Karen: IVES
Kaffee-Kantate / Coffee cantata -> Schweigt stille, plaudert
  nicht, S. 211: J.S.BACH
Kaffeklatsch, Der -> Stücke, musical clock, H.XIX (No. 6):
  J.HAYDN
Kafka-Lieder -> Lieder nach Worten von Franz Kafka: KŘENEK
Kaiserhymne -> Gott erhalte Franz den Kaiser: J.HAYDN
Kaiserquartett / Emperor quartet / Erdödy quartets -> Quar-
  tet, strings, no. 78, op. 76, no. 3, C major: J.HAYDN
Kaiser-Wilhelm-Polonaise -> Fest-Polonaise, orchestra: JO-
  HANN STRAUSS
Kaiserstadt-Polka -> S' gibt nur a Kaiserstadt: JOHANN
  STRAUSS
Kakadu-Quadrille <- Vert-vert: JOSEPH STRAUSS
Kakadu variations -> Variationen über Ich bin der Schneider
  Kakadu, piano trio, op. 121a: BEETHOVEN
Kammer-Fantasie über Carmen / Chamber fantasy on Carmen /

Sonatina super Carmen -> Sonatina, piano, no. 6: BUSONI
Kampf, Der, D. 594 <- Freigeisterei der Leidenschaft: SCHU-
BERT
Kanarienvogel, Der / The canary -> Deutsche Tanze, orchestra,
K. 600 (No. 5): MOZART
Kanarienvogel-Kantate / Canary cantata -> Cantate oder Trau-
er-Music eines kunsterfahrenen Canarien-Vogels: TELEMANN
Kantat vid Reformationsfesten i Uppsala <- Reformationskan-
taten: ALFVÉN
Kantat vid Svenska Röda korsets högtidsammankomst <- Röda
kors-kantaten: ALFVÉN
Kantat vid Sveriges Rigsdags 500-års minnesfest <- Rigsdags-
kantaten: ALFVÉN
Kantat vid Uppsala universitets 450-ars-jubileum <- Univer-
sitetskantaten: ALFVÉN
Kantate von der Vergnügsamkeit -> Ich bin in mir vergnügt,
S. 204: J.S.BACH
Kantate zum Geburtstag des Sängers J.M. Vogl, D. 666 <- Der
Frühlingsmorgen: SCHUBERT
Kantate zum Geburtstag des Prof. Watteroth -> Prometheus-
Kantate, D. 451: SCHUBERT
Kantate zur Feier der Genesung des Fräulein Irene von Kiese-
wetter, D. 936 <- Die Erde und der Frühling / Genesungs-
Kantate: SCHUBERT
Karelia's fate -> Patriotic march: SIBELIUS
Karnevalslied -> Tout n'est qu'images fugitives: WAGNER
Katerina Ismailova -> Lady Macbeth of Mstensk: SHOSTAKOVICH
Katherinentänze -> Minuets, orchestra, H.IX,11: J.HAYDN
Keats settings -> Choral settings of poems by John Keats:
CASTELNUOVO-TEDESCO
Keeper of the garden, The / Örtagårmästaren / Hortulanus ->
Symphony, no. 5: ROSENBERG
Kegelstatt trio -> Trio, piano, clarinet & viola, K. 498, Eb
major: MOZART
Keltic sonata -> Sonata, piano, no. 4, op. 59: MACDOWELL
Kennst du das Land -> Gesänge, op. 75 (Mignon): BEETHOVEN
Kentuckiana <- Divertissement sur 20 airs de Kentucky: MIL-
HAUD
Kentucky concerto <- Louisville concerto: LUENING
Kerner-Lieder -> Gedichte, op. 35: SCHUMANN
Key to dreams, The -> Juliette: MARTINU
Khaldis <- Concerto, piano, 4 trumpets & percussion: HOVA-
NESS
Khoro, violin & piano <- Fantasy on a Bulgarian dance theme,
op. 18: VLADIGEROV
Kid songs -> I hate music: BERNSTEIN
Kinder concerto -> Concerto, piano, K. 456, Bb major: MOZART
Kinderball -> Ball-Scenen, op. 109: SCHUMANN

Kindermarsch / Children's march -> March, piano, 4 hands, D.
  928, G major: SCHUBERT
Kindersonate -> Sonaten fur die Jugend, piano, op. 118 (No.
  1): SCHUMANN
Kindersinfonie / Toy symphony / Sinfonia Berchtolsgadensis:
  J.HAYDN -> Cassation, 2 horns, string & toy instruments,
  C major (Selections): LEOPOLD MOZART
Kinderstück / The joyous peasant -> Lieder ohne Worte, op.
  102 (No. 5): MENDELSSOHN
King Arthur <- The British worthy: ARNE
King James II suite -> Why, why are all the muses mute? (Se-
  lections) : PURCELL
King Kojata <- Tamara: BAX
King of Denmark's galliard, The <- The battle galliard: DOW-
  LAND
King of Prussia quartets / Preussische Quartette / Prussian
  quartets -> Quartet, strings, K. 575, D major; K. 589, Bb
  major; K. 590, F major: MOZART
King shall rejoice, The <- Wedding anthem: BOYCE
King's jewel, The -> Alman, keyboard instrument, H. 36: GIB-
  BONS
Kirchensonaten / Church sonatas / Epistle sonatas / Festival
  sonatas -> Sonata, organ & orchestra, K. 263, C major; K.
  271e (278) C major; K. 317a (329) C major; Sonata, organ &
  string orchestra, K. 41h (67) Eb major; K. 41i '68) Bb major; K. 41k (69) D major; K. 124a (144) D major; K. 124b
  (145) F major; K. 212, Bb major; K. 241, G major; K. 241a
  (224) F major; K. 241b (225) A major; K. 244, F major: K.
  245, D major; K. 271d (274) G major; K. 317c (328) C ma-
  jor; K. 336d (336) C major: MOZART
Kirgiz suite, violin & piano <- Suite, violin & piano, op.
  73: HOVANESS
Kismet -> Quartet, strings, no. 2, D major: BORODIN
Klänge aus Mähren -> Moravian duets, op. 32: DVOŘÁK
Klärchen-Lieder -> Egmont (Die Trommel); Egmont (Freudvoll
  und Leidvoll): BEETHOVEN
Klärchens Lied, D. 210 <- Die Liebe: SCHUBERT
Klage -> Der Leidende, D. 432: SCHUBERT
Klagendes Lied / Elegie -> Lieder ohne Worte, op. 85 (No. 4):
  MENDELSSOHN
Klavierstimmer, Der -> Wiener Frauen: LEHÁR
Klavierstucke, op. 76 <- Capricci and Intermezzi, op. 76:
  BRAHMS
Kleine Blasmusik / Little wind music -> Bagatelles, piano,
  4 hands [arr.]: KŘENEK
Kleine Dreigroschenmusik -> Die Dreigroschenoper (Suite):
  WEILL
Kleine Freimaurer-Kantate, Eine / A little freemason canta-

ta -> Laut verkunde unsre Freude, K. 623: MOZART
Kleine geistliche Concerte <- Geistliche Concerte: SCHÜTZ
Kleine geistliche Concerte (Sei gegrüsset, Maria) <- Annun-
   ciation cantata: SCHÜTZ
Kleine Hausmusik -> Suite, violin & piano, op. 103a, A minor
   (Selections; arr.): REGER
Kleine Kantate / Little cantata -> Un lieto brindisi: BEET-
   HOVEN
Kleine Magnificat / Little Magnificat -> Magnificat, S. Anh.
   21, A minor: J.S.BACH
Kleine Nachtmusik, Eine <- Serenade, K. 525, G major: MOZART
Kleine Orgelmesse / Little organ mass / Missa brevis Sancti
   Joanni de Deo -> Mass, H.XXII,7, B♭ major: J.HAYDN
Kleine Symphonie / Little symphony -> Symphony, op. 44, G
   major: PFITZNER
Kling leise, mein Lied <- Ständchen / Serenade: LISZT
Knotting song -> Hears not my Phyllis: PURCELL
Koke no niwa <- Moss garden / A magic garden: HOVANESS
Kolysanka -> La berceuse d'Aïtacho Enia: SZYMANOWSKI
Komisches musikalisches Sendschreiben <- Brief an Danzi: WE-
   BER
Komm, Gott Schöpfer, heiliger Geist / Leipzig chorales ->
   Chorale prelude, S. 667: J.S.BACH
Komm heiliger Geist, Herre Gott / Leipzig chorales -> Cho-
   rale prelude, S. 651; Chorale prelude, S. 652: J.S.BACH
Komm, lieber Mai <- Sehnsucht nach dem Frühlinge: MOZART
Kommet her, ihr frechen Sünder <- Passionslied: MOZART
Kommst du nun, Jesu / Schübler chorales -> Chorale prelude,
   S. 650: J.S.BACH
Komplimentierungs-Quartett / Compliment quartet -> Quartet,
   strings, no. 2, op. 18, no. 2, G major: BEETHOVEN
Konstitutionslied -> Am Geburtstage des Kaisers, D. 748:
   SCHUBERT
Kontertänze -> Ecossaisen, piano: WEBER
Kontretanz, K. 534 <- Das Donnerwetter / The thunderstorm:
   MOZART
Kontretanz, K. 535 <- La bataille / Die Belagerung Belgrads
   / The siege of Belgrade: MOZART
Kontretanz, K. 587 <- Der Sieg vom Helden Coburg / The vic-
   tory of the hero of Coburg: MOZART
Konzertsolo, piano <- Concerto pathétique: LISZT
Konzertstück, op. 92 -> Introduction und Allegro appassiona-
   to, piano & orchestra, op. 92: SCHUMANN
Kosa <- Gypsy song: GLINKA
Kreutzer quartet -> Quartet, strings, no. 1: JANÁČEK
Kreutzer sonata -> Sonata, violin & piano, no. 9, op. 47, A
   major: BEETHOVEN
Kreuzstab-Kantate -> Ich will den Kreuzstab gerne tragen, S.

56: J.S.BACH
Kriegsgöttin, Die -> Bellona-Polka, orchestra: JOSEPH STRAUSS
Kriegslied der Österreicher -> Ein grosses deutsches Volk
    sind wir: BEETHOVEN
Krönungskonzert / Coronation concerto -> Concerto, piano, K.
    537, C major: MOZART
Krönungsmesse / Coronation mass -> Mass, K. 317, C major:
    MOZART
Kujawiak <- Mazurka, violin & piano, op. 3, A minor: WIENI-
    AWSKI
Kulavy / Prague mazurka -> Mazurka, piano, op. posth., G ma-
    jor: CHOPIN
Kurfürstensonaten -> Sonata, piano, K. 47, no. 1, E♭ major;
    K. 47, no. 2, F minor; K. 47, no. 3, D major: BEETHOVEN

Laberinto armonico, Il / The labyrinth -> L'arte del vio-
    lino (Concerto, no. 12, D major (Capriccio)): LOCATELLI
Labyrinth, The / Il laberinto armonico -> L'arte del violi-
    no (Concerto, no. 12, D major (Capriccio)): LOCATELLI
Lach-Polka -> Patti-Polka, orchestra: JOSEPH STRAUSS
Lachrimae <- Seven tears: DOWLAND
Ladies' game, The / How to get your way with men without
    them finding out -> Le astuzie femminili: CIMAROSA
Lady Hatton's galliard -> Galliard, keyboard instrument, H.
    20: GIBBONS
Lady Macbeth of Mstensk <- Katerina Ismailova: SHOSTAKOVICH
Ländler, violin, D. 374 <- Wildbacher Landler: SCHUBERT
Ländlerische Tänze -> Tänze, 2 violins & double bass, K. 15:
    BEETHOVEN
Ländliche Hochzeit / Rustic wedding symphony -> Symphony, op.
    26, E♭ major: GOLDMARK
Laetantur coeli <- Motet de St. Barthelémy: COUPERIN
Lager-Szene -> Marches, piano, op. 76: SCHUMANN
Lagrima, Una -> Preghiera: DONIZETTI
Lake of Van sonata, piano <- Sonata, piano, op. 175: HOVA-
    NESS
Lambacher-Sinfonie -> Symphony, K. 42a (76) F major: MOZART
Lament for string orchestra -> Serious song, string orches-
    tra: FINE
Lamentatio sanctae matris ecclesiae Constantinopolitanae <-
    O tres piteulx: DUFAY
Lamentation of a sinner, The -> O Lord, turn not away thy
    face: DOWLAND
Lamentatione / Weihnachtssymphonie / Christmas symphony ->
    Symphony, M. 26, D minor: J.HAYDN
Lamentationes Jeremiae prophetae -> Threni: STRAVINSKY
Lamentations of Job, The -> Sacrae lectiones novem ex prophet
    Job: LASSUS

Lamento, Il -> Etudes de concert, piano (No. 1): LISZT
Lamento d'Arianna [Aria] <- L'Arianna: MONTEVERDI
Lancaster symphony -> Symphony, no. 17: COWELL
Lancione, La -> Arie musicali, 1. libro (Begli occhi io non
   provo): FRESCOBALDI
Land of hope and glory -> Pomp and circumstance, no. 1 (Lar-
   gamente): ELGAR
Landende Orest, Der -> Orest auf Tauris, D. 548: SCHUBERT
Landsknechtständchen -> Libro de villanelle, moresche et al-
   tre canzoni (Matona mia cara): LASSUS
Landwehrmarsch / York'scher Marsch -> March, band, K. 18, F
   major: BEETHOVEN
Langues de feu, Les -> Messe de la Pentecôte (Entrée): MES-
   SIAEN
Largo, piano, op. posth., Eb major [arr.] <- Hymn to Poland:
   CHOPIN
Largo quartet / Erdödy quartets -> Quartet, strings, no. 80,
   op. 76, no. 5, D major: J.HAYDN
Lark quartet / Lerchenquartett / Hornpipe quartet / Tost
   quartets -> Quartet, strings, no. 68, op. 64, no. 5, D ma-
   jor: J.HAYDN
Lass Fürstin, lass noch einen strahl, S. 198 <- Funeral ode /
   Trauer-Ode: J.S.BACH
Lass of Richmond Hill, The -> Sonata, harp, F major: DUSSEK
Lasst uns sorgen, lasst uns wachen, S. 213 <- Hercules auf
   dem Scheidewege / Glückwunschkantate: J.S.BACH
Last hope, The <- Religious meditation: GOTTSCHALK
Last musical thought, The / Der letzter musikalischer Ge-
   danke -> Andante maestoso, piano, K. 62, C major: BEETHO-
   VEN
Last rose of summer, The -> Fantasy, piano, op. 15: MENDELS-
   SOHN
Late swallows -> Quartet, strings, no. 2: DELIUS
Lauda Jerusalem <- Motet pour l'année dernière: COUPERIN
Laudate pueri Dominum <- Graduale in Festo SS. Innocentium
   die Dominica: M.HAYDN
Laudon symphony -> Symphony, M. 69, C major: J.HAYDN
Laurinda, La -> Il biante: STRADELLA
Laut verkünde unsre Freude, K. 623 <- Eine kleine Freimau-
   rer-Kantate / A little freemason cantata: MOZART
Lazarus <- Die Feier der Auferstehung / Easter cantata: SCHU-
   BERT
Leander -> The forsaken nymph: HÄNDEL
Leaves be green, The -> Browning: BYRD
Lebensbilder -> Lebenslied, D. 425; Lebenslied, D. 508: SCHU-
   BERT
Lebensglück / Vita felice -> Das Glück der Freundschaft:
   BEETHOVEN

Lebenslied, D. 425 <- Lebensbilder: SCHUBERT
Lebenslied, D. 508 <- Lebensbilder: SCHUBERT
Lebenslust / Im traulichen Kreise -> Die Geselligkeit, D.
609: SCHUBERT
Lebensreise -> Lied zur Gesellenreise: MOZART
Lebensstürme <- Charakteristisches Allegro: SCHUBERT
Left alone / Ballade / After the battle -> Forgotten: MUSOR-
GSKY
Legend, op. 29 <- Baba-Yaga: RIMSKY-KORSAKOV
Légendes <- St. Francis legends: LISZT
Legends <- Lemminkäinen suite: SIBELIUS
Leggierezza, La -> Études de concert, piano (No. 2): LISZT
Leib-Quartett -> Quartet, strings, no. 13, op. 130, B♭ ma-
jor: BEETHOVEN
Leicester <- Le château de Kenilworth: AUBER
Leichenfantasie -> Fantasia, piano, 4 hands, D. 1, G major:
SCHUBERT
Leiden der Trennung, D. 509 <- Sehnsucht / Artaserse: SCHU-
BERT
Leidende, Der, D. 432 <- Klage: SCHUBERT
Leiermann, Der / The organ grinder -> Deutsche Tänze, K. 602
(No. 4): MOZART
Leipzig chorales -> Chorale prelude, S. 651; S. 652; S. 653;
S. 654; S. 655; S. 656; S. 657; S. 658; S. 659; S. 660; S.
661; S. 662; S. 663; S. 664; S. 665; S. 666; S. 667; S.
668: J.S.BACH
Leipzig gigue -> Gigue, piano, K. 574, G major: MOZART
Leise, leise lasst uns singen, D. 635 <- Nächtliches Ständ-
chen / Ruhe: SCHUBERT
Lélio <- Le retour à la vie / The return to life: BERLIOZ
Lemminkainen suite -> Legends: SIBELIUS
Lenau-Lieder -> Gedichte, op. 90: SCHUMANN
Lenda amerindia (Erosão) <- The origins of the Amazon / The
sun and the moon: VILLA-LOBOS
Leningrad symphony -> Symphony, no. 7, op. 60: SHOSTAKOVICH
Lenore -> Symphony, no. 5, op. 177, E major: RAFF
Leonora / Elda / Daila / L'ange de Niside -> La favorite:
DONIZETTI
Leonore -> Fidelio: BEETHOVEN
Lerchenquartett / Lark quartet / Hornpipe quartet / Tost
quartets -> Quartet, strings, no. 68, op. 64, no. 5, D ma-
jor: J.HAYDN
Lethe <- Esop in the shades: ARNE
Lettera amorosa / Love letter -> Madrigals, book 7 (Se i
languidi): MONTEVERDI
Letzte Walzer -> Waltzes, piano, D. 146: SCHUBERT
Letzten Leiden des Erlösers, Die <- Passion cantata: C.P.E.
BACH

Letzter musikalischer Gedanke, Der / The last musical thought
  -> Andante maestoso, piano, K. 62, C major: BEETHOVEN
Leyenda -> Suite española, piano, no. 1 (Asturias): ALBÉNIZ
Li veri amici -> La Candace: VIVALDI
Liberated queen, The -> The captive queen: SIBELIUS
Libro de villanelle, moresche et altre canzoni (Matona mia
  cara) <- Landsknechtständchen: LASSUS
Licht und Liebe, D. 352 <- Nachtgesang: SCHUBERT
Licorne, La <- The triumph of chastity: IBERT
Lidice <- Memorial to Lidice: MARTINŮ
Liebe, Die -> Klärchens Lied, D. 210: SCHUBERT
Liebe und Wahrheit -> Das Geheimnis: BEETHOVEN
Liebende, Der, D. 207 <- Die Schiffende / Lied eines Lieben-
  den: SCHUBERT
Liebesgötter auf dem Markte -> Wer kauft Liebesgötter?, D.
  261: SCHUBERT
Liebesklage -> Arietten, op. 82 (T'intendo, sì, mio cor):
  BEETHOVEN
Liebesläuschen, D. 698 <- Des Fräuleins Liebesläuschen: SCHU-
BERT
Liebeslied -> Myrthen (Widmung): SCHUMANN
Liebestraum / Canzona -> O Lieb', so lang du lieben kannst:
  LISZT
Liebesverbot, Das <- Die Novize von Palermo: WAGNER
Lied der Mignon -> Sehnsucht, D. 310; D. 359; D. 481; D. 656;
  Gesänge aus Wilhelm Meister, D. 877, no. 2-4: SCHUBERT
Lied der Nacht / Song of the night -> Symphony, no. 7: MAHLER
Lied des Orpheus, D. 474 <- Orpheus: SCHUBERT
Lied eines Kriegers, D. 822 <- Reiterlied: SCHUBERT
Lied eines Liebenden / Die Schiffende -> Der Liebende, D.
  207: SCHUBERT
Lied eines Schiffers an die Dioskuren, D. 360 <- Schiffers
  Nachtlied: SCHUBERT
Lied zur Gesellenreise <- Lebensreise: MOZART
Lieder, op. 2 <- German songs, op. 2: GRIEG
Lieder, op. 4 <- Heine-Lieder: PFITZNER
Lieder, op. 9 <- Eichendorff-Lieder: PFITZNER
Lieder, op. 15 <- Hebräische Melodien: BUSONI
Lieder, op. 40 <- Chamisso-Lieder: SCHUMANN
Lieder, op. 48 <- Gellert-Lieder: BEETHOVEN
Lieder, op. 48 (Die Ehre Gottes aus der Natur) <- Creation's
  hymn: BEETHOVEN
Lieder, op. 75 (Aus Goethes Faust) <- Mephisto's flea song:
  BEETHOVEN
Lieder, op. 80 (Sehnsucht) <- Weihnachtslied: WEBER
Lieder, op. 107 (Mädchenlied) <- Nacht in der Spinnstube:
  BRAHMS
Lieder nach Worten von Franz Kafka <- Kafka-Lieder: KŘENEK

Lieder ohne Worte, op. 19 (No. 1) <- Sweet remembrance: MEN-
DELSSOHN
Lieder ohne Worte, op. 19 (No. 2) <- Regrets: MENDELSSOHN
Lieder ohne Worte, op. 19 (No. 3) <- Jägerlied/ Hunting song:
MENDELSSOHN
Lieder ohne Worte, op. 19 (No. 5) <- Restlessness: MENDELS-
SOHN
Lieder ohne Worte, op. 19 (No. 6) <- Venezianisches Gondel-
lied / Venetian gondola song: MENDELSSOHN
Lieder ohne Worte, op. 30 (No. 2) <- Without repose: MEN-
DELSSOHN
Lieder ohne Worte, op. 30 (No. 3) <- Contemplation: MENDELS-
SOHN
Lieder ohne Worte, op. 30 (No. 4) <- The wanderer: MENDELS-
SOHN
Lieder ohne Worte, op. 30 (No. 5) <- A rivulet: MENDELSSOHN
Lieder ohne Worte, op. 30 (No. 6) <- Venezianisches Gondel-
lied / Venetian gondola song: MENDELSSOHN
Lieder ohne Worte, op. 38 (No. 1) <- The evening star: MEN-
DELSSOHN
Lieder ohne Worte, op. 38 (No. 2) <- Lost happiness: MENDELS-
SOHN
Lieder ohne Worte, op. 38 (No. 3) <- The harp of the poet:
MENDELSSOHN
Lieder ohne Worte, op. 38 (No. 4) <- Hope: MENDELSSOHN
Lieder ohne Worte, op. 38 (No. 5) <- Appassionata: MENDELS-
SOHN
Lieder ohne Worte, op. 53 (No. 1) <- On the shore: MENDELS-
SOHN
Lieder ohne Worte, op. 53 (No. 2) <- Fleecy clouds / Night
vision: MENDELSSOHN
Lieder ohne Worte, op. 53 (No. 3) <- Agitation: MENDELSSOHN
Lieder ohne Worte, op. 53 (No. 4) <- The sorrowful soul:
MENDELSSOHN
Lieder ohne Worte, op. 53 (No. 5) <- Folk song / Volkslied /
Triumphal chant: MENDELSSOHN
Lieder ohne Worte, op. 53 (No. 6) <- The flight: MENDELSSOHN
Lieder ohne Worte, op. 62 (No. 1) <- May breezes: MENDELS-
SOHN
Lieder ohne Worte, op. 62 (No. 2) <- The departure: MENDELS-
SOHN
Lieder ohne Worte, op. 62 (No. 3) <- Trauermarsch / Funeral
march: MENDELSSOHN
Lieder ohne Worte, op. 62 (No. 4) <- Morning song: MENDELS-
SOHN
Lieder ohne Worte, op. 62 (No. 5) <- Venezianisches Gondel-
lied / Venetian gondola song: MENDELSSOHN
Lieder ohne Worte, op. 62 (No. 6) <- Frühlingslied / Spring

Camberwell Green: MENDELSSOHN
Lieder ohne Worte, op. 67 (No. 1) <- Lost illusion: MENDELS-
SOHN
Lieder ohne Worte, op. 67 (No. 3) <- The pilgrims: MENDELS-
SOHN
Lieder ohne Worte, op. 67 (No. 4) <- The bee's wedding /
Spinnerlied / Spinning song: MENDELSSOHN
Lieder ohne Worte, op. 67 (No. 5) <- The shepherd's com-
plaint: MENDELSSOHN
Lieder ohne Worte, op. 85 (No. 1) <- Reverie: MENDELSSOHN
Lieder ohne Worte, op. 85 (No. 2) <- L'adieu: MENDELSSOHN
Lieder ohne Worte, op. 85 (No. 3) <- Passion: MENDELSSOHN
Lieder ohne Worte, op. 85 (No. 4) <- Elegie / Klagendes Lied:
MENDELSSOHN
Lieder ohne Worte, op. 85 (No. 5) <- The return: MENDELSSOHN
Lieder ohne Worte, op. 85 (No. 6) <- Song of the traveler:
MENDELSSOHN
Lieder ohne Worte, op. 102 (No. 3) <- Retrospection: MEN-
DELSSOHN
Lieder ohne Worte, op. 102 (No. 5) <- Kinderstück / The joy-
ous peasant: MENDELSSOHN
Lieder ohne Worte, op. 102 (No. 6) <- Belief / Faith: MEN-
DELSSOHN
Lieder und Gesänge, op. 63 (Ich sah als Knabe) <- Heimweh,
no. 3: BRAHMS
Lieder und Gesänge, op. 63 (Meine Liebe ist grün) <- Junge
Lider, no. 1: BRAHMS
Lieder und Gesänge, op. 63 (O wüsst' ich doch den Weg zu-
rück) <- Heimweh, no. 2: BRAHMS
Lieder und Gesänge, op. 63 (Wenn um den Hollunder) <- Junge
Lieder, no. 2: BRAHMS
Lieder und Gesänge, op. 63 (Wie traulich war) <- Heimweh, no.
1: BRAHMS
Lieder von Rückert <- Rückert-Lieder: MAHLER
Lieder-Quadrille <- Melange-Quadrille: JOHANN STRAUSS
Lieto brindisi, Un <- Kleine Kantate / Little cantata: BEET-
HOVEN
Life for the czar, A <- Ivan Susanin: GLINKA
Light of life, The <- Lux Christi: ELGAR
Like Laura's ghost / O komm' im Traum -> Oh, quand je dors:
LISZT
Lilliburlero -> A new Irish tune, harpsichord, G major: PUR-
CELL
Linz symphony -> Symphony, K. 425, C major: MOZART
Lira concerti / Lirenkonzerte -> Concerto, 2 hurdy-gurdies,
H.VIIh,1, C major; H.VIIh,2, G major; H.VIIh,3, G major;
H.VIIh,4, F major; H.VIIh,5, F major: J.HAYDN
Lirenkonzerte / Lira concerti -> Concerto, 2 hurdy-gurdies,

H.VIIh,1, C major; H.VIIh,2, G major; H.VIIh, 3, G major;
    H.VIIh,4, F major; H.VIIh,5, F major: J.HAYDN
Lisa -> Sissy [Lisa]: KREISLER
Litanei -> Ora pro nobis: LISZT
Litanei auf das Fest Aller Seelen -> Am Tage Aller Seelen,
    D. 343: SCHUBERT
Little C major symphony -> Symphony, D. 589, C major: SCHU-
    BERT
Little cantata / Kleine Kantate -> Un lieto brindisi: BEET-
    HOVEN
Little cantata on romantic texts -> Die Serenaden: HINDEMITH
Little E minor prelude -> Prelude and fugue, organ, S. 533,
    E minor: J.S.BACH
Little freemason cantata, A / Eine kleine Freimaurer Kanta-
    te -> Laut verkunde unsre Freude, K. 623: MOZART
Little G minor symphony -> Symphony, K. 173dB (183) G minor:
    MOZART
Little gypsy, The -> May-day: ARNE
Little husband, little wife / Petit mari, petite femme /
    Playing house -> Jeux d'enfants (Duo): BIZET
Little Kären -> Kären: IVES
Little Magnificat / Kleine Magnificat -> Magnificat, S. Anh.
    21, A minor: J.S.BACH
Little organ mass / Kleine Orgelmesse / Missa brevis Sancti
    Joanni de Deo -> Mass, H.XXII,7, Bb major: J.HAYDN
Little Russian symphony / Ukrainian symphony -> Symphony,
    no. 2, op. 17, C minor: TCHAIKOVSKY
Little slippers, The <- Oxana's caprices: TCHAIKOVSKY
Little suite -> Duets, violins (Selections; arr.): BARTÓK
Little symphony -> Trio, flutes & violoncello, H.IV,1, C ma-
    jor [arr.]: J.HAYDN
Little symphony / Kleine Symphonie -> Symphony, op. 44, G
    major: PFITZNER
Little train of the Brazilian countryman, The -> Bachianas
    brasileiras, no. 2 (Toccata: O tremzinho do caipira):
    VILLA-LOBOS
Little trumpet piece -> Scherzo, piano, B minor: MENDELSSOHN
Little wind music / Kleine Blasmusik -> Bagatelles, piano, 4
    hands [arr.]: KRENEK
Liturgic symphony / Symphonie liturgique -> Symphony, no. 3:
    HONEGGER
Livietta e Tracollo <- La contadina astuta: PERGOLESI
Llamadas <- Sinfonia proletario: CHAVEZ
Lob der Einsamkeit -> Die Einsiedelei, D. 337: SCHUBERT
Lobe den Herrn, meine Seele, S. 69a <- Ratswahlkantate: J.S.
    BACH
Lobet den Herren, S. 137 <- Ratswahlkantate: J.S.BACH
Lobet Gott in seinen Reichen, S. 11 <- Himmelfahrts-Oratori-

um / Ascension oratorio: J.S.BACH
Lobgesang <- Symphony, no. 2, op. 52, B♭ major: MENDELSSOHN
Lobgesang der Maria / Magnificat -> Motets, op. 69 (Mein
   Herz erhebet Gott): MENDELSSOHN
Lobgesang der Simeon -> Motets, op. 69 (Herr, nun lässest
   du): MENDELSSOHN
Lobkowitz cantata / Birthday cantata -> Es lebe unser teurer
   Fürst: BEETHOVEN
Lobkowitz quartets -> Quartet, strings, no. 1, op. 18, no.
   1, F major; no. 3, op. 18, no. 3, D major; no. 4, op. 18,
   no. 4, C minor; no. 5, op. 18, no. 5, A major; no. 6, op.
   18, no. 6, B♭ major: BEETHOVEN
Lobkowitz quartets -> Quartet, strings, no. 82, op. 77, no.
   1, G major; no. 83, op. 77, no. 2, F major: J.HAYDN
Locanda, La <- Il fanatico in Berlina: PAISIELLO
Locandiera, La -> Mirandolina: MARTINŮ
Lodron concerto -> Concerto, 3 pianos, K. 242, F major: MO-
   ZART
Lodronische Nachtmusik -> Divertimento, K. 287, B♭ major:
   MOZART
Lombardi alla prima crociata, I <- Gerusalemme / Jerusalem:
   VERDI
London -> Upon Westminster Bridge: CASTELNUOVO-TEDESCO
London chaconne -> Chaconne, strings, G minor: PURCELL
London sonatas -> Sonata, piano, no. 50, C major; no. 51, D
   major; no. 52, E♭ major: J.HAYDN
London sonatas -> Sonata, piano, K. 10, B♭ major; K. 11, G
   major; K. 12, A major; K. 13, F major; K. 14, C major; K.
   15, B♭ major: MOZART
London symphonies / Salomon symphonies -> Symphony, M. 93, D
   major; M. 94, G major; M. 95, C minor; M. 96, D major; M.
   97, C major; M. 98, B♭ major; M. 99, E♭ major; M. 100, D
   major; M. 101, D major; M. 102, B♭ major; M. 103, E♭ ma-
   jor; M. 104, D major: J.HAYDN
London symphony / Salomon symphonies / London symphonies ->
   Symphony, m. 104, D major: J.HAYDN
London symphony -> Symphony, no. 2, G major: VAUGHAN WILLIAMS
London trios -> Divertimento, H.IV, 1 C major; H.IV,2, C ma-
   jor; H.IV,3, G major; H.IV,4, G major: J.HAYDN
Londoner Quadrille -> Festival Quadrille: JOHANN STRAUSS
Look down harmonious Saint <- Praise of harmony: HÄNDEL
Lord bee thanked, The <- A thanksgiving: DOWLAND
Lord Canterbury's pavan -> Pavan, keyboard instrument, T. 57:
   TOMKINS
Lord d'Isle's galliard -> Sir Robert Sidney his galliard:
   DOWLAND
Lord have mercy upon us <- Zum Abendsegen: MENDELSSOHN
Lord Salisbury's galliard -> Galliard, keyboard instrument,

H. 19: GIBBONS
Lord Salisbury's pavan -> Pavan, keyboard instrument, H. 18:
  GIBBONS
Lord Viscount Lisle his galliard, The <- Sir Robert Sidney
  his galliard: DOWLAND
Lord Willoughby's welcome home <- Rowland: BYRD
Lost happiness -> Lieder ohne Worte, op. 38 (No. 2): MEN-
  DELSSOHN
Lost illusion -> Lieder ohne Worte, op. 67 (No. 1): MENDELS-
  SOHN
Louischen <- Nitschewo-Polka: JOHANN STRAUSS
Louisville concerto -> Kentucky concerto: LUENING
Louisville symphony -> Symphony, no. 7: BADINGS
Lousadzak / The coming of light -> Concerto, piano & string
  orchestra, no. 1, op. 48: HOVANESS
Love and glory -> Britannia: ARNE
Love in Bath -> Operas (Selections; arr.): HÄNDEL
Love in the stocks -> Hugh the drover: VAUGHAN WILLIAMS
Love letter / Lettera amorosa -> Madrigals, book 7 (Sei lan-
  guidi): MONTEVERDI
Love song -> Serestas (Modinha): VILLA-LOBOS
Love triumphant <- Nature will prevail: PURCELL
Lovely yet ungrateful swain <- Vauxhall songs: J.C.BACH
Lover, The -> Sonata, harpsichord, K. 213 (L. 108) D minor:
  D.SCARLATTI
Love's goddess sure was blind <- Ode for Queen Mary's birth-
  day [1692]: PURCELL
Lucio Silla overture -> Symphony, op. 18, no. 2, Bb major:
  J.C.BACH
Lucio Silla (Overture) <- Symphony, K. 135, D major: MOZART
Lucretia, La -> O numi eterni: HÄNDEL
Lucullo, Il -> L'humanità nelle fiere: A.SCARLATTI
Lützow concerto -> Concerto, piano, K. 246, C major: MOZART
Lumagne, La -> Sonata, flute & continuo, op. 2, no. 4, G mi-
  nor: BLAVET
Lunz / Wallfahrtsarie -> Abschied, D. 475: SCHUBERT
Lustige Suite, string orchestra, C major <- La bouffonne /
  Suite, string orchestra, C5, C major: TELEMANN
Lutheran masses -> Mass, S. 233, F major; S. 234, A major;
  S. 235, G minor; S. 236, G major: J.S.BACH
Lux Christi -> The light of life: ELGAR
Lyra, La -> Suite, string orchestra, Es3, Eb major: TELEMANN
Lyric symphony -> Symphony, no. 7, E major: BRUCKNER

Ma mie Margot -> Concertos comiques (No. 10): CORRETTE
Ma tante Aurore <- Le roman impromptu: BOIELDIEU
Macedonian mountain dance, piano, op. 144b <- Mountain dance,
  piano, no. 2: HOVANESS

Mad Bess -> Bess of Bedlam: PURCELL
Madama l'umorista <- Gli stravaganti: PAISIELLO
Maddalena alla croce -> Arie musicali, 1. libro (A piè della
   gran croce): FRESCOBALDI
Madras sonata, piano, op. 176 <- Sonata, piano, op. 176; HO-
   VANESS
Madras symphony -> Symphony, no. 13: COWELL
Madrigali amorosi -> Madrigali guerrieri e amorosi: MONTE-
   VERDI
Madrigali guerrieri e amorosi <- Madrigali amorosi: MONTE-
   VERDI
Madrigals, book 7 (Se i languidi) <- Lettera amorosa / Love
   letter: MONTEVERDI
Madrigals, book 9 (Bel pastor) <- Dialogue of a nymph and a
   shepherd: MONTEVERDI
Madrigals, mixed voices, unacc. [1939] <- Czech madrigals:
   MARTINŮ
Mädchen, Das -> Blanka, D. 631: SCHUBERT
Maestri di cappella, Il <- Die Generalprobe / The dress re-
   hearsal: CIMAROSA
Maestro e lo scolare, Il -> Variations, piano, 4 hands, H.
   XVIIa,1: J.HAYDN
Magd, ein' Dienerin, Ein' -> Cantilena pro Adventu, A major:
   J.HAYDN
Magelone songs -> Romanzen aus L. Tiecks Magelone, op. 33:
   BRAHMS
Magic garden, A / Moss garden -> Koke no niwa: HOVANESS
Magie di Merlina e Zoroastro, Le <- Le pazzie di Stellidaura
   e Zoroastro: CIMAROSA
Magnificat / Lobgesang der Maria -> Motets, op. 69 (Mein
   Herz erhebet Gott): MENDELSSOHN
Magnificat, S. Anh. 21, A minor <- Kleine Magnificat / Lit-
   tle Magnificat: J.S.BACH
Magyar dallok (No. 9) <- Rhapsody on Hungarian songs: LISZT
Magyar rondo / Hungarian rondo -> Régi magyar katonadalok:
   KODÁLY
Magyarokhoz, A <- Song of faith: KODÁLY
Maid of Cashmere, The / La courtisane amoureuse -> Le dieu
   et la bayadère: AUBER
Maiden quartets / Jungfernquartette / Russian quartets ->
   Quartet, strings, no. 38, op. 33, no. 1, B minor; no. 39,
   op. 33, no. 2, E♭ major; no. 40, op. 33, no. 3, C major;
   no. 41, op. 33, no. 4, B♭ major; no. 42, op. 33, no. 5, G
   major; no. 43, op. 33, no. 6, D major: J.HAYDN
Maiden's seasons, The -> Arioso: SIBELIUS
Mailänder-Quartette / Milanese quartets / Italian quartets
   -> Quartet, strings, K. 134b (156) G major; K. 157, D major; K. 158, F major; K. 159, B♭ major; K. 159a (160) E♭

major: MOZART

Mailied, D. 503 <- Frühlingslied: SCHUBERT

Maillotins, Les -> Pièces de clavecin, 3. livre, 18. ordre (Le tic-toc-choc): COUPERIN

Maj -> Vårsång: ALFVÉN

Majnun -> Symphony, no. 24, op. 273: HOVANESS

Majority <- The masses: IVES

Majos enamorados, Los -> Goyescas [Piano work]: GRANADOS

Man and wife / Mann und Weib / Der Geburtstag / Birthday divertimento -> Divertimento, H.II,11, C major: J.HAYDN

Man in the moon, The -> Il mondo della luna: J.HAYDN

Maunaun's birthing <- The birth of Manaunaun / Irewee's shoothree: COWELL

Maniscalco, Il <- Der gelehrte Hufschmied: DITTERSDORF

Mann und Weib / Man and wife / Der Geburtstag / Birthday divertimento -> Divertimento, H.II,11, C major: J.HAYDN

March, band, K. 18, F major <- Landwehrmarsch / York'scher Marsch: BEETHOVEN

March, orchestra, Ab major <- Turkish march: MUSORGSKY

March, orchestra, H.VIII,3, Eb major <- Prince of Wales march: J.HAYDN

March, orchestra, K. 249, D major <- Haffner march: MOZART

March, piano, 4 hands, D. 928, G major <- Children's march / Kindermarsch: SCHUBERT

March, wood-winds & horn, K. 29, Bb major <- Grenadiermarsch: BEETHOVEN

March and canzona, 4 trumpets, Z. 860, F minor <- Funeral march / The Queen's funeral march: PURCELL

March for the Sultan Abdul Medjid -> Marcia militare: ROSSINI

March in homage of Ludwig II of Bavaria -> Huldingungsmarsch: WAGNER

Marche des Gardes a Cheval / Tscherkessen-Marsch -> Russischer Marsch, orchestra: JOHANN STRAUSS

Marche des gibaros -> Souvenir de Porto Rico: GOTTSCHALK

Marche écossaise sur un thème populaire, piano, 4 hands <- The Earl of Ross march: DEBUSSY

Marche festivale -> Marche réligieuse, orchestra: GOUNOD

Marche française -> Joyeuse marche, orchestra: CHABRIER

Marche hongroise / Hungarian march -> Ungarischer Sturm-Marsch, piano: LISZT

Marche pontificale, piano <- Marche romaine: GOUNOD

Marche réligieuse, orchestra <- Marche festivale: GOUNOD

Marche romaine -> Marche pontificale, piano: GOUNOD

Marches, piano, op. 76 <- Lager-Szene: SCHUMANN

Marches, wood-winds & brasses, H.VIII,1-2 <- Derbyshire marches: J.HAYDN

Marches héroïques / Heroic marches -> Musique héroïque: TE-

LEMANN
Marcia militare <- March for the Sultan Abdul Medjid: ROSSINI
Marco Spada <- La fille du bandit: AUBER
Margarethe -> Faust: GOUNOD
Margoton -> Concertos comiques (No. 3): CORRETTE
Mari battu, Le -> Rita: DONIZETTI
Maria di Rohan <- Il Conte di Chalais: DONIZETTI
Maria Stuarda <- Buondelmonte: DONIZETTI
Maria Theresa symphony / Sturm und Drang symphonies -> Symphony, M. 48, C major: J.HAYDN
Marian motets -> Benedicta es caelorum regina; Alma redemptoris mater; Illibata Dei virgo nutrix; O virgo virginum; Missus est Gabriel; Ave nobilissima creatura: DEPRÈS
Mariazeller-Messe / Missa Cellensis -> Mass, H.XXII,8, C major: J.HAYDN
Mariengarten -> Quasi cedrus: LISZT
Marina del Granatello, La -> La Zelmira: PAISIELLO
Marine <- La chanson de matelot: BIZET
Marito disperato, Il <- Il marito geloso / L'amante disperato: CIMAROSA
Marito geloso, Il / L'amante disperato -> Il marito disperato: CIMAROSA
Mark Twain overture -> Tom Sawyer: ANTHEIL
Marquis de Tulipano, Le / Il matrimonio inaspettato -> La finte contesse: PAISIELLO
Married beau, The <- The curious impertinent: PURCELL
Martyrs, Les <- Il Poliuto: DONIZETTI
Masaniello -> La muette de Portici: AUBER
Mascarade royale / Le grand Porte-diadème -> Le carnaval: LULLY
Maskenzug <- Trapp-Polka: JOHANN STRAUSS
Masonic ritual music / Onward ye brethren -> Musique réligieuse, voice, chorus & organ, op. 113: SIBELIUS
Mass, Bb minor <- Missa solemnis: BRUCKNER
Mass, C major <- Missa venerationis: CALDARA
Mass, Eb major <- Chorale mass: BRUCKNER
Mass, Eb major <- Unfinished mass: JANÁČEK
Mass, Eb major <- Grosse Jugendmesse: WEBER
Mass, D. 452, C major <- Benedictus mass: SCHUBERT
Mass, D. 678, Ab major <- Missa solemnis: SCHUBERT
Mass, D. 872, Bb major <- German mass / Deutsche Messe: SCHUBERT
Mass, H.XXII,2, D minor <- Missa, Sunt bona mixta malis: J. HAYDN
Mass, H.XXII,3, G major <- Missa, Rorate coeli desuper: J. HAYDN
Mass, H.XXII,4, Eb major<- Great organ mass / Grosse Orgelmesse: J.HAYDN

Mass, H.XXII,5, C major <- Cäcilienmesse / Missa Sanctae
    Caeciliae / Saint Cecilia mass / Cantata mass: J.HAYDN
Mass, H.XXII,6, G major <- Missa Sancti Nicolai / Nicolai-
    messe / St. Joseph mass: J.HAYDN
Mass, H.XXII,7, B♭ major <- Kleine Orgelmesse / Little organ
    mass / Missa brevis Sancti Joanni de Deo: J.HAYDN
Mass, H.XXII,8, C major <- Mariazeller-Messe / Missa Cellen-
    sis: J.HAYDN
Mass, H.XXII,9, C major <- Mass in time of war / Missa in
    tempore belli / Paukenmesse: J.HAYDN
Mass, H.XXII,10, B♭ major <- Heiligmesse / Missa Sancti Ber-
    nardi de Offida: J.HAYDN
Mass, H.XXII,11, D minor <- Imperial mass / Nelson mass /
    Missa in augustiis / Coronation mass: J.HAYDN
Mass, H.XXII,12, B♭ major <- Theresienmesse: J.HAYDN
Mass, H.XXII,13, B♭ major <- Creation mass / Schöpfungsmes-
    se: J.HAYDN
Mass, H.XXII,14, B♭ major <- Harmoniemesse / Wind-band mass:
    J.HAYDN
Mass, K. 47a (139) C minor <- Orphanage mass / Waisenhaus-
    messe: MOZART
Mass, K. 66, C major <- Dominicus mass / Missa Dominica: MO-
    ZART
Mass, K. 167, C major <- Missa trinitatis / Trinity mass:
    MOZART
Mass, K. 246a (262) C major <- Missa longa: MOZART
Mass, K. 257, C major <- Credo mass: MOZART
Mass, K. 258, C major <- Piccolomini mass: MOZART
Mass, K. 317, C major <- Coronation mass / Krönungsmesse:
    MOZART
Mass, K. 337, C major <- Missa solemnis: MOZART
Mass, no. 1 <- Missa, Domine Dominus noster: LECHNER
Mass, no. 1, op. 75a, E♭ major <- Freischützmesse: WEBER
Mass, no. 2 <- Missa, Non fu mai cervo: LECHNER
Mass, no. 2, G major <- Messe pour les sociétés chorales:
    GOUNOD
Mass, no. 2, op. 76, G major <- Jubelmesse: WEBER
Mass, no. 3 <- Missa, Non e lasso martire: LECHNER
Mass, no. 3, G major <- Messe aux communautés réligieuses:
    GOUNOD
Mass, no. 6, G major <- Messe aux cathédrales: GOUNOD
Mass, no. 7, C major <- Messe aux chapelles: GOUNOD
Mass, no. 8, C major <- Messe dit de Clovis: GOUNOD
Mass, no. 11, A major <- Coronation mass: CHERUBINI
Mass, op. 123, D major -> Missa solemnis: BEETHOVEN
Mass, op. 147, C minor <- Missa sacra: SCHUMANN
Mass, S. 233, F major <- Lutheran masses: J.S.BACH
Mass, S. 234, A major <- Lutheran masses: J.S.BACH

Mass, S. 235, G minor <- Lutheran masses: J.S.BACH
Mass, S. 236, G major <- Lutheran masses: J.S.BACH
Mass, alto, 2 horns & organ, C major <- Short chorale mass /
    Windhager Messe: BRUCKNER
Mass, 10 voices & orchestra, F major <- Missa romana: PERGO-
    LESI
Mass in time of war / Missa in tempore belli / Paukenmesse
    -> Mass, H.XXII,9, C major: J.HAYDN
Masses, The -> Majority: IVES
Master of Clamency, The <- Colas Breugnon: KABALEVSKY
Matilde di Shabran <- Bellezza e cuor di ferro / Matilde e
    Corradino: ROSSINI
Matilde e Corradino / Bellezza e cuor di ferro -> Matilde di
    Shabran: ROSSINI
Matin, Le -> Symphony, M. 6, D major: J.HAYDN
Matinée, La -> Sonata, piano, op. 25, no. 2, D major: DUSSEK
Matrimoni impensati, I <- La bella greca: CIMAROSA
Matrimoni in ballo, I <- La baronessa stramba: CIMAROSA
Matrimonio inaspettato, Il / Le marquis de Tulipano -> Le
    finte contesse: PAISIELLO
Matrimonio per raggiro, Il <- La donna bizzarra: CIMAROSA
Matrimonio per susurro, Il -> Angiolina: SALIERI
Matrimonio raggirato, Il -> L'apprensivo raggirato: CIMAROSA
Max und Moritz reisen ins Schlaraffenland -> Peter und Paul
    reisen im Schlaraffenland: LEHÁR
May breezes -> Lieder ohne Worte, op. 62 (No. 1): MENDELSSOHN
May Day / First of May -> Symphony, no. 3, op. 20: SHOSTAKO-
    VICH
May-day <- The little gypsy: ARNE
Maytime in Sussex -> Morning song: BAX
Mazurka, piano <- Homage to Paderewski: MARTINŮ
Mazurka, piano, op. 59, no. 1, A minor <- Cracow mazurka:
    CHOPIN
Mazurka, piano, op. posth., A minor <- The nightingale: CHO-
    PIN
Mazurka, piano, op. posth., G major <- Kulavy /Prague mazur-
    ka: CHOPIN
Mazurka, violin & piano, op. 3, A minor -> Kujawiak: WIENI-
    AWSKI
Mazurka, violin & piano, op. 12, no. 1, D major <- Sielanka:
    WIENIAWSKI
Mazurka, violin & piano, op. 12, no. 2, G major <- Le ménet-
    rier: WIENIAWSKI
McKonkey's Ferry <- Washington at Trenton: ANTHEIL
Medea <- The cave of the heart: BARBER
Meditation <- Album leaf: MUSORGSKY
Méditation sur le premier prélude de bach <- Ave Maria: GOU-
    NOD

Meditations for organ / Nine meditations for organ -> La na-
tivité du Seigneur: MESSIAEN
Méditations symphoniques -> L'Ascension: MESSIAEN
Megkésett melódiák -> Songs, op. 6: KODÁLY
Meine Seele erhebet den Herrn / Schübler chorales -> Chorale
prelude, S. 648: J.S.BACH
Meistersinger sonata / Thun sonata -> Sonata, violin & piano,
no. 2, op. 100, A major: BRAHMS
Melancholischer Walzer -> Caprice-valse, piano, no. 2: LISZT
Melancholy nymph, The <- Tha faithful maid: HÄNDEL
Melange-Quadrille -> Lieder-Quadrille: JOHANN STRAUSS
Melk concerto -> Concerto, violin, H.VIIa,3, A major: J.HAYDN
Mélodies, op. 2 <- Irlande: BERLIOZ
Mélodies, op. 2 (Le coucher de soleil) <- Rêverie: BERLIOZ
Mélodies, op. 2 (L'origine du harpe) <- Ballade: BERLIOZ
Mélodies hébraïques <- Chants hébraïques: RAVEL
Memento -> Gedenkblatter: JOSEPH STRAUSS
Memoria de Mozart, A -> Sinfonietta, no. 1: VILLA-LOBOS
Memorial to Lidice -> Lidice: MARTINŮ
Ménetrier, Le -> Mazurka, violin & piano, op. 12, no. 2, G
major: WIENIAWSKI
Menuet du boeuf / Ochsenmenüett -> Minuet, orchestra, H.IX,
27: J.HAYDN
Mephisto waltz, no. 1 -> Episoden aus Lenaus Faust (Der Tanz
in der Dorfschenke): LISZT
Mephistopheles' serenade -> Song of the flea: MUSORGSKY
Mephisto's flea song -> Lieder, op. 75 (Aus Goethes Faust):
BEETHOVEN
Mercato di Malmantile, Il -> La vanitâ delusa: CIMAROSA
Mercure <- The adventures of Mercury: SATIE
Mercury symphony -> Symphony, M. 43, Eb major: J.HAYDN
Mère au berceau de son fils, La -> La ninna-nonna: DONIZETTI
Merope, La -> L'oracolo in Messenia: VIVALDI
Merry workshop / Fröhliche Werkstatt -> Sonatina, wood-winds
& brasses, no. 2, Eb major: R.STRAUSS
Merrymaking / Tavern song -> Mulató gajd: KODÁLY
Messa concertata -> Musiche sacre (Mass): CAVALLI
Messa da requiem -> Requiem: VERDI
Messe aux cathédrales -> Mass, no. 6, G major: GOUNOD
Messe aux chapelles -> Mass, no. 7, C major: GOUNOD
Messe aux communautés réligieuses -> Mass, no. 3, G major:
GOUNOD
Messe de la Pentecôte (Communion) <- Les oiseaux et les
sources: MESSIAEN
Messe de la Pentecôte (Consécration) <- Le don de sagesse:
MESSIAEN
Messe de la Pentecôte (Entrée) <- Les langues de feu: MESSI-
AEN

Messe de la Pentecôte (Offertoire) <- Les choses visibles et
   invisibles: MESSIAEN
Messe de la Pentecôte (Sortie) <- Le vent de l'Esprit: MESSI-
   AEN
Messe de Requiem <- Requiem: CAMPRA
Messe dit de Clovis -> Mass, no. 8, C major: GOUNOD
Messe pour les sociétés chorales -> Mass, no. 2, G major:
   GOUNOD
Messe solennelle -> Petite messe solennelle: ROSINI
Messe solennelle à Sainte Cécile <- St. Cecilia mass: GOUNOD
Metamorfosi di Pasquale, Le <- Tutto è illusione nel mondo:
   SPONTINI
Metamorphosen-Sinfonien / Ovid symphonies -> Symphony, K. 73;
   K. 74; K. 75; K. 76; K. 77; K. 78; K. 79; K. 80; K. 81; K.
   82; K. 83; K. 84: DITTERSDORF
Métamorphoses nocturnes -> Quartet, strings, no. 1: LIGETI
Metrical psalms -> Psalmen Davids [1628]: SCHÜTZ
Metropolitan Museum fanfare -> Portraits (Parades; arr.):
   THOMSON
Mi chomocho <- Israel: HARRIS
Midas élu pour Juge entre Pan et Apollon / Metamorphosen-
   Sinfonien / Ovid symphonies -> Symphony, K. 83: DITTERSDORF
Midi, Le -> Symphony, M. 7, C major: J.HAYDN
Midsommarvaka -> Swedish rhapsody, orchestra, no. 1, op. 19:
   ALFVÉN
Midst silent shades <- Vauxhall songs: J.C.BACH
Mighty Casey, The [Cantata] <- Baseball cantata / Casey at
   the bat: SCHUMAN
Mignon -> Lieder, op. 75 (Kennst du das Land): BEETHOVEN
Milanese quartets / Mailänder-Quartette / Italian quartets
   -> Quartet, strings, K. 134b (156) G major; K. 157, D ma-
   jor; K. 158, F major; K. 159, Bb major; K. 159a (160) Eb
   major: MOZART
Military concerto -> Concerto, piano, op. 40, Bb major: DUS-
   SEK
Military polonaise -> Polonaise, piano, op. 40, no. 1, A ma-
   jor: CHOPIN
Military septet / Grand military septet -> Septet, piano,
   winds & strings, op. 114, C major: HUMMEL
Military symphony / London symphonies / Salomon symphonies
   -> Symphony, M. 100, D major: J.HAYDN
Minerve, La -> Pièces de clavecin, 3. livre, 15. ordre (La
   régente): COUPERIN
Miniatures -> Music for children [arr.]: WALTON
Minimax <- Repertorium für Militärmusik: HINDEMITH
Minnesång -> Gustaf Vasa: ALFVÉN
Minnesang -> Huldigung, D. 240: SCHUBERT
Minuet, orchestra, H.IX,1, C major <- Rococo minuet: J.HAYDN

Minuet, orchestra, H.IX,27 <- Menuet de boeuf / Ochsenmenü-
   ett: J.HAYDN
Minuet, orchestra, K. 3, Eb major <- Gratulations-Menüett:
   BEETHOVEN
Minuets, orchestra, H.IX,11 <- Katherinentänze: J.HAYDN
Minuets, orchestra, K. 10 <- Gesellschaftsmenüette: BEETHOVEN
Minute waltz / Dog waltz -> Waltz, piano, op. 64, no. 1, Db
   major: CHOPIN
Mirabilia testimonia tua <- Tabescere me fecit: COUPERIN
Miracle, The -> Symphony, M. 96, D major: J.HAYDN
Miracle de la femme laide, Le -> Dolorès: JOLIVET
Mirandolina <- La locandiera: MARTINŮ
Mircath <- Viking battle-song: BAX
Mirliton, Le -> Concertos comiques (No. 1): CORRETTE
Miserere mei, Deus <- Penitential psalms: LASSUS
Miserly knight, The <- The covetous knight: RACHMANINOFF
Missa, Ad bene placitum -> Missa, Illumina ocules meos: PA-
   LESTRINA
Missa, Beschaffens Glück <- Missa, Il me suffit: LASSUS
Missa brevis, K. 186h (194) D major <- Counterpoint mass:
   MOZART
Missa brevis, K. 196b (220) C major <- Spatzenmesse / Spar-
   row mass: MOZART
Missa brevis, K. 258, C major <- Spaur mass: MOZART
Missa brevis, K. 259, C major <- Organ solo mass: MOZART
Missa brevis Sancti Joanni de Deo / Kleine Orgelmesse / Lit-
   tle organ mass -> Mass, H.XXII,7, Bb major: J.HAYDN
Missa Cellensis / Mariazeller-Messe -> Mass, H.XXII,8, C ma-
   jor: J.HAYDN
Missa cinque vocum pro defunctis <- Requiem: LASSUS
Missa, De beata Virgine [1570] <- Missa, Vel domenicalis:
   PALESTRINA
Missa, Domine Dominus noster -> Mass, no. 1: LECHNER
Missa Dominica / Dominicus mass -> Mass, K. 66, C major: MO-
   ZART
Missa, Frère Thibault -> Missa sine nomine: LASSUS
Missa, Il me suffit -> Missa, Beschaffens Gluck: LASSUS
Missa, Illumina oculos meos <- Missa, Ad bene placitum: PA-
   LESTRINA
Missa in augustiis / Nelson mass / Imperial mass / Corona-
   tion mass -> Mass, H.XXII,11, D minor: J.HAYDN
Missa in tempore belli / Mass in time of war / Paukenmesse
   -> Mass, H.XXII,9, C major: J.HAYDN
Missa longa -> Mass, K. 246a (262): MOZART
Missa, Non e lasso martire -> Mass, no. 3: LECHNER
Missa, Non fu mai cervo -> Mass, no. 2: LECHNER
Missa oratorio -> Vidapura: VILLA-LOBOS
Missa pro defunctis <- Requiem: CIMAROSA

Missa pro defuncto Archiepiscopo Sigismundo <- Requiem so-
  lemne [1771]: M.HAYDN
Missa romana -> Mass, 10 voices & orchestra, F major: PERGO-
  LESI
Missa, Rorate coeli desuper -> Mass, H.XXII,3, G major: J.
  HAYDN
Missa sacra -> Mass, op. 147, C minor: SCHUMANN
Missa Sanctae Caeciliae / Cäcilienmesse / Saint Cecilia mass
  / Cantata mass -> Mass, H.XXII,5, C major: J.HAYDN
Missa Sancti Bernardi de Offida / Heiligmesse -> Mass, H.
  XXII,10, B♭ major: J.HAYDN
Missa Sancti Nicolai / Nicolaimesse / St. Joseph mass ->
  Mass, H.XXII,6, G major: J.HAYDN
Missa sine nomine <- Missa, Frère Thibault: LASSUS
Missa sine nomine <- Je suis déshéritée: PALESTRINA
Missa solemnis <- Mass, op. 123, D major: BEETHOVEN
Missa solemnis -> Mass, B♭ minor: BRUCKNER
Missa solemnis / Schöpfungsmesse / Creation mass -> Mass, H.
  XXII,13, B♭ major: J.HAYDN
Missa solemnis -> Mass, K. 337, C major: MOZART
Missa solemnis -> Mass, D. 678, A♭ major: SCHUBERT
Missa solennis <- Graner Messe / Festival mass: LISZT
Missa, Sunt bona mixta malis -> Mass, H.XXII,2, D minor: J.
  HAYDN
Missa trinitatis / Trinity mass -> Mass, K. 167, C major:
  MOZART
Missa, Ut, re, mi, fa, sol, la <- Hexachord mass: PALESTRINA
Missa, Vel domenicalis -> Missa, De beata Virgine [1570]:
  PALESTRINA
Missa venerationis -> Mass, C major: CALDARA
Missus est Gabriel <- Marian motets: DEPRÈS
Mit Gott / Geistervariationen -> Andante, piano, G major:
  SCHUMANN
Moda, La <- Gli scompigli domestici: DITERSDORF
Moda, La <- I scompigli domestici: SALIERI
Modista raggiatrice, La -> La scuffiara: PAISIELLO
Mödlinger Tänze / Viennese dances -> Tänze, orchestra, K. 17:
  BEETHOVEN
Moeurs du bon vieux temps, Les -> Aucassin et Nicolette:
  GRÉTRY
Mohrenkönig, Der -> Don Gayseros, D. 93: SCHUBERT
Moïse / Le passage de la mer Rouge -> Moïse et Pharaon: ROS-
  SINI
Moïse et Pharaon <- Le passage de la mer Rouge / Moïse: ROS-
  SINI
Molinara, La <- La bella molinara / L'amor contrastato: PAI-
  SIELLO
Mollares, las <- Danse andalouse / Andalusian dance: GLINKA

Molly Mog <- The fair maid of the inn: HÄNDEL
Mombreuil et Merville -> Le pari: BOIELDIEU
Moments musicaux, piano, D. 780 (No. 6) <- Air russe: SCHU-
    BERT
Mon salut! -> An der Wolga: JOHANN STRAUSS
Monde renversé, Le -> L'isle de Merlin: GLUCK
Mondenschein, D. 875 <- Vollmondnacht: SCHUBERT
Mondo della luna, Il <- The man on the moon: J.HAYDN
Mondschein sonata / Moonlight sonata / Arbor sonata / Sunset
    sonata -> Sonata, piano, no. 14, op. 27, no. 2, C# minor:
    BEETHOVEN
Monsieur Choufleuri chez lui le... <- Salon Pitzelberger:
    OFFENBACH
Monsieur de Pourceaugnac <- Le divertissement de Chambord:
    LULLY
Montanhas do Brasil -> Symphony, no. 6: VILLA-LOBOS
Months, The, op. 37a -> Les saisons: TCHAIKOVSKY
Moonlight sonata / Mondschein sonata / Arbor sonata / Sunset
    sonata -> Sonata, piano, no. 14, op. 27, no. 2, C# minor:
    BEETHOVEN
Moor's revenge, The -> Abdelazer: PURCELL
Mora <- Game of chance: HOVANESS
Moravian duets, op. 32 <- Klänge aus Mähren: DVOŘÁK
Morceaux de fantaisie, piano, op. 3 (Prélude) <- The bells
    of Moscow: RACHMANINOFF
Morgenfantasie -> Der Flüchtling, D. 67; Der Flüchtling, D.
    402: SCHUBERT
Morning is charming, The <- Hunting song: HÄNDEL
Morning song <- Maytime in Sussex: BAX
Morning song -> Lieder ohne Worte, op. 62 (No. 4): MENDELS-
    SOHN
Moro di Venezia, Il -> Otello: ROSSINI
Moro per amore / Rodrigo -> Floridoro: STRADELLA
Morta di S. Giuseppe, La <- La fenice sul rogo: PERGOLESI
Morto redivivo, Il <- San Antonio: CALDARA
Morzin symphonies -> Symphony, M. 1, D major; M. 2, C major;
    M. 4, D major; M. 10, D major; M. 15, D major; M. 18, G
    major; M. 37, C major: J.HAYDN
Mosaic -> Quartet, strings, no. 3: COWELL
Mosè in Egitto <- Moses: ROSSINI
Moses -> Mosè in Egitto: ROSSINI
Moses fantasy / Fantasia on the G-string -> Sonata a preghi-
    era con variazioni, violin & orchestra: PAGANINI
Moss garden / A magic garden -> Koke no niwa: HOVANESS
Motet de l'année dernière -> Lauda Jerusalem: COUPERIN
Motet de St. Augustin -> Jucunda vox ecclesiae: COUPERIN
Motet de St. Barthelémy -> Laetantur coeli: COUPERIN
Motet de Ste. Anne -> Festiva laetis cantibus: COUPERIN

Motet de Ste. Suzanne -> Veni, veni sponsa Christi: COUPERIN
Motet pour le jour de Pâques -> Victoria! Christo resurgenti:
    COUPERIN
Motets [1563] (Dies sanctificatus) <- In festo nativitatis
    Domini: PALESTRINA
Motets, op. 69 (Herr, nun lässest du) <- Lobgesang der Sime-
    on: MENDELSSOHN
Motets, op. 69 (Mein Herz erhebet Gott) <- Lobgesang der Ma-
    ria / Magnificat: MENDELSSOHN
Mountain dance, piano, no. 2 -> Macedonian mountain dance,
    piano, op. 144b: HOVANESS
Mountain maid, The -> Haugtussa: GRIEG
Mountain symphony / Bergsymphonie -> Ce qu'on entend sur la
    montagne: LISZT
Moy Mell <- An Irish tone poem / The pleasant plain: BAX
Mozart variations -> Variationen und Fuge über ein Thema von
    Mozart, 2 pianos: REGER
Mozartiana -> Suite, orchestra, no. 4, op. 61, G major:
    TCHAIKOVSKY
Mpeca scoperta, La <- L'imbroglio scoperto: LEO
Müllerlieder -> Die schöne Müllerin: SCHUBERT
Muette de Portici, La <- Masaniello: AUBER
Mulató gajd <- Tavern song / Merrymaking: KODÁLY
Murillo <- La corde du pendu: MEYERBEER
Muse de Monaco, La -> Pièces de clavecin, 3. livre, 15. ord-
    re (La princesse de Chabeuil): Couperin
Muse ménagère, La <- Household suite: MILHAUD
Muse Urania e Clio, Le -> Sole, Urania e Clio: A.SCARLATTI
Musette, La -> Suite, string orchestra, g1, G minor: TELE-
    MANN
Music for children -> Summer day suite, orchestra: PROKOFIEV
Music for children [arr.] <- Miniatures: WALTON
Music for radio <- Saga of the prairie / Prairie journal:
    COPLAND
Music for the royal fireworks / The royal fireworks -> Fire-
    works music: HÄNDEL
Music in London -> Symphony, no. 1, Bb major: BOYCE
Musica notturna delle strade di Madrid, La -> Quartet,
    strings, G. 324, C major: BOCCHERINI
Musical joke, A / Ein musikalischer Spass / Alster overture
    -> Suite, orchestra, F11, F major: TELEMANN
Musicalische Exequien <- German requiem: SCHÜTZ
Musiche sacre (Mass) <- Messa concertata: CAVALLI
Musik zu einer Pantomime, string orchestra, K. 416d (446) <-
    Pantalon und Columbine: MOZART
Musikalischer Scherz -> Perpetuum mobile: JOHANN STRAUSS
Musikalischer Spass, Ein, K. 522 <- Bauernsinfonie / Dorfmu-
    sikanten-Sextett: MOZART

Musikalischer Spass, Ein / A musical joke / Alster overture
-> Suite, orchestra, F11, F major: TELEMANN
Musique héroïque <- Marches héroïques / Heroic marches: TELE-
MANN
Musique réligieuse, voice, chorus & organ, op. 113 <- Masonic
ritual music / Ye onward brethren:SIBELIUS
My beloved is mine / Canticle I -> Canticle in memory of Dick
Sheppard: BRITTEN
My country -> Josef Kajetán Tyl (Overture): DVOŘÁK
My heart is inditing of a good matter <- Coronation anthem:
PURCELL
My Lisochek -> Songs, op. 54 (Lullaby): TCHAIKOVSKY
My Lord of Oxenford's maske / The Earl of Oxford's march ->
The battell (The march before the battle): BYRD
Myrthen (Widmung) <- Liebeslied: SCHUMANN
Myrthen (Zum Schluss;arr.) <- Zur Trauerfeier: SCHUMANN
Myrthen-Kränze-Walzer, orchestra <- Elisabethsklänge: JOHANN
STRAUSS
Mysterious mountain -> Symphony, no. 2, op. 132: HOVANESS
Mystery sonatas / Rosenkranz-Sonaten / Rosary sonatas / Bib-
lical sonatas -> Sonata, violin & continuo [Bayerische
Staatsbibliothek: Mus. Ms. 4123] no. 1, D minor; no. 2, A
major; no. 3, B minor; no. 4, D minor; no. 5, A major; no.
6, C minor; no. 7, F major; no. 8, Bb major; no. 9, A minor; no. 10, G minor; no. 11, G major; no. 12, C major; no.
13, D minor; no. 14, D major; no. 15, C major; no. 16, G
minor: BIBER

Nachklänge von Ossian <- Ossian overture: GADE
Nacht in der Spinnstube -> Lieder, op. 107 (Mädchenlied):
BRAHMS
Nachtgesang -> Licht und Liebe, D. 352: SCHUBERT
Nachtigall, Die -> Seufzer, D. 198: SCHUBERT
Nachtmusique -> Serenade, K. 388, C minor: MOZART
Nachtwächterbass-Serenade / Nightwatchman's call serenade ->
Serenade, string orchestra, C major: BIBER
Nächtliches Ständchen / Ruhe -> Leise, leise lasst uns sing-
en, D. 635: SCHUBERT
Näherin und Trompeter -> Fleurette: OFFENBACH
Närrischer Traum, Ein <- Der Traum: M.HAYDN
Naila / Soir de fête -> La source: DELIBES
Naissance d'Osiris, La <- La fête pamilie: RAMEAU
Namensfeier für Franz Michael Vierthaler, D. 294 <- Gratula-
tions-Kantate: SCHUBERT
Namensfeier-Ouvertüre / Zur Namensfeier -> Overture, op. 115,
C major: BEETHOVEN
Nanga Parvat -> Symphony, no. 7, band, op. 178: HOVANESS
Nativité du Seigneur, La <- Meditations for organ / Nine me-

ditations for organ: MESSIAEN

Nativity, The /Christmas oratorio / The Christmas story /
  Weihnachtshistorie -> Historia von der Geburt Jesu Christi:
  SCHÜTZ

Nature et patrie -> Callias: GRÉTRY

Nature will prevail -> Love triumphant: PURCELL

Neapolitan folk dance -> Sonata, K. 487 (L. 205) C major: D.
  SCARLATTI

Neapolitanische Lieder <- Canzoni 'e copp' 'o tammurro: HENZE

Negra, La <- La nouvelle Ourika: DONIZETTI

Neige, La <- Le nouvel Éginard: AUBER

Nel chiuso centro -> L'Orfeo: PERGOLESI

Nelson mass / Imperial mass / Missa in augustiis / Coronation
  mass -> Mass, H.XXII, 11, D minor: J.HAYDN

Nelson-Arie / Pindarick ode -> The battle of the Nile: J.
  HAYDN

Nemici generosi, I <- Il duello per complimento: CIMAROSA

Nénies <- Dirges, op. 9a: BARTÓK

Nereid <- Ideala: BAX

Nerone, Il <- Sopra un' eccelsa torre: STRADELLA

Neue Gutsherr, Der -> Der Schiffspatron: DITTERSDORF

Neue Lambacher-Sinfonie: WOLFGANG AMADEUS MOZART -> Symphony,
  G major, no. 16: LEOPOLD MOZART

Neue Satanella-Polka -> Diabolin-Polka, orchestra: JOHANN
  STRAUSS

Neumodische Liebhaber, Der <- Die Satyrn in Arcadien: TELE-
  MANN

New England symphony, A -> Three places in New England: IVES

New hopes / At the open window -> Songs, op. 63 (I opened the
  window): TCHAIKOVSKY

New Irish tune, A <- Lilliburlero: PURCELL

New World symphony / From the New World -> Symphony, no. 9,
  op. 95, E minor: DVOŘÁK

New Year's greeting <- Christmas carol: KODÁLY

Nicolaimesse / Missa Sancti Nicolai / St. Joseph mass ->
  Mass, H.XXII,6, G major: J.HAYDN

Nigella e Clori -> Cantata pastorale eroica: CALDARA

Night / La nuit -> Etude, piano, op. 31, no. 3, E major: GLA-
  ZUNOV

Night piece -> Paris: DELIUS

Night thoughts <- Homage to Ives: COPLAND

Nightingale, The -> Mazurka, piano, op. posth., A minor: CHO-
  PIN

Nightwatchman's call serenade / Nachtwächterbass-Serenade ->
  Serenade, string orchestra, C major: BIBER

Nimm einen Strahl der Sonne <- Ihr Auge: LISZT

Nina <- La pazza per amore: PAISIELLO

Nina -> Tre giorni son che Nina: PERGOLESI

Nina e Martuffo -> Chi dell' altrui si veste presto si spoglia: CIMAROSA
Nine enchanted stags, The / The giant stags -> Cantata profana: BARTÓK
Nine meditations for organ / Meditations for organ -> La nativité du Seigneur: MESSIAEN
1942 symphony -> Symphony, no. 4: ANTHEIL
1905 symphony / The year 1905 -> Symphony, no. 11, op. 103:
SHOSTAKOVICH
1917 symphony / The year 1917 / To the memory of Lenin ->
Symphony, no. 12, op. 112: SHOSTAKOVICH
1933 symphony -> Symphony, no. 1: HARRIS
1922 suite, piano <- Suite, piano, op. 26: HINDEMITH
Ninfa e il pastore, La -> Serenata a tre: VIVALDI
Ninna-Nanna <- Per Giuliana: CASTELNUOVO-TEDESCO
Nonna-nonna, La <- La mère au berceau de son fils: DONIZETTI
Nitschewo-Polka -> Louischen: JOHANN STRAUSS
No, non turbarti <- La tempestà: BEETHOVEN
No se emenderà jamas <- Cantata spagnuola: HÄNDEL
No wit like a woman's -> Sir Barnaby Wigg: PURCELL
Noble famous Queen, The -> While Phoebus us'd to dwell: BYRD
Nocturne -> At twilight: FIBICH
Nocturne, piano, op. 27, no. 1, C# minor <- Reminiscence:
CHOPIN
Noël allemande -> Concertos de Noël (No. 5): CORRETTE
Non più, tutto ascoltai -> Non temer, amato bene, K. 490: MO-
ZART
Non temer, amato bene, K. 490 <- Non più, tutto ascoltai: MO-
ZART
Nonet, mixed voices & orchestra <- Impressão rapida de todo o
Brasil: VILLA-LOBOS
Nordic symphony -> Symphony, no. 1, op. 21, E minor: HANSON
Nordland-Suite / Swedish suite -> Suite, orchestra, no. 2,
op. 89: BRUCH
Norse sonata -> Sonata, piano, no. 3, op. 57: MACDOWELL
Northern symphony -> Symphony, no. 3: BAX
Norwegian folk dances -> Slåtter, piano, op. 72: GRIEG
Notebook for Wilhelm Friedemann Bach -> Clavier-Büchlein vor
Wilhelm Friedemann Bach: J.S.BACH
Notenbuch der Anna Magdalena Bach <- Clavierbüchlein der Anna
Magdalena Bach: J.S.BACH
Notte, La -> Concerto, bassoon & string orchestra, R. 501, Bb
major; Concerto, flute & string orchestra, R. 439, G minor;
Concerto, orchestra, R. 28, G minor: VIVALDI
Notturno, op. 148 -> Adagio, piano trio, D. 897, Eb major:
SCHUBERT
Notturno, 4 orchestras, K. 269a (286) D major <- Notturno
serenade: MOZART

Notturno, viola & piano, op. 42, D major -> Serenade, string trio, op. 8, D major [arr.]: BEETHOVEN

Notturno elegiaco -> Elegy, horn & organ, op. 5: ALFVÉN

Notturno serenade -> Notturno, 4 orchestras, K. 269a (286) D major: MOZART

Nous nous marirons dimanche -> Concertos comiques (No. 20): CORRETTE

Nouveau séducteur, Le -> Le timide: AUBER

Nouvel Éginard, Le -> La neige: AUBER

Nouvelle mariée, La / The bride's complaint -> Songs, op. 47 (Was I not a little blade of grass?): TCHAIKOVSKY

Nouvelle Ourika, La -> La negra: DONIZETTI

Novae aliquot et ante <- Bicinia: LASSUS

Novelettes, piano [arr.] -> Short story: GERSHWIN

Novize von Palermo, Die -> Das Liebesverbot: WAGNER

Now does the glorious day appear <- Ode for Queen Mary's birthday [1689]: PURCELL

Now that the sun hath veiled his light <- Evening hymn: PUR-CELL

Nozani-na orekna / Pica-pao -> Chôros, no. 3: VILLA-LOBOS

Nozze con l'inimico, Le <- L'Analinda: A.SCARLATTI

Nürnberger Partita -> Concentus musico-instrumentalis (No.7): FUX

Nuit, La / Night -> Etude, piano, op. 31, no. 3, E major: GLA-ZUNOV

Nuit des tropiques, La <- Symphony, no. 1: GOTTSCHALK

Nuits d'été (Au cimetière) <- Clair de lune: BERLIOZ

Nuits d'été (L'îsle inconnu) <- Barcarolle: BERLIOZ

Nullte Symphonie -> Symphony, D minor: BRUCKNER

Nun danket alle Gott / Leipzig chorales -> Chorale prelude, S. 657: J.S.BACH

Nun danket den Herre Gott, S. 252 <- Trauungschoräle / Wedding chorales: J.S.BACH

Nun komm der Heiden Heiland / Leipzig chorales -> Chorale prelude, S. 659; Chorale prelude, S. 660; Chorale prelude, S. 661: J.S.BACH

Nun lasst uns den Leib begraben, D. 168 <- Begräbnislied: SCHUBERT

Nuovo Don Chisciotte, Il -> Il fantastico: LEO

Nuovo Pourceaugnac, Il -> Il Giovedi Grasso: DONIZETTI

Nurmahal <- Das Rosenfest von Cashmir: SPONTINI

Nursery, The <- Enfantines: MUSORGSKY

Nut-brown maid, The -> Henry and Emma: ARNE

Nymphe de Diane, La -> Sylvia: DELIBES

Nymphes de Diane, Les -> Zéphire: RAMEAU

Nymphes des bois, déesses des fontaines -> La déploration de Jehan Ockeghem: DEPRÈS

Nymphs of the ocean -> The Oceanides: SIBELIUS

O be joyful in the Lord <- Chandos jubilate: HÄNDEL
O beata et benedicta -> Zum Feste der Dreieinigkeit: MENDELS-
SOHN
O divine redeemer -> Repentir: GOUNOD
O Ewigkeit, du Donnerwort, S. 60 <- Dialogus zwischen Furcht
und Hoffnung: J.S.BACH
O heilige Nacht <- Weihnachtslied: LISZT
O holder Tag, S. 210 <- Hochzeits-Kantate / Wedding cantata:
J.S.BACH
O imprevisto -> Symphony, no. 1: VILLA-LOBOS
O komm' im Traum / Like Laura's ghost -> Oh, quand je dors:
LISZT
O la, o che bon eccho <- Echo song: LASSUS
O lamm Gottes, unschuldig / Leipzig chorales -> Chorale pre-
lude, S. 656: J.SBACH
O Lieb', so lang du lieben kannst <- Canzona / Liebestraum:
LISZT
O Lord of whom I do depend <- The humble sute of a sinner:
DOWLAND
O Lord, turn not away thy face <- The lamentation of a sin-
ner: DOWLAND
O numi eterni! -> La Lucretia: HÄNDEL
O thou moonlit night / In this summer night -> Songs, op. 73
(In this moonlight): TCHAIKOVSKY
O tres piteulx -> Lamentatio Sanctae Matris ecclesiae Con-
stantinopolitanae: DUFAY
O virgo virginum <- Marian motets: DEPRÈS
Obertura republicana <- Chapultepec: CHAVEZ
Occasione fa il ladro, L' <- Il cambia della valigia: ROSSINI
Océan -> Symphony, no. 2, op. 42, C major: RUBINSTEIN
Ocean etude -> Etude, piano, op. 25, no. 12, C minor: CHOPIN
Ocean moods -> Childhood memories of ocean moods: HARRIS
Oceanides, The <- Nymphs of the ocean: SIBELIUS
Ochsenmenüett / Menuet du boeuf -> Minuet, orchestra, H.IX,
27: J.HAYDN
Octave etude -> Grandes études de Paganini, piano (No. 2):
LISZT
Octaves etude -> Etude, piano, op. 25, no. 10, B minor: CHO-
PIN
October symphony / To October -> Symphony, no. 2, op. 14:
SHOSTAKOVICH
Ode, orchestra <- An elegiac song: STRAVINSKY
Ode an die Freude / Ode to joy -> Symphony, no. 9, op. 125,
D minor (Presto): BEETHOVEN
Ode for Mr. Louis Maidwell's school <- Celestial music: PUR-
CELL
Ode for Queen mary's birthday [1689] -> Now does the glori-

ous day appear: PURCELL

Ode for Queen Mary's birthday [1690] -> Arise, my muse: PUR-
CELL

Ode for Queen Mary's birthday [1691] -> Welcome, welcome glorious morn: PURCELL

Ode for Queen Mary's birthday [1692] -> Love's goddess sure
was blind: PURCELL

Ode for Queen Mary's birthday [1693] -> Celebrate this festival: PURCELL

Ode for Queen Mary's birthday [1694] -> Come, ye sons of art:
PURCELL

Ode for Saint Cecilia's Day [1683] -> Welcome to all the
pleasures: PURCELL

Ode for Saint Cecilia's Day [1695] -> Raise, raise the voice:
PURCELL

Ode on the death of Queen Caroline -> Funeral anthem: HÄNDEL

Ode to joy / Ode an die Freude -> Symphony, no. 9, op. 125,
D minor (Presto): BEETHOVEN

Ode to Queen mary [1690] -> High on a throne of glittering
ore: PURCELL

Ode to thunder / Donnerode -> Wie ist dein Name so gross:
TELEMANN

Ode to women -> An die Frauen: J.HAYDN

Odisséia da paz -> Symphony, no. 7: VILLA-LOBOS

Odysseus symphony -> Symphony, no. 25, op. 275: HOVANESS

Örtagårsmästaren / Hortulanus / The keeper of the garden ->
Symphony, no. 5: ROSENBERG

Österreichische Quartette / Austrian quartets / Wiener Quartette / Viennese quartets -> Quartet, strings, K. 168, F
major; K. 169, A major; K.170, C major; K. 171, E♭ major;
K.172, B♭ major; K. 173, D minor: MOZART

Offertorium de B.V. Maria, K. 277 -> Alma Dei creatoris: MO-
ZART

Office du samedi matin -> Service sacré pour le samedi matin: MILHAUD

Officium defunctorum (Missa pro defunctis) <- Requiem: VIC-
TORIA

Officium hebdomadae sanctae (Passio secundum Ioannem) <-
Passion according to St. John / St. John Passion: VICTORIA

Oh, my lovely maiden -> Bolero, piano: GLINKA

Oh, quand je dors <- Like Laura's ghost / O komm im Traum:
LISZT

Oiseaux et les sources, Les -> Messe de la Pentecôte (Communion): MESSIAEN

Ojos criollos <- Danse cubaine: GOTTSCHALK

Old English carols <- Christmas carols: HOLST

Old flame, An <- A retrospect: IVES

Old man's song <- The harper's song / Song of the old man:

MUSORGSKY
Olimpia -> Alceste in Ebuda: PAISIELLO
Ombra felice -> Io ti lascio, e questo addio: MOZART
Omphale, L' -> Suite, string orchestra, e8, E minor: TELEMANN
On Sjølund's fair plains -> Symphony, no. 1, op. 5, C minor: GADE
On the Dnieper <- Yarema's song: MUSORGSKY
On the shore -> Lieder ohne Worte, op. 53 (No. 1): MENDELS-
SOHN
Once I passed through a populous city <- Idyll: DELIUS
Once upon a time -> Eventyr: DELIUS
One small word / Sweet maid, answer me -> Songs, op. 28 (The
fearful minute): TCHAIKOVSKY
135th Street -> Blue Monday: GERSHWIN
Ongaku <- Gagaku / Impressions of court music: COWELL
Onward ye brethren / Masonic ritual music -> Musique réligi-
euse, voice, chorus & organ, op. 113: SIBELIUS
Opayayie <- La reine des îles: OFFENBACH
Opera of operas <- Tom Thumb the great: ARNE
Operas (Selections) <- Christopher Columbus: OFFENBACH
Operas (Selections; arr.) <- The great elopement: HÄNDEL
Operas (Selections; arr.) <- Love in Bath: HÄNDEL
Operas (Selections; arr.) <- Les patineurs: MEYERBEER
Operas (Selections; arr.) <- Gaieté parisienne: OFFENBACH
Operettas (Selections; arr.) <- Bouffes parisiennes: OFFEN-
BACH
Ora pro nobis <- Litanei: LISZT
Oracolo in Messenia, L' <- La Merope: VIVALDI
Oratio, L' -> Le gare dell' amor paterno: STRADELLA
Oratorio per la Passione di nostro Signore Gesù Cristo <-
Passion oratorio: A.SCARLATTI
Orb and sceptre <- Coronation march [1953]: WALTON
Orchester-Lieder, op. 4 <- Altenberg-Lieder: BERG
Orchestervariationen über ein Thema von N. Paganini <- Paga-
nini-Variationen: BLACHER
Orchestra song, The <- The band song: SCHUMAN
Orchestral variations -> Variations, piano [arr.]: COPLAND
Orest auf Tauris, D. 548 <- Der landende Orest: SCHUBERT
Orfeo, L' <- Nel chiuso centro: PERGOLESI
Orfeo ed Euridice -> L'anima del filosofo: J.HAYDN
Organ grinder, The / Der Leiermann -> Deutsche Tänze, K. 602
(No. 4): MOZART
Organ solc mass -> Missa brevis, K. 259, C major: MOZART
Organ symphony -> Symphony, no. 1 [1924]: COPLAND
Organ symphony -> Symphony, no. 3, op. 78, C minor: SAINT-
SAËNS
Organoeida ad missam lectam <- Silent mass: KODÁLY
Oriental fantasy / Fantaisie orientale -> Islamey: BALAKIREV

Oriental song -> Songs, op. 2 (The rose and the nightingale):
RIMSKY-KORSAKOV
Oriental suite -> Beni Mora: HOLST
Origin of fire, The <- Ukko the firemaker: SIBELIUS
Originaltänze, piano, D. 365 <- Erste Walzer / First waltzes,
op. 9: SCHUBERT
Originaltänze, piano, D. 365 (No. 2) <- Sehnsuchtwalzer /
Trauerwalzer: SCHUBERT
Origins of the Amazon, The / The sun and the moon -> Lenda
amerindie (Erosão): VILLA-LOBOS
Orione <- Diana vendicata: J.C.BACH
Orismene, L' -> Dalli sdegni d'amore: LEO
Orlando <- La gelosa pazzia: A.SCARLATTI
Orphanage mass / Waisenhausmesse -> Mass, K. 47a (139) C mi-
nor: MOZART
Orphée et Euridice / Metamorphosen-Sinfonien / Ovid sympho-
nies -> Symphony, K. 84: DITTERSDORF
Orpheus -> Lied des Orpheus, D. 474: SCHUBERT
Os bichinhos -> Prole do bebê, no. 2: VILLA-LOBOS
Ossian overture -> Nachklänge von Ossian: GADE
Osterkantate / Easter cantata -> Der Himmel lacht, die Erde
jubiliert, S. 31: J.S.BACH
Osterlied -> Jesus Christus unser Heiland, D. 168A: SCHUBERT
Ostwind / Glückliches Geheimnis -> Suleika, D. 720: SCHUBERT
Otello <- Il moro di Venezia: ROSSINI
Ottavina, L' -> Concerto, violin & string orchestra, R. 763,
A major: VIVALDI
Otto mesi in due ore <- Gli esiliati in Siberia: DONIZETTI
Ottone, re d'Italia -> Adelaida di Borgogna: ROSSINI
Ours, L' / The bear / Paris symphonies -> Symphony, M. 82, C
major: J.HAYDN
Ouverture à la burlesque -> Suite, string orchestra, F10, F
major: TELEMANN
Ouverture à la pastorelle -> Suite, string orchestra, F7, F
major: TELEMANN
Ouverture burlesque -> Suite, string orchestra, B8, Bb major:
TELEMANN
Over the pavements -> Scherzo, band: IVES
Overtura chinesa, op. 37 / Chinese overture -> Turandot (O-
verture): WEBER
Overture [1954] <- Holland Festival overture: BADINGS
Overture, D. 590, D major <- Italian overtures: SCHUBERT
Overture, D. 591, C major <- Italian overtures: SCHUBERT
Overture, K. 311a (Anh. 8) Bb major <- Paris overture: MOZART
Overture, K. 333, C major <- Costantino overture: FUX
Overture, op. 42, Bb major <- American overture: PROKOFIEV
Overture, op. 101, C major <- Trumpet overture: MENDELSSOHN
Overture, op. 115, C major <- Namensfeier-Ouvertüre / Zur

Namensfeier: BEETHOVEN
Overture in the French style -> Partita, harpsichord, S. 831,
    B minor: J.S.BACH
Overture on Hebrew themes, piano, clarinet & string quartet
    <- Hebrew overture: PROKOFIEV
Overture solennelle -> 1812 overture: TCHAIKOVSKY
Ovid symphonies / Metamorphosen-Sinfonien -> Symphony, K. 73;
    K. 74; K. 75; K. 76; K. 77; K. 78; K. 79; K; 80; K. 81; K.
    82; K. 83; K. 84: DITTERSDORF
Oxana's caprices -> The little slippers: TCHAIKOVSKY
Oxford symphony -> Symphony, M. 92, G major: J.HAYDN

Pacsirta, A <- Wo die Lerche singt: LEHÁR
Paganini etudes -> Grandes études de Paganini, piano: LISZT
Paganini studies / Paganini variations -> Studien, piano,
    op. 35: BRAHMS
Paganini studies -> Studien nach Capricen von Paganini, pi-
    ano, op. 3: SCHUMANN
Paganini variations -> Orchestervariationen über ein Thema
    von N. Paganini: BLACHER
Paganini variations / Paganini studies -> Studien, piano,
    op. 35: BRAHMS
Paganini variations -> Variations sur un thème de Paganini,
    violin & orchestra: YSAŸE
Palindrom-Sinfonie / Sturm und Drang symphonies -> Symphony,
    M. 47, G major: J.HAYDN
Pampeana, no. 3 <- A pastoral symphony: GINASTERA
Pantalon und Columbine -> Musik zu einer Pantomime, string
    orchestra, K. 416d (446): MOZART
Pantins, Les -> Concertos comiques (No. 17): CORRETTE
Papsthymnus, Der -> Pio IX: LISZT
Paraphrases de concert (Rigoletto) <- Rigoletto paraphrase:
    LISZT
Pardon de Ploërmel, Le <- Dinorah: MEYERBEER
Pari, le <- Mombreuil et Merville: BOIELDIEU
Paride sull' Ida <- Gli amori di Paride con Enone: CALDARA
Paris <- Night piece: DELIUS
Paris overture -> Overture, K. 311a (Anh. 8) Bb major: MOZART
Paris sonatas -> Sonata, piano, K. 300d (300) A minor; K.
    300h (330) C major; K. 300i (331) A major; K. 300k (332) F
    major; K. 315c (333) Bb major: MOZART
Paris suite / Impressions of Paris -> Suite symphonique:
    IBERT
Paris symphonies -> Symphony, M. 82, C major; M. 83, G minor;
    M. 84, Eb major; M. 85, Bb major; M. 86, D major; M. 87, A
    major: J.HAYDN
Paris symphony -> Symphony, K. 300a (297) D major: MOZART
Parisian quartets -> Quartet, flute, strings & continuo

[1738] No. 1, G major; no. 2, D major; no. 3, A major; no. 4, G minor; no. 5, E minor; no. 6, D major; no. 7, D major; no. 8, A minor; no. 9, G major; no. 10, B minor; no. 11, A major; no. 12, E minor: TELEMANN

Parnasse, La <- L'apothéose de Corelli: COUPERIN

Partenza -> Stelle, perfide stelle: HÄNDEL

Partenza del reggimento, La -> Rataplan: DONIZETTI

Partita, harpsichord, S. 825, B♭ major <- German suites: J.S. BACH

Partita, harpsichord, S. 826, C minor <- German suites: J.S. BACH

Partita, harpsichord, S. 827, A minor <- German suites: J.S. BACH

Partita, harpsichord, S. 828, D major <- German suites: J.S. BACH

Partita, harpsichord, S. 829, G major <- German suites: J.S. BACH

Partita, harpsichord, S. 830, E minor <- German suites: J.S. BACH

Partita, harpsichord, S. 831, B minor <- Overture in French style: J.S.BACH

Pas de fleurs -> Valse: DELIBES

Passage de la mer Rouge, Le / Moïse -> Moïse et Pharaon: ROSSINI

Passio Domini nostri Jesu Christi secundum Joannem <- St.John Passion: LASSUS

Passio Domini nostri Jesu Christi secundum Lucam <- St. Luke Passion: LASSUS

Passio Domini nostri Jesu Christi secundum Marcum <- St.Mark Passion: LASSUS

Passio Domini nostri Jesu Christi secundum Matthaeum <- St. Matthew Passion: LASSUS

Passion -> Lieder ohne Worte, op. 85 (No. 3): MENDELSSOHN

Passion [ca. 1716] <- The Passion of Christ / Brockes Passion: HÄNDEL

Passion [St. John] <- Historia des Leidens und Sterbens unsers Herrn Jesu Christi, nach dem Evangelisten St. Johannem / St. John Passion: SCHÜTZ

Passion [St. Luke] <- St. Luke Passion: SCHÜTZ

Passion [St. Luke: 1744] <- St. Luke Passion: TELEMANN

Passion [St. Matthew] <- St. Matthew Passion / Historia des Leidens und Sterbens unsers Herrn Jesu Christi, nach dem Evangelisten S. Matheus: SCHÜTZ

Passion [St. Matthew: 1730] <- St. Matthew Passion: TELEMANN

Passion according to St. John, The / St. John Passion -> Gradualia, book 1 (Turbarum voces in passione Domini): BYRD

Passion according to St. John, The / St. John Passion -> Officium hebdomadae sanctae (Passio secundum Ioannem): VICTORIA

Passion according to St. Luke <- St. Luke Passion: PENDERECKI
Passion cantata -> Die letzten Leiden des Erlösers:C.P.E.
  BACH
Passion of Christ, The / Brockes Passion -> Passion [ca.
  1716]: HÄNDEL
Passion oratorio -> Oratorio per la Passione di nostro Sig-
  nore Gesù Cristo: A.SCARLATTI
Passione, la / Sturm und Drang symphonies -> Symphony, M.
  49, F minor: J.HAYDN
Passionskantate -> Grabmusik, K. 35a (42): MOZART
Passionslied -> Kommet her, ihr frechen Sünder: MOZART
Pastor fido, Il <- Sonata, flute & harpsichord, op. 13, no.
  1, C major; no. 2, C major; no. 3, G major; no. 4, A major;
  no. 5, C major; no. 6, G minor: VIVALDI
Pastoral concerto / Concerto alla rustica -> Concerto, violin
  & string orchestra, R. 151, G major: VIVALDI
Pastoral concerto for the Nativity / Christmas concerto ->
  Concerto grosso, op. 8, no. 6, G minor: TORELLI
Pastoral coronation song, A -> While Thirsis, wrapt in downy
  sleep: PURCELL
Pastoral elegy on the death of John Playford / Elegy on the
  death of John Playford -> Gentle shepherds, you that know:
  PURCELL
Pastoral sonata -> Sonata, piano, no. 15, op. 28, D major:
  BEETHOVEN
Pastoral sonata -> Sonata, harpsichord, K. 9 (L. 413) D mi-
  nor: D.SCARLATTI
Pastoral symphony / Pastorale -> Symphony, no. 6, op. 68, F
  major: BEETHOVEN
Pastoral symphony -> Pampeana, no. 3: GINASTERA
Pastoral symphony -> Symphony, no. 7, op. 77, F major: GLA-
  ZUNOV
Pastoral symphony -> Symphony, op. 4, no. 2, D major: STAMITZ
Pastoral symphony -> Symphony, no. 3: VAUGHAN WILLIAMS
Pastorale / Pastoral symphony -> Symphony, no. 6, op. 68, F
  major: BEETHOVEN
Pastorale -> Symphonie pour petit orchestre, no. 2: MILHAUD
Pastorale, piano <- Hungarian Christmas song / Ungarisches
  Weihnachtslied: DOHNÁNYI
Pastorale per il santissimo Natale, op. 2, no. 12 <- Christ-
  mas concerto: MANFREDINI
Pastorale, theme and variations, harp, B. 161, G minor <-
  Theme and variations, harp: HÄNDEL
Pastorale Watteau -> Ruses d'amour: GLAZUNOV
Pastoral-Sonate -> Sonata, organ, no. 3, op. 88, G major:
  RHEINBERGER
Pastorella, La, D. 513 <- Il filosofo di campagna: SCHUBERT
Pastorella, La -> Concerto, orchestra, R. 95, D major: VIVALDI

Pastorella riconosciuta, La -> La villana riconosciuta: CIMA-
ROSA

Pastorelle, La <- Il faut aimer: COUPERIN

Pastourelle <- L'éventail de Jeanne: POULENC

Pathétique sonata -> Sonata, piano, no. 8, op. 13, C minor:
BEETHOVEN

Pathétique symphony -> Symphony, no. 6, op. 74, B minor:
TCHAIKOVSKY

Patineurs, Les -> Operas (Selections; arr.): MEYERBEER

Patriotic march <- Karelia's fate: SIBELIUS

Patriotische König, Der -> Alfred, König der Angelsachsen: J.
HAYDN

Patti-Polka, orchestra <- Lach-Polka: JOSEPH STRAUSS

Paukenmesse / Mass in time of war / Missa in tempore belli
-> Mass, XXII,9, C major: J.HAYDN

Paukenschlag-Symphonie / Surprise symphony / London symphonies / Salomon symphonies -> Symphony, M. 94, G major: J.
HAYDN

Paukenwirbel-Symphonie / Drum-roll symphony / London symphonies / Salomon symphonies -> Symphony, M. 103, E♭ major: J.
HAYDN

Paulus <- St. Paul oratorio: MENDELSSOHN

Pavan, keyboard instrument, H. 18 <- Lord Salisbury's pavan:
GIBBONS

Pavan, keyboard instrument, T. 41 <- Earl Stafford's pavan:
TOMKINS

Pavan, keyboard instrument, T. 43 <- Earl Stafford's pavan:
TOMKINS

Pavan, keyboard instrument, T. 57 <- Lord Canterbury's pavan: TOMKINS

Pavan, 5 viols, A minor <- Deleroye pavan: GIBBONS

Pavan and galliard, virginal, MB 59 < Pavana bray; Galliarda
bray: BYRD

Pavana bray -> Pavan and galliard, virginal, MB 59: BYRD

Paysans changes a grenouilles, Les / Metamorphosen-Sinfonien
/ Ovid symphonies -> Symphony, K. 78: DITTERSDORF

Paz, A -> Symphony, no. 5: VILLA-LOBOS

Pazza per amore, La -> Nina: PAISIELLO

Pazzia in trono, La <- Caligola delirante: CAVALLI

Pazzie di Stellidaura e Zoroastro, Le -> Le magie di Merlina
e Zoroastro: CIMAROSA

Pazzo apposto, Lo <- Il finto pazzo: LEO

Peacock variations / Felszállott a páva -> Variations on a
Hungarian folksong, orchestra: KODÁLY

Peasant cantata / Bauernkantate -> Mer hahn en neue oberkeet,
S. 212: J.S.BACH

Peasant's lullaby, A / Sleep, son of peasants -> Cradle song:
MUSORGSKY

Peascod time <- The hunt's up: GIBBONS
Pedagogic overture <- Doctor Syntax: WALTON
Pélage <- Le roi de la paix: SPONTINI
Pèlerins de la Mecque, Les -> La rencontre imprévue: GLUCK
Pellerins, Les (La marche) <- Au temple d'amour: COUPERIN
Penitential psalms -> Psalmi Davidici: A.GABRIELI
Penitential psalms -> Domine, ne in furore tuo; Miserere mei,
    Deus: LASSUS
People's choice, The -> Transatlantic: ANTHEIL
Per Giuliana -> Ninna-Nanna: CASTELNUOVO-TEDESCO
Perpetuum mobile <- Musikalischer Scherz: JOHANN STRAUSS
Perpetuum mobile -> Suite, string orchestra, D12, D major:
    TELEMANN
Pescatore, Il <- Balle il bronzo; Era l'ora: DONIZETTI
Pescatrice, La <- L'erede riconosciuta: PICCINNI
Pesther Carneval / Carneval de Pesth -> Rhapsodie hongroise,
    piano, no. 9: LISZT
Peter und Paul reisen im Schlaraffenland <- Max und Moritz
    reisen ins Schlaraffenland: LEHÁR
Petite Marguerite <- En avril: BIZET
Petite messe solennelle <- Messe solennelle: ROSSINI
Petites études, piano <- Short etudes: PEPIN
Petites pièces enfantines -> Villageoises: POULENC
Petites prières de Saint François d'Assise <- Prayers of
    Saint Francis of Assisi: POULENC
Petöfi symphony -> Symphony, no. 4, op. 119: HUBAY
Petrarca sonnets -> Années de pelerinage, 2. année (Sonetto
    47 del petrarca); (Sonetto 104 del Petrarca); (Sonetto 123
    del petrarca): LISZT
Petroushka (Fête populaire de la semaine grasse) <- Danse de
    la foire: STRAVINSKY
Pfauenkirchfahrt, Die / Die Bauernkirchfahrt -> Sonata, 3
    violins, 2 violas & continuo, B♭ major: BIBER
Pfingstoratorium / Whitsun oratorio -> Spiritus intelligen-
    tiae sanctus: KRENEK
Phantasie trio -> Trio, piano & strings, no. 1, A minor:
    IRELAND
Phantasy, oboe & strings, op. 2 <- Fantasy quartet: BRITTEN
Phénix <- Concerto, 3 bassoons & continuo: CORRETTE
Philemon und Baucis <- Jupiters Reise auf die Erde: J.HAYDN
Philosopher, The -> Symphony, M. 22, E major: J.HAYDN
Philosophic symphony -> Symphony, no. 6, A major: BRUCKNER
Phinée avec ses amis changés en rochers / Metamorphosen-
    Sinfonien / Ovid symphonies -> Symphony, K. 77: DITTERS-
    DORF
Phoebus und Pan / Der Streit zwischen Phoebus und Pan / The
    contest between Phoebus and Pan -> Geschwinde, geschwinde
    ihr wirbelnden Winde, S. 201: J.S.BACH

Piacere, Il / Concerto, op. 8, no. 6, C minor -> Il cimento
  dell' armonia e dell' inventione (No. 6): VIVALDI
Piano playin' Jazzbo Brown <- Jasbo Brown blues: GERSHWIN
Pianto d'Arianna, Il / Ariadne's lament -> Concerto a quattro,
  string orchestra, op. 7, no. 6: LOCATELLI
Pica-pao / Nozani-na orekna -> Choros no. 3: VILLA-LOBOS
Piccolo divertimento -> Variations, piano, H.XVII,6, F minor:
  J.HAYDN
Piccolomini mass -> Mass, K. 258, C major: MOZART
Picture, The <- The cuckold in conceit: ARNE
Pièce a tretous, La -> Pièces de clavecin, 3. livre, 19. or-
  dre (Les calotins et les calotines): COUPERIN
Pièce en forme de habanera / Habanera -> Vocalise en forme
  de habanera: RAVEL
Pieces, organ, op. 14 <- In memory of Gallén-Kallela: SIBE-
  LIUS
Pieces, piano, op. 17 <- Sarcasms: PROKOFIEV
Pieces, piano, op. 101 <- Romantic compositions: SIBELIUS
Pieces, piano, op. 103 <- Characteristic impressions: SIBE-
  LIUS
Pièces brèves, piano <- Feuillets d'album: FAURÉ
Pièces brèves, violin, violoncello & piano -> Trio, piano &
  strings, no. 1: MARTINŮ
Pièces de clavecin, 1. livre, 1. ordre (La fleurie) <- La
  tendre: COUPERIN
Pièces de clavecin, 2. livre, 9. ordre (Le petit-denil) <-
  Les trois veuves: COUPERIN
Pièces de clavecin, 2. livre, 11. ordre (L'etincalante) <-
  La bontemps: COUPERIN
Pièces de clavecin, 3. livre, 13. ordre (Les folies françoi-
  ses) <- Les dominos: COUPERIN
Pièces de clavecin, 3. livre, 15. ordre (Le dodo) <- L'amour
  au berceau: COUPERIN
Pièces de clavecin, 3. livre, 15. ordre (La princesse de Cha-
  beuil) <- La muse de Monaco: COUPERIN
Pièces de clavecin, 3. livre, 15. ordre (La régente) <- La
  minerve: COUPERIN
Pièces de clavecin, 3, livre, 16. ordre (Les graces incompa-
  rables) <- La conti: COUPERIN
Pièces de clavecin, 3. livre, 17. ordre (La superbe) <- La
  forqueray: COUPERIN
Pièces de clavecin, 3. livre, 18. ordre (Le tic-toc-choc) <-
  Les maillotins: COUPERIN
Pièces de clavecin, 3. livre, 19. ordre (Les calotins et les
  calotines) <- La pièce a tretous: COUPERIN
Pièces de clavecin, 4. livre, 20. ordre (Les cherubins) <-
  L'aimable lazure: COUPERIN
Pièces de clavecin, 4. livre, 24. ordre (Divine Babiche) <-

Pièces enfantines -> De la musique avant toute chose: FRAN-
  ÇAIX
Pièces enfantines -> Chansons naïves: JOLIVET
Pièces faciles, piano, 4 hands [1915; arr.] <- Suite, orch-
  estra, no. 2: STRAVINSKY
Pièces faciles, piano, 4 hands [1917] (Selections; arr.) <-
  Suite, orchestra, no. 1: STRAVINSKY
Pièces hébraïques, violin & piano <- Suite hébraïque: BLOCH
Pièces impromptus -> Suite, piano, no. 3, op. 18: ENESCO
Pièces pittoresques, piano (Selections; arr.) <- Suite pas-
  torale: CHABRIER
Pièces romantiques / Fantastic pieces, op. 12 -> Fantasie-
  stücke, piano, op. 12: SCHUMANN
Pièces tirées de la Temple de Shakespeare -> Chansons d'Ariel:
  MARTIN
Pietro il Grande, czar delle Russie -> Il falegname di Livo-
  nia: DONIZETTI
Piezas caracteristicàs, piano (Barcarolle) <- Ciel sans nu-
  ages: ALBÉNIZ
Pikanterien-Walzer -> Asklepios-Walzer, orchestra: LEHÁR
Pilade e Oreste -> La forza dell' amicizia: CALDARA
Pilgrims, The -> Lieder ohne Worte, op. 67 (No. 3): MENDELS-
  SOHN
Pilgrim's song / To the forest -> Songs, op. 47 (I bless you,
  forests): TCHAIKOVSKY
Pimpinone <- Die ungleiche Heirat: TELEMANN
Pindarick ode / Nelson-Arie -> The battle of the Nile: J.HAYDN
Pio IX <- Der Papsthymnus: LISZT
Piper's dance -> Havana hornpipe: COWELL
Pirati, I -> Chiare e Serafina: DONIZETTI
Pirro e Demetrio <- La forza della fedeltà: A.SCARLATTI
Pisendel concerto -> Concerto, violin & string orchestra, B♭
  major, no. 3: TELEMANN
Pisendel concerto -> Concerto, violin & string orchestra, R.
  340, A major: VIVALDI
Plaisir des dames, Le -> Concertos comiques (NO. 6): CORRETTE
Plaisirs, Les -> Suite, flute & string orchestra, A minor:
  TELEMANN
Plappermäulchen <- Die Plaudertasche: JOSEPH STRAUSS
Platée <- Junon jalouse: RAMEAU
Plaudertasche, Die -> Plappermaulchen: JOSEPH STRAUSS
Playera -> Danzas españolas, piano, op. 37 (No. 5): GRANADOS
Playing house / Little husband, little wife / Petit mari, pe-
  tite femme -> Jeux d'enfants (Duo): BIZET
Pleasant plain, The / An Irish tone poem -> Moy Mell: BAX
Pli selon pli (Improvisation sur Mallarmé, no. 1) <- La vi-
  erge, le vivace et le bel aujourd'hui: BOULEZ
Pli selon pli (Improvisation sur Mallarmé, no. 2) <- Une den-

telle s'abolit: BOULEZ

Ploughboy, The -> Concerto, piano, op. 15, E♭ major (Rondo): DUSSEK

Pluie de diamants <- Goldregen / The golden rain / Pluie d'or: WALDTEUFEL

Pluie d'or / Goldregen / The golden rain -> Pluie de diamants: WALDTEUFEL

Poem of fire -> Prometheus: SKRIABIN

Poème dansé -> Jeux: DEBUSSY

Poème mystique <- Sonata, violin & piano, no. 2: BLOCH

Poems <- Balmont songs: STRAVINSKY

Poems of Verlaine -> Songs, op. 9: STRAVINSKY

Poet's song -> Song [E.E. Cummings]: COPLAND

Poisoned kiss, The <- The empress and the necromancer: VAUGHAN WILLIAMS

Polacca brillante, piano, op. 72, E major <- L'hilarité: WEBER

Poland's downfall -> Polonaise, piano, op. 40, no. 2, C minor: CHOPIN

Poland's greatness / Military polonaise -> Polonaise, piano, op. 40, no. 1, A major: CHOPIN

Polish ballade -> Ballade, piano, no. 1, op. 23, G minor: CHOPIN

Polish fantasy / Fantasia on Polish airs -> Grande fantaisie sur des airs polonais, piano & orchestra, op. 13: CHOPIN

Polish symphony -> Symphony, no. 3, op. 29, D major: TCHAIKOVSKY

Political overture, A -> Slava: BERNSTEIN

Poliuto, Il <- Les martyrs: DONIZETTI

Polka pomnenka, piano, C major <- Forget-me-not polka: DVOŘÁK

Polonaise, op. 74 -> Concerto, clarinet, no. 2, op. 74, E♭ major (Alla polacca): WEBER

Polonaise, piano, op. 26, no. 2, E♭ major <- Siberian polonaise: CHOPIN

Polonaise, piano, op. 40, no. 1, A major <- Military polonaise / Poland's greatness: CHOPIN

Polonaise, piano, op. 40, no. 2, C minor <- Poland's downfall: CHOPIN

Polonaise, piano, op. 44, F# minor <- Tragic polonaise: CHOPIN

Polonaise, piano, op. 53, A♭ major <- Heroic polonaise / Polonaise héroïque: CHOPIN

Polonaise, piano & orchestra, op. 22, E♭ major <- Andante spianato et grande polonaise brillante: CHOPIN

Polonaise, violin & orchestra, op. 4, D major <- Concert polonaise: WIENIAWSKI

Polonaise brillante -> Introduction et polonaise brillante, violoncello & piano, op. 3, C major: CHOPIN

Polonaise héroïque / Heroic polonaise -> Polonaise, piano,
  op. 53, Ab major: CHOPIN
Polonaise-fantaisie, piano, op. 61, Ab major <- Fantaisie
  polonaise: CHOPIN
Pomone <- Herbstweisen: WALDTEUFEL
Pomp and circumstance, no. 1 (Largamente) <- Land of hope
  and glory: ELGAR
Poor shepherd, The -> The sun was sunk: HÄNDEL
Porgy and Bess (Selections; arr.) <- Catfish row: GERSHWIN
Portrait of Georges Hugnet -> Portraits (Barcarolle): THOM-
  SON
Portrait of Lise Deharme -> Portraits (In a bird cage): THOM-
  SON
Portrait of Mlle. Alvarez de Toledo -> Portraits (Tango lull-
  aby): THOMSON
Portrait of Nicolas de Chatelain -> Portraits (Cantabile):
  THOMSON
Portraits (Barcarolle) <- Portrait of Georges Hugnet: THOM-
  SON
Portraits (Cantabile) <- Portrait of Nicolas de Chatelain:
  THOMSON
Portraits (In a bird cage) <- Portrait of Lise Deharme: THOM-
  SON
Portraits (Portrait of Max Kahn) <- Fanfare for France: THOM-
  SON
Portraits (Tango lullaby) <- Portrait of Mlle. Alvarez de
  Toledo: THOMSON
Poseidon sonata, piano, op. 191 <- Sonata, piano, op. 191:
  HOVANESS
Posiana, La -> Rondo, piano, op. 5, F major: CHOPIN
Posthorn concerto / Il corneto da posta -> Concerto, violin
  & string orchestra, R. 363, Bb major: VIVALDI
Posthorn serenade -> Serenade, K. 320, D major: MOZART
Potpourri, orchestra <- Greenwich Village potpourri / Im-
  pressions of bohemian life: SCHUMAN
Poule, La / The hen / Paris symphonies -> Symphony, M. 83,
  G minor: J.HAYDN
Poupée, La / The doll -> Jeux d'enfants (Berceuse): BIZET
Power of music, The -> Alexander's feast: HÄNDEL
Präludium und Fuge über den Namen Bach, organ <- Fantasy and
  fugue on B.A.C.H.: LISZT
Prague mazurka / Kulavy -> Mazurka, piano, op. posth., G ma-
  jor: CHOPIN
Prague symphony -> Symphony, K. 504, D major: MOZART
Prague Te Deum -> Te Deum: CALDARA
Prairie journal / Saga of the prairie -> Music for radio:
  COPLAND
Praise of harmony -> Look down harmonious saint: HÄNDEL

Praise to the Lord -> Stücke, organ, op. 145 (Dankpsalm):
  REGER
Prater canons -> Gehn wir in Prater, K. 558: MOZART
Prayer -> Dettingen Te Deum (Verlich uns Herr): HÄNDEL
Prayers of Saint Francis of Assisi -> Petites prières de
  Saint François d'Assise: POULENC
Precamur, sancte Domine -> Christe, qui lux: BYRD
Precauzione inutile, La -> Il barbiere di Siviglia: PAISIELLO
Preghiera <- Una lagrima: DONIZETTI
Preis der Tonkunst -> Der glorreiche Augenblick: BEETHOVEN
Preise, Jerusalem, den Herrn, S. 119 <- Ratswahlkantate: J.S.
  BACH
Preiset den Herrn <- Festkantate / Festive cantata: BRUCKNER
Prelude, keyboard instrument, H. 1 <- Running fantasia: GIB-
  BONS
Prelude, piano, op. 28, no. 8, F# minor <- Desperation: CHO-
  PIN
Prelude, piano, op. 28, no. 15, Db major <- Raindrop prelude:
  CHOPIN
Prelude, piano, op. 28, no. 20, C minor <- Funeral march pre-
  lude: CHOPIN
Prelude, string quartet <- Recueillement: BLOCH
Prelude and fugue, organ, S. 522, Eb major <- St. Anne fugue:
  J.S.BACH
Prelude and fugue, organ, S. 533, E minor <- Little E minor
  prelude: J.S.BACH
Prelude and fugue, organ, S. 539, D minor <- Fiddle fugue:
  J.S.BACH
Prelude and fugue, organ, S. 546, C minor <- Arnstadt pre-
  lude: J.S.BACH
Prelude and fugue, organ, S. 548, E minor <- Great E minor
  prelude / Wedge fugue: J.S.BACH
Preludes, orchestra <- Household music: VAUGHAN WILLIAMS
Preussische Quartette / Prussian quartets -> Quartet, strings,
  no. 45, op. 50, no. 1, Bb major; no. 46, op. 50, no. 2, C
  major; no. 47, op. 50, no. 3, Eb major; no. 48, op. 50,
  no. 4, F minor; no. 49, op. 50, no. 5, F major; no. 50,
  op. 50, no. 6, D major; J.HAYDN
Preussische Quartette / Prussian quartets / King of Prussia
  quartets -> Quartet, strings, K. 575, D major; K. 589, Bb
  major; K. 590, F major: MOZART
Preussische Sonaten / Prussian sonatas -> Sonata, harpsichord, W. 48, no. 1, F major; W. 48, no. 2, Bb major; W.
  48, no. 3, E major; W. 48, no. 4, C minor; W. 48, no. 5, C
  major; W. 48, no. 6, A major: C.P.E.BACH
Primavera, La / Spring / Concerto, op. 8, no. 1, E major ->
  Il cimento dell' armonia e dell' inventione (No. 1): VI-
  VALDI

Primo omicidio, Il -> Cain: A.SCARLATTI
Prince of Wales march -> March, orchestra, H.VIII,3, E♭ major: J.HAYDN
Prince troubadour, Le <- Le grand trompeur de dames: MÉHUL
Princess of Persia, The -> Distressed innocence: PURCELL
Printemps, Le / Spring symphony -> Symphony, no. 4, op. 52:
   LAJTHA
Printemps, Le / Spring symphony -> Symphonie pour petit orchestre, no. 1: MILHAUD
Printemps, women's voices & orchestra <- Salut printemps:
   DEBUSSY
Prinz Methusalem (Selections; arr.) <- Ballnacht in Florenz:
   JOHANN STRAUSS
Probesonaten / Easy sonatas / Essay sonatas -> Sonata, harpsichord, W. 63, no. 1, C major; W. 63, no. 2, D minor; W.
   63, no. 3, A major; W. 63, no. 4, B minor; W. 63, no. 5,
   E♭ major; W. 63, no. 6, F minor: C.P.E.BACH
Prole de bebê, no. 2 <- Os bichinhos: VILLA-LOBOS
Prole de bebê, no. 3 <- Esportes: VILLA-LOBOS
Proletarians, unite! -> Symphony, no. 1: KABALEVSKY
Promesse imprudente, La -> Emma: AUBER
Prometheus -> Die Geschöpfe des Prometheus: BEETHOVEN
Prometheus <- Poem of fire: SKRIABIN
Prometheus-Kantate, D. 451 <- Kantate zum Geburtstag des
   Prof. Watteroth: SCHUBERT
Prophetess, The <- The history of Dioclesian: ARNE
Prophetess, The -> Dioclesian: PURCELL
Prophets, The -> Concerto, violin, no. 2: CASTELNUOVO-TEDESCO
Proscritto, Il / Settimio -> L'esule di Roma: DONIZETTI
Protée -> Suite symphonique, no. 2: MILHAUD
Proteo, Il -> Concerto, violin, violoncello & string orchestra, R. 572, F major: VIVALDI
Prude, La -> Suite, string orchestra, h3, B minor: TELEMANN
Prussian quartets / Preussische Quartette -> Quartet,
   strings, no. 45, op. 50, no. 1, B♭ major; no. 46, op. 50,
   no. 2, C major; no. 47, op. 50, no. 3, E♭ major; no. 48,
   op. 50, no. 4, F minor; no. 49, op. 50, no. 5, F major;
   no. 50, op. 50, no. 6, D major: J.HAYDN
Prussian quartets / Preussische Quartette / King of Prussia
   quartets -> Quartet, strings, K. 575, D major; K. 589, B♭
   major; K. 590, F major: MOZART
Prussian sonatas / Preussische Sonaten -> Sonata, harpsichord, W. 48, no. 1, F major; W. 48, no. 2, B♭ major; W.
   48, no. 3, E major; W. 48, no. 4, C minor; W. 48, no. 5, C
   major; W. 48, no. 6, A major: C.P.E.BACH
Psalm symphony -> Symphony, no. 6: BADINGS
Psalmen Davids [1619] (Jauchzet den Herren alle Welt) <- Echo
   psalm: SCHÜTZ

Psalmen Davids [1628] <- Metrical psalms: SCHÜTZ
Psalmi Davidici <- Penitential psalms: A.GABRIELI
Psiche <- Amore innamorato: A.SCARLATTI
Psyche and Eros -> Psyché (Apothéose): FRANCK
Puchberg divertimento -> Divertimento, K. 563, E♭ major: MO-
  ZART
Puneña, no. 2 <- Hommage à Paul Sacher: GINASTERA

Quadrille en quator, Le -> Concertos comiques (No. 4):
  CORRETTE
Quando amor vuol ferirmi <- Cupid's game is deceitful: A.
  SCARLATTI
Quarante voleurs, Les -> Ali Baba: CHERUBINI
Quarter-tone chorale -> Chorale, string orchestra: IVES
Quartet, flute, strings & continuo [1738] no. 1, G major <-
  Parisian quartets: TELEMANN
Quartet, flute, strings & continuo [1738] no. 2, D major <-
  Parisian quartets: TELEMANN
Quartet, flute, strings & continuo [1738] no. 3, A major <-
  Parisian quartets: TELEMANN
Quartet, flute, strings & continuo [1738] no. 4, G minor <-
  Parisian quartets: TELEMANN
Quartet, flute, strings & continuo [1738] no. 5, E minor <-
  Parisian quartets: TELEMANN
Quartet, flute, strings & continuo [1738] no. 6, D major <-
  Parisian quartets: TELEMANN
Quartet, flute, strings & continuo [1738] no. 7, D major <-
  Parisian quartets: TELEMANN
Quartet, flute, strings & continuo [1738] no. 8, A minor <-
  Parisian quartets: TELEMANN
Quartet, flute, strings & continuo [1738] no. 9, G major <-
  Parisian quartets: TELEMANN
Quartet, flute, strings & continuo [1738] no. 10, B minor <-
  Parisian quartets: TELEMANN
Quartet, flute, strings & continuo [1738] no. 11, A major <-
  Parisian quartets: TELEMANN
Quartet, flute, strings & continuo [1738] no. 12, E minor <-
  Parisian quartets: TELEMANN
Quartet, strings, D minor <- Juvenile quartet: SUK
Quartet, strings, D. 703, C minor <- Quartettsatz: SCHUBERT
Quartet, strings, D. 810, D minor <- Death and the maiden /
  Der Tod und das Mädchen: SCHUBERT
Quartet, strings, G. 223, G major <- La tiranna: BOCCHERINI
Quartet, strings, G. 276, D major <- L'uccelliera: BOCCHE-
  RINI
Quartet, strings, G. 324, C major <- La musica notturna del-
  le strade di Madrid: BOCCHERINI
Quartet, strings, K. 73f (80) G major <- Italian quartets:

MOZART
Quartet, strings, K. 134a (155) D major <- Italian quartets:
MOZART
Quartet, strings, K. 134b (156) G major <- Italian quartets
/ Mailänder-Quartette / Milanese quartets: MOZART
Quartet, strings, K. 157, D major <- Italian quartets / Mai-
länder-Quartette / Milanese quartets: MOZART
Quartet, strings, K. 158, F major <- Italian quartets / Mai-
länder-Quartette / Milanese quartets: MOZART
Quartet, strings, K. 159, Bb major <- Italian quartets / Mai-
länder-Quartette / Milanese quartets: MOZART
Quartet, strings, K. 159a (160) Eb major <- Italian quartets
/ Mailänder-Quartette / Milanese quartets: MOZART
Quartet, strings, K. 168, F major <- Austrian quartets / Ös-
terreichische Quartette: MOZART
Quartet, strings, K. 169, A major <- Austrian quartets / Ös-
terreichische Quartette: MOZART
Quartet, strings, K. 170, C major <- Austrian quartets / Ös-
terreichische Quartette: MOZART
Quartet, strings, K. 171, Eb major <- Austrian quartets / Ös-
terreichische Quartette: MOZART
Quartet, strings, K. 172, Bb major <- Austrian quartets / Ös-
terreichische Quartette: MOZART
Quartet, strings, K. 173, D minor <- Austrian quartets / Ös-
terreichische Quartette: MOZART
Quartet, strings, K. 387, G major <- Frühlings-Quartett /
Spring quartet / Haydn quartets: MOZART
Quartet, strings, K. 417b (421) D minor <- Haydn quartets:
MOZART
Quartet, strings, K. 421b (428) Eb major <- Haydn quartets:
MOZART
Quartet, strings, K. 458, Bb major <- Hunt quartet / Jagd-
quartett / Haydn quartets: MOZART
Quartet, strings, K. 464, A major <- Drum quartet / Haydn
quartets: MOZART
Quartet, strings, K. 465, C major <- Dissonanzen-Quartett /
Haydn quartets: MOZART
Quartet, strings, K. 499, D major <- Hoffmeister quartet:
MOZART
Quartet, strings, K. 575, D major <- Cello quartet / Preus-
sische Quartette / Prussian quartets / King of Prussia
quartets: MOZART
Quartet, strings, K. 589, Bb major <- Preussische Quartette
/ Prussian quartets / King of Prussia quartets: MOZART
Quartet, strings, K. 590, F major <- Preussische Quartette
/ Prussian quartets / King of Prussia quartets: MOZART
Quartet, strings, no. 1 <- From the Salvation Army / A re-
vival service: IVES

Quartet, strings, no. 1 <- Kreutzer quartet: JANÁČEK
Quartet, strings, no. 1 <- Métamorphoses nocturnes: LIGETI
Quartet, strings, no. 1 -> Rispetti e strambotti: MALIPIERO
Quartet, strings, no. 1, E minor <- From my life: SMETANA
Quartet, strings, no. 1, op. 1, no. 1, B♭ major <- La chasse
  / Hunt quartet: J.HAYDN
Quartet, strings, no. 1, op. 18, no. 1, F major <- Lobkowitz
  quartets: BEETHOVEN
Quartet, strings, no. 2 <- Late swallows: DELIUS
Quartet, strings, no. 2 <- Intimate pages: JANÁČEK
Quartet, strings, no. 2 <- Stornelli e ballate: MALIPIERO
Quartet, strings, no. 2, D major <- Kismet: BORODIN
Quartet, strings, no. 2, D major <- Doric quartet: RESPIGHI
Quartet, strings, no. 2, op. 18, no. 2, G major <- Compliment
  quartet / Komplimentierungsquartett / Lobkowitz quartets:
  BEETHOVEN
Quartet, strings, no. 3 <- Mosaic: COWELL
Quartet, strings, no. 3 <- Cantari alla madrigalesca: MALI-
  PIERO
Quartet, strings, no. 3 <- Quartetto pastorale: ROSENBERG
Quartet, strings, no. 3, op. 18, no. 3, D major <- Lobkowitz
  quartets: BEETHOVEN
Quartet, strings, no. 3, op. 26 <- Slavonic quartet: GLAZUNOV
Quartet, strings, no. 4 <- United quartet: COWELL
Quartet, strings, no. 4 <- Hyperboles: PEPIN
Quartet, strings, no. 4, op. 18, no. 4, C minor <- Lobkowitz
  quartets: BEETHOVEN
Quartet, strings, no. 5 <- Variationen über einen divergier-
  enden c-moll Dreiklang: BLACHER
Quartet, strings, no. 5 <- Quartetti dei capricci: MALIPIERO
Quartet, strings, no. 5 <- Brazilian quartet no. 1: VILLA-
  LOBOS
Quartet, strings, no. 5, op. 18, no. 5, A major <- Lobkowitz
  quartets: BEETHOVEN
Quartet, strings, no. 6 <- L'arca di Noè: MALIPIERO
Quartet, strings, no. 6 <- Brazilian quartet no. 2: VILLA-
  LOBOS
Quartet, strings, no. 6, op. 18, no. 6, B major <- Lobkowitz
  quartets: BEETHOVEN
Quartet, strings, no. 6, op. 192, no. 1 <- Suite in älterer
  Form / Suite in the older form: RAFF
Quartet, strings, no. 7, op. 59, no. 1, F major <- Rasumov-
  sky quartets: BEETHOVEN
Quartet, strings, no. 7, op. 107, C major <- Hommage au pas-
  sé: GLAZUNOV
Quartet, strings, no. 7, op. 192, no. 2 <- Die schöne Müller-
  in: RAFF
Quartet, strings, no. 8, op. 59, no. 2, E minor <- Rasumov-

sky quartets: BEETHOVEN

Quartet, strings, no. 8, op. 110 [arr.] <- Chamber symphony: SHOSTAKOVICH

Quartet, strings, no. 9, op. 59, no. 3, C major <- Helden-quartett / Rasumovsky quartets: BEETHOVEN

Quartet, strings, no. 10 <- Birthday quartet: MILHAUD

Quartet, strings, no. 10, op. 74, E♭ major <- Harfenquartett / Harp quartet: BEETHOVEN

Quartet, strings, no. 11, op. 67, no. 2, E♭ major <- Recoll-ections: MIASKOVSKY

Quartet, strings, no. 11, op. 95, F minor <- Quartetto seri-oso: BEETHOVEN

Quartet, strings, no. 11, op. 111 <- Quartetto rustico: HOLM-BOE

Quartet, strings, no. 12 < In memory of Fauré: MILHAUD

Quartet, strings, no. 12 <- Quartetto riepilogo: ROSENBERG

Quartet, strings, no. 12, op. 96, F major <- American quar-tet: DVOŘÁK

Quartet, strings, no. 12, op. 127, E♭ major <- Galitzin quar-tets: BEETHOVEN

Quartet, strings, no. 13, op. 130, B♭ major <- Leib-Quartett / Galitzin quartets: BEETHOVEN

Quartet, strings, no. 15, op. 132, A minor <- Faust quartets / Galitzin quartets: BEETHOVEN

Quartet, strings, no. 16, op. 135, F major <- Faust quartets: BEETHOVEN

Quartet, strings, no. 18, op. 3, no. 5, F major / Serenade quartet: J.HAYDN -> Quartet, strings, op. 3, no. 5, F ma-jor: ROMAN HOFFSTETTER

Quartet, strings, no. 32, op. 20, no. 1, E♭ major <- Sonnen-quartette / Sun quartets: J.HAYDN

Quartet, strings, no. 33, op. 20, no. 2, C major <- Sonnen-quartette / Sun quartets: J.HAYDN

Quartet, strings, no. 34, op. 20, no. 3, G minor <- Sonnen-quartette / Sun quartets: J.HAYDN

Quartet, strings, no. 35, op. 20, no. 4, D major <- Sonnen-quartette / Sun quartets: J.HAYDN

Quartet, strings, no. 36, op. 20, no. 5, F minor <- Sonnen-quartette / Sun quartets: J.HAYDN

Quartet, strings, no. 37, op. 20, no. 6, D major <- Sonnen-quartette / Sun quartets: J.HAYDN

Quartet, strings, no. 38, op. 33, no. 1, B minor <- Russian quartets / Jungfernquartette / Maiden quartets: J.HAYDN

Quartet, strings, no. 39, op. 33, no. 2, E♭ major <- The joke Der Scherz / Russian quartets / Jungfernquartette / Maiden quartets: J.HAYDN

Quartet, strings, no. 40, op. 33, no. 3, C major <- Vogel-quartett / Bird quartet / Russian quartets / Jungfernquar-

tette / Maiden quartets: J.HAYDN
Quartet, strings, no. 41, op. 33, no. 4, Bb major <- Russian
  quartets / Jungfernquartette / Maiden quartets: J.HAYDN
Quartet, strings, no. 42, op. 33, no. 5, G major <- Russian
  quartets / Jungfernquartette / Maiden quartets: J.HAYDN
Quartet, strings, no. 43, op. 33, no. 6, D major <- Russian
  quartets / Jungfernquartette / Maiden quartets: J.HAYDN
Quartet, strings, no. 45, op. 50, no. 1, Bb major <- Preus-
  sische Quartette / Prussian quartets: J.HAYDN
Quartet, strings, no. 46, op. 50, no. 2, C major <- Preus-
  sische Quartette / Prussian quartets: J.HAYDN
Quartet, strings, no. 47, op. 50, no. 3, Eb major <- Preus-
  sische Quartette / Prussian quartets: J.HAYDN
Quartet, strings, no. 48, op. 50, no. 4, F minor <- Preus-
  sische Quartette / Prussian quartets: J.HAYDN
Quartet, strings, no. 49, op. 50, no. 5, F major <- Traum-
  Quartett / Dream quartet / Preussische Quartette / Prus-
  sian quartets: J.HAYDN
Quartet, strings, no. 50, op. 50, no. 6, D major <- Frosch-
  Quartett / Frog quartet / Preussische Quartette / Prussian
  quartets: J.HAYDN
Quartet, strings, no. 58, op. 54, no. 1, G major <- Tost
  quartets: J.HAYDN
Quartet, strings, no. 59, op. 54, no. 2, C major <- Tost
  quartets: J.HAYDN
Quartet, strings, no. 60, op. 54, no. 3, F major <- Tost
  quartets: J.HAYDN
Quartet, strings, no. 61, op. 55, op. 1, A major <- Tost
  quartets: J.HAYDN
Quartet, strings, no. 62, no. 55, no. 2, F major <- Rasier-
  messer-Quartett / Razor quartet / Tost quartets: J.HAYDN
Quartet, strings, no. 63, op. 55, no. 3, B major <- Tost
  quartets: J.HAYDN
Quartet, strings, no. 64, op. 64, no. 1, C major <- Tost
  quartets: J.HAYDN
Quartet, strings, no. 65, op. 64, no. 2, B minor <- Tost
  quartets: J.HAYDN
Quartet, strings, no. 66, op. 64, no. 3, B major <- Tost
  quartets: J.HAYDN
Quartet, strings, no. 67, op. 64, no. 4, G major <- Tost
  quartets: J.HAYDN
Quartet, strings, no. 68, op. 64, no. 5, D major <- Lerchen-
  quartett / Lark quartet / Hornpipe quartet / Tost quartets:
  J.HAYDN
Quartet, strings, no. 69, op. 64, no. 6, E major <- Tost
  quartets: J.HAYDN
Quartet, strings, no. 70, op. 71, no. 1, B major <- Apponyi
  quartets: J.HAYDN

Quartet, strings, no. 71, op. 71, no. 2 D, major <- Apponyi
quartets: J.HAYDN
Quartet, strings, no. 72, op. 71, no. 3, E♭ major <- Apponyi
quartets: J.HAYDN
Quartet, strings, no. 73, op. 74, no. 1, C major <- Apponyi
quartets: J.HAYDN
Quartet, strings, no. 74, op. 74, no. 2, F major <- Apponyi
quartets: J.HAYDN
Quartet, strings, no. 75, op. 74, no. 3, G minor <- Reiter-
quartett / Horseman quartet / Apponyi quartets: J.HAYDN
Quartet, strings, no. 76, op. 76, no. 1, G major <- Erdödy
quartets: J.HAYDN
Quartet, strings, no. 77, op. 76, no. 2, D minor <- Bell
quartet / Quinten-Quartett / Erdödy quartets: J.HAYDN
Quartet, strings, no. 77, op. 76, no. 2, D minor (Minuet) <-
Hexenmenüett / Witches' minuet: J.HAYDN
Quartet, strings, no. 78, op. 76, no. 3, C major <- Emperor
quartet / Kaiser-Quartett / Erdödy quartets: J.HAYDN
Quartet, strings, no. 78, op. 76, no. 3, C major (Poco can-
tabile) <- Emperor variations: J.HAYDN
Quartet, strings, no. 79, op. 76, no. 4, B♭ major <- Sonnen-
aufgang-Quartett / Sunrise quartet / Erdödy quartets: J.
HAYDN
Quartet, strings, no. 80, op. 76, no. 5, D major <- Largo
quartet / Erdödy quartets: J.HAYDN
Quartet, strings, no. 81, op. 76, no. 6, E♭ major <- Erdödy
quartets: J.HAYDN
Quartet, strings, no. 82, op. 77, no. 1, G major <- Lobko-
witz quartets: J.HAYDN
Quartet, strings, no. 83, op. 77, no. 2, F major <- Lobko-
witz quartets: J.HAYDN
Quartet, strings, no. 84, op. 103, B♭ major <- Schwanenge-
sang / Unfinished quartet: J.HAYDN
Quartet, strings, op. 3, no. 5, F major: ROMAN HOFFSTETTER
<- Quartet, strings, no. 18, op. 3, no. 5, F major / Sere-
nade quartet: J.HAYDN
Quartet, strings, op. 6, no. 2, B♭ major <- Figaro quartet:
DANZI
Quartet, strings, op. 56, D minor -> Voces intimae: SIBELIUS
Quartetti dei capricci -> Quartet, strings, no. 5: MALIPIERO
Quartetto pastorale -> Quartet, strings, no. 3: ROSENBERG
Quartetto riepilogo -> Quartet, strings, no. 12: ROSENBERG
Quartetto rustico -> Quartet, strings, no. 11, op. 111:
HOLMBOE
Quartetto serioso -> Quartet, strings, no. 11, op. 95, F mi-
nor: BEETHOVEN
Quartettsatz -> Quartet, strings, D. 703, C minor: SCHUBERT
Quasars -> Symphony, no. 3: PEPIN

Quatre âges du monde, Les / Metamorphosen-Sinfonien / Ovid
   symphonies -> Symphony, K. 73: DITTERSDORF
Quattro invenzioni <- La festa degli indolenti: MALIPIERO
Quattro stagioni, Le -> Contesa delle stagioni: D.SCARLATTI
Quattro stagioni, Le / The four seasons -> Il cimento dell'
   armonia e dell' inventione (No. 1-4): VIVALDI
Queen Esther -> Esther: HÄNDEL
Queene Elizabeth, her galliard <- K. Darcies galliard: DOW-
   LAND
Queen's funeral march, The / Funeral march -> March and can-
   zona, 4 trumpets, Z. 860, F minor: PURCELL
Querelleuse, La -> Suite, string orchestra, G8, G major:
   TELEMANN
Quest, The <- A concert-march passacaglia: HARRIS
Questo silenzio <- Il sonno: A.SCARLATTI
Qui latuit in virgine <- Je suis povene de leesse: DUFAY
Quinten-Quartett / Bell quartet / Erdödy quartets -> Quar-
   tet, strings, no. 77, op. 76, no. 2, D minor: J.HAYDN
Quintet, clarinet & strings, K. 581, A major <- Stadler
   quintet: MOZART
Quintet, oboe, clarinet & strings, op. 39 [arr.] <- Trapeze:
   PROKOFIEV
Quintet, piano & strings, D. 667, A major <- Forellen-Quin-
   tett / Trout quintet: SCHUBERT
Quintet, piano & strings, G. 409, C major [arr.] <- La riti-
   rata di Madrid: BOCCHERINI
Quintet, strings, op. 29, C major <- Storm quintet / Sturm-
   Quintett: BEETHOVEN
Quintet, strings, op. 88, F major <- Frühlings-Quintett /
   Spring quintet: BRAHMS
Quintet, violins, viola & violoncellos, G. 275, E major <-
   Bull quintet: BOCCHERINI
Quintet, violins, viola & violoncellos, G. 324, C major <-
   La musica notturna delle strade di Madrid: BOCCHERINI

Rage over the lost penny / Die Wut über den verlorenen Gro-
   schen -> Rondo a capriccio, piano, op. 129, G major: BEET-
   HOVEN
Rain sonata / Regen-Sonate -> Sonata, violin & piano, no. 1,
   op. 78, G major: BRAHMS
Raindrop prelude -> Prelude, piano, op. 28, no. 15, D♭ major:
   CHOPIN
Raise, raise the voice <- Ode for Saint Cecilia's Day [1695]:
   PURCELL
Rakastava <- Den Älskande: SIBELIUS
Råkóczi march -> Rhapsodie hongroise, piano, no. 15: LISZT
Rambling lady, The -> Sir Anthony Love: PURCELL
Rapsodie sur un thème de Paganini, piano & orchestra (Vari-

ation, no. 24) <- Crème de menthe variation: RACHMANINOFF

Rasch tritt der Tod <- Gesang der Mönche: BEETHOVEN

Rasiermesser-Quartett / Razor quartet / Tost quartets ->
   Quartet, strings, no. 62, op. 55, no. 2, F major: J.HAYDN

Rasumovsky quartets -> Quartet, strings, no. 7, op. 59, no.
   1, F major; no. 8, op. 59, no. 2, E minor; no. 9, op. 59,
   no. 3, C major: BEETHOVEN

Rataplan <- La partenza del reggimento: DONIZETTI

Ratswahlkantate -> Ihr Tore zu Zion, S. 193; Lobe den Herrn,
   meine Seele, S. 69a; Lobet den Herren, S. 137; Preise Jerusalem, den Herrn, S. 119: J.S.BACH

Razor quartet / Rasiermesser-Quartett / Tost quartets ->
   Quartet, strings, no. 62, op. 55, no. 2, F major: J.HAYDN

Re Cervo, Il <- Die Irrfahrten der Wahrheit: HENZE

Recitativ sonata / Sturm-Sonate / Tempest sonata -> Sonata,
   piano, no. 17, op. 31, no. 2, D minor: BEETHOVEN

Recollections -> Quartet, strings, no. 11, op. 67, no. 2, Eb
   major: MIASKOVSKY

Reconnaissance -> Die Zeitlose: JOHANN STRAUSS

Recueillement -> Prelude, string quartet: BLOCH

Recuerdos de Castilla / Spanish overture, no. 2 -> Souvenir
   d'une nuit d'été: GLINKA

Reformation cantata -> Gott, der Herr ist Sonn' und Schild,
   S. 79; Ein feste Burg ist unser Gott, S. 80: J.S.BACH

Reformation symphony -> Symphony, no. 5, op. 107, D minor:
   MENDELSSOHN

Reformationskantaten -> Kantat vid Reformationsfesten i Uppsala: ALFVÉN

Refrainlieder (Die Unterscheidung) <- Gehorsam / Gretchen gehorsam: SCHUBERT

Regen-Sonate / Rain sonata -> Sonata, violin & piano, no. 1,
   op. 78, G major: BRAHMS

Régi magyar katonadalok < Magyar rondo / Hungarian rondo: KO-
   DÁLY

Regrets -> Lieder ohne Worte, op. 19 (No. 2): MENDELSSOHN

Regulus <- The faction of Carthage: PURCELL

Rehearsal, The <- Bays in petticoats: BOYCE

Reine, La / Paris symphonies -> Symphony, M. 85, Bb major: J.
   HAYDN

Reine de Saba, La <- Irene: GOUNOD

Reine des îles, La -> Opayayie: OFFENBACH

Reine Nefertiti, La -> Bas-relief: CASTELNUOVO-TEDESCO

Reiter, Der -> Symphony, op. 6, no. 7, D major: STAMITZ

Reiterlied -> Lied eines Kriegers, D. 822: SCHUBERT

Reiterquartett / Horseman quartet / Apponyi quartets -> Quartet, strings, no. 75, op. 74, no. 3, G minor: J.HAYDN

Rejoice in the lamb <- Festival cantata, op. 30: BRITTEN

Rejoice in the Lord alway <- Bell anthem: PURCELL

Religious meditation -> The last hope: GOTTSCHALK
Reliquie / Unfinished sonata -> Sonata, piano, D. 840, C major: SCHUBERT
Remember November <- Election day is action day: HARRIS
Reminiscence -> Nocturne, piano, op. 27, no. 1, C# minor: CHOPIN
Reminiscences de Don Juan <- Don Juan fantasy: LISZT
Remorse -> Songs, op. 57 (On the golden cornfields): TCHAIKOVSKY
Rencontre imprévue, La <- Les pelèrins de la Mecque: GLUCK
Rendez-vous de chasse -> Fanfare de chasse: ROSSINI
Repentir <- O divine redeemer: GOUNOD
Repertorium für Militärmusik -> Minimax: HINDEMITH
Réponds moi <- Danse cubaine: GOTTSCHALK
Requiem -> Rest with the holy ones: BALAKIREV
Requiem <- Grande messe des morts: BERLIOZ
Requiem -> Ein deutsches Requiem: BRAHMS
Requiem -> Messe de Requiem: CAMPRA
Requiem -> Missa pro defunctis: CIMAROSA
Requiem -> Missa cinque vocum pro defunctis: LASSUS
Requiem <- Messa da requiem: VERDI
Requiem 1583 -> Missa pro defunctis: VICTORIA
Requiem 1605 -> Officium defunctorum (Missa pro defunctis): VICTORIA
Requiem and Kyrie, F major -> Introitus and Kyrie, F major: J.C.BACH
Requiem for those we love, A / American requiem / Fliederrequiem -> When lilacs in the door-yard bloom'd: HINDEMITH
Requiem solemne [1771] -> Missa pro defuncto Archiepiscopo Sigismundo: M.HAYDN
Rest with the holy ones <- Requiem: BALAKIREV
Restlessness -> Lieder ohne Worte, op. 19 (No. 5): MENDELSSOHN
Ressurection, The / The Easter story -> Historia von der Auferstehung Jesu Christi: SCHÜTZ
Ressurection symphony / Auferstehungs-Symphonie -> Symphony, no. 2, C minor: MAHLER
Retour à la vie, Le / Return to life -> Lélio: BERLIOZ
Retour à Paris, Le -> Sonata, piano, op. 70, Ab major: DUSSEK
Retrospect, A -> An old flame: IVES
Retrospection -> Lieder ohna Worte, op. 102 (No. 3): MENDELSSOHN
Return, The -> Lieder ohne Worte, op. 85 (No. 5): MENDELSSOHN
Return to life / Le retour à la vie -> Lélio: BERLIOZ
Revelation of St. John, The / Johannis uppenbarelse -> Symphony, no. 4: ROSENBERG
Revenant, Le -> Le barbier de village: GRÉTRY
Rêverie -> Mélodies, op. 2 (Le coucher de soleil); La cap-

tive: BERLIOZ
Reverie -> Lieder ohne Worte, op. 85 (No. 1): MENDELSSOHN
Rêverie sur un motif de l'opéra Roméo et Juliette <- Les ad-
    ieux: LISZT
Revival service, A / From the Salvation Army -> Quartet,
    strings, no. 1: IVES
Révolution grecque, La -> Scène héroique: BERLIOZ
Revolutionary etude -> Etude, piano, op. 10, no. 12, C minor:
    CHOPIN
Rhapsodie hongroise, piano, no. 5 <- Héroïde-elégique: LISZT
Rhapsodie hongroise, piano, no. 9 <- Carneval de Pesth /
    Pesther Carneval: LISZT
Rhapsodie hongroise, piano, no. 15 <- Råkóczi march: LISZT
Rhapsodisk ouverture <- En fantasirejse til Farøerne: NIELSEN
Rhapsody, alto, men's voices & orchestra, op. 53 <- Altrhap-
    sodie: BRAHMS
Rhapsody on Hungarian songs -> Magyar dallok (No. 9): LISZT
Rhapsody-concerto -> Concerto rhapsody, violoncello & orch-
    estra: KHACHATURIAN
Rhenisch symphony -> Symphony, no. 3, op. 97, Eb major: SCHU-
    MANN
Rhodanienne -> Symphony, no. 8, D: MILHAUD
Rhumba -> Archipelago: ANTHEIL
Rhumba -> Cuban overture: GERSHWIN
Ricciardo e Zoraide <- La Zoraide: ROSSINI
Richmond heiress, The <- A woman once in the right: PURCELL
Ridente la calma <- Der Sylphe des Friedens: MOZART
Rien de trop <- Les deux paravents: BOIELDIEU
Rigoletto paraphrase -> Paraphrases de concert (Rigoletto):
    LISZT
Riksdagskantaten -> Kantat vid Sveriges Rigsdags 500-års
    minnesfest: ALFVÉN
Riposo, Il -> Concerto, violin & string orchestra, R. 270, E
    major: VIVALDI
Rire du diable, Le / The devil's chuckle -> Caprice, violin,
    op. 1, no. 13, Bb major: PAGANINI
Rispetti e strambotti <- Quartet, strings, no. 1: MALIPIERO
Rita <- Le mari battu: DONIZETTI
Rite of spring, The -> Le sacre du printemps: STRAVINSKY
Ritirata di Madrid, La -> Quintet, piano & strings, G. 409,
    C major: BOCCHERINI
Ritiro, Il -> Concerto, violin, R. 256, Eb major; Concerto,
    3 violins & string orchestra, R. 294a, F major: VIVALDI
Ritorno di Don Calandrino, Il <- Armidoro e Laurina: CIMAROSA
Ritratto dell ' amore -> Les goûts réunis (Concert, no. 9):
    COUPERIN
Ritter von Blaubart und seine Sechste -> Barbe-bleu: OFFEN-
    BACH

Rival queens, The <- The death of Alexander the Great: ARNE
Rival sisters, The <- The violence of love: PURCELL
Rive d'amour -> La rose et l'abeille: BIZET
Rivulet, A -> Lieder ohne Worte, op. 30 (No. 5): MENDELSSOHN
Robe de dissention, La <- Le faux prodigue: RAMEAU
Roberto Devereux <- Il conte di Essex: DONIZETTI
Robin et Marion -> Le jeu de Robin et Marion: ADAM DE LA
    HALLE
Rococo minuet -> Minuet, orchestra, X.IX,8, no. 1, C major:
    J.HAYDN
Rococo variations -> Variations on a rococo theme, violoncel-
    lo & orchestra: TCHAIKOVSKY
Rodrigo / Moro per amore -> Floridoro: STRADELLA
Röda kors-kantaten -> Kantat vid Svenska Röda korsets hög-
    tidssammankomst: ALFVÉN
Roi de la paix, Le -> Julie; Pélage: SPONTINI
Roman impromptu, Le -> Ma tante Aurore: BOIELDIEU
Roman symphony / Symphonie romane -> Symphony, organ, no. 10,
    op. 73: WIDOR
Romances sans paroles, op. 7 -> Romanzen: VIEUXTEMPS
Romantic compositions, piano -> Pieces, piano, op. 101: SIBE-
    LIUS
Romantic sonata -> Sonata, piano, no. 4, op. 184, F# minor:
    RHEINBERGER
Romantic symphony -> Symphony, no. 4, Eb major: BRUCKNER
Romantic symphony / Sinfonia romantica -> Symphony, no. 4:
    CHAVEZ
Romantic symphony -> Symphony, no. 2, op. 30: HANSON
Romantic symphony / Symphonie romantique -> Symphony, no. 11:
    MILHAUD
Romanze des Richard Löwenherz, D. 907 <- Crusader's return:
    SCHUBERT
Romanzen aus L. Tiecks Magelone, op. 33 <- Magelone songs:
    BRAHMS
Rondo, piano, op. 1, C minor <- L'adieu a Varsovie: CHOPIN
Rondo, piano, op. 5, F major <- La Posiana: CHOPIN
Rondo, piano, op. 11, Eb major <- Rondo favori: HUMMEL
Rondo a capriccio, piano, op. 129, G major <- Rage over the
    lost penny / Die Wut über den verlorenen Groschen: BEET-
    HOVEN
Rondo arlecchinesco, orchestra <- Harlekins Reigen: BUSONI
Rondo brillante, piano, op. 62, E major <- La gaité: WEBER
Rondo élégante -> Introduction and Rondo, piano, op. 16, Eb
    major: CHOPIN
Rondo fantastique sur un thème espagnol, piano <- El contra-
    bandista: LISZT
Rondo favori -> Rondo, piano, op. 11, Eb major: HUMMEL
Rosalia von Montanver -> Das Fräulein im Turme, D. 114: SCHU-

BERT
Rosamunde overture -> Die Zauberharfe (Overture): SCHUBERT
Rosary sonatas / Rosenkranz-Sonaten / Mystery sonatas / Bib-
   lical sonatas -> Sonata, violin & continuo [Bayerische
   Staatsbibliothek: Mus. Ms. 4123] no. 1, D minor; no. 2, A
   major; no. 3, B minor; no. 4, D minor; no. 5, A major; no.
   6, C minor; no. 7, F major; no. 8, Bb major; no. 9, A mi-
   nor; no. 10, G minor; no. 11, G major; no. 12, C major;
   no. 13, D minor; no. 14, D major; no. 15, C major; no. 16,
   G minor: BIBER
Rosaura, La -> Gli equivoci in amore: A.SCARLATTI
Rose et l'abeille, La <- Rive d'amour: BIZET
Rosemary -> Danse pensée, piano: ELGAR
Rosenband, Der, D. 280 <- Cidli: SCHUBERT
Rosenfest von Cashmir, Das -> Nurmahal: SPONTINI
Rosenkranz-Sonaten / Rosary sonatas / Mystery sonatas / Bib-
   lical sonatas -> Sonata, violin & continuo [Bayerische
   Staatsbibliothek: Mus. Ms. 4123] no. 1, D minor; no. 2, A
   major; no. 3, B minor; no. 4, D minor; no. 5, A major; no.
   6, C minor; no. 7, F major; no. 8, Bb major; no. 9, A mi-
   nor; no. 10, G minor; no. 11, G major; no. 12, C major;
   no. 13, D minor; no. 14, D major; no. 15, C major; no. 16,
   G minor: BIBER
Rosière républicaine, La <- La fête de la vertu: GRÉTRY
Rosmene <- L'infedeltà fedele: A.SCARLATTI
Rote Käppchen, Das <- Hilft's nicht so schadt's nicht: DIT-
   TERSDORF
Rouet, Le <- Chanson de rouet: RAVEL
Rowland -> Lord Willoughby's welcome home: BYRD
Roxana / Alexander in India -> Alessandro: HÄNDEL
Roxolane, La -> Symphony, M. 63, C major: J.HAYDN
Royal fanfare -> Vive le roy: DEPRÈS
Royal fireworks, The / Music for the royal fireworks -> Fire-
   works music: HANDEL
Royal martyr, The -> Tyrannic love: PURCELL
Roze, La -> Les festes de l'Hymen: RAMEAU
Rübezahl <- Der Berggeist / Schicksal und Treue: DANZI
Rübezahl -> Der Beherrscher der Geister: WEBER
Rückert-Lieder -> Lieder von Rückert: MAHLER
Ruhe / Nächtliches Ständchen -> Leise, leise lasst uns sin-
   gen, D. 635: SCHUBERT
Ruins, The <- Huszt: KODÁLY
Running fantasia -> Prelude, keyboard instrument, H. 1: GIB-
   BONS
Rural symphony / Symphonie rurale -> Symphony, no. 12: MIL-
   HAUD
Ruralia hungarica (No. 2) <- Gypsy andante: DOHNÁNYI
Ruses d'amour <- Pastorale Watteau: GLAZUNOV

Russian Easter overture <- Great Russian Easter overture:
RIMSKY-KORSAKOV
Russian fantasy -> Fantaisie de concert sur des thèmes rus-
ses, violin & orchestra, op. 33: RIMSKY-KORSAKOV
Russian quartets / Jungfernquartette / Maiden quartets ->
Quartet, strings, no. 38, op. 33, no. 1, B minor; no. 39,
op. 33, no. 2, E♭ major; no. 40, op. 33, no. 3, C major;
no. 41, op. 33, no. 4, B♭ major; no. 42, op. 33, no. 5, G
major; no. 43, op. 33, no. 6, D major: J.HAYDN
Russian symphony -> Symphony, no. 5, op. 107, G minor: RUBIN-
STEIN
Russischer Marsch, orchestra <- Tscherkessen-Marsch / Marche
des gardes a cheval: JOHANN STRAUSS
Rustic march -> Under Blaník: SUK
Rustic wedding symphony / Ländliche Hochzeit -> Symphony,
op. 26, E♭ major: GOLDMARK

S' gibt nur a Kaiserstadt <- Kaiserstadt-Polka: JOHANN
STRAUSS
Sacrae lectiones novem ex prophet Iob <- The lamentations of
Job: LASSUS
Sacre du printemps, Le <- The rite of spring: STRAVINSKY
Sacre du printemps, Le (Les augures printaniers) <- Danse
des adolescents: STRAVINSKY
Sacred and profane dances / Danses sacrée et profane -> Dan-
ses, harp & string orchestra: DEBUSSY
Sacred concertos -> Symphoniae sacrae: SCHÜTZ
Saga of the prairie / Prairie journal -> Music for radio:
COPLAND
Sailor's return, The -> Thomas and Sally: ARNE
St. Anne fugue -> Prelude and fugue, organ. S. 552, E♭ major:
J.S.BACH
St. Anthony chorale -> Feldpartiten, H.II,46: J.HAYDN
St. Cecilia mass -> Messe solennelle à Sainte Cécile: GOUNOD
St. Cecilia mass / Cantata mass / Cäcilienmesse / Missa
Sactae Caeciliæ -> Mass, H.XXII,5, C major: J.HAYDN
St. Francis legends -> Légendes: LISZT
St. John Passion / The Passion according to St. John -> Gra-
dualia, book 1 (Turbarum voces in passione Domini): BYRD
St. John Passion -> Passio Domini nostri Jesu Christi sec-
undum Joannem: LASSUS
St. John Passion / Historia des Leidens und Sterbens unsers
Herrn Jesu Christ nach dem Evangelisten St. Johannem ->
Passion (St. John): SCHÜTZ
St. John Passion / Passion according to St. John -> Officium
hebdomadae sanctae (Passio secundum Ioannem): VICTORIA
St. Joseph mass / Missa Sancti Nicolai / Nicolaimesse ->
Mass, H.XXII,6, G major: J.HAYDN

St. Luke Passion -> Passio Domini nostri Jesu Christi sec-
undum Lucam: LASSUS
St. Luke Passion -> Passion according to St. Luke: PENDERECKI
St. Luke Passion -> Passion [St. Luke]: SCHÜTZ
St. Luke Passion -> Passion [St. Luke: 1744]: TELEMANN
St. Mark concerto -> Trattenimenti armonici per camera, op.
6 (No. 11): ALBINONI
St. Mark Passion -> Passio Domini nostri Jesu Christi sec-
undum Marcum: LASSUS
St. Matthew Passion -> Passio Domini nostri Jesu Christi
secundum Matthaeum: LASSUS
St. Matthew Passion / Historia des Leidens und Sterbens un-
sers Herrn Jesu Christi, nach dem Evangelisten St. Matthe-
us -> Passion [St. Matthew]: SCHÜTZ
St. Matthew Passion -> Passion [St. Matthew: 1730]: TELEMANN
St. Paul oratorio -> Paulus: MENDELSSOHN
Saint Vartan symphony <- Symphony, op. 180: HOVANESS
Saisons, les <- Album of miniatures: ALBÉNIZ
Saisons, Les <- The months, op. 37a: TCHAIKOVSKY
Saisons, Les (Novembre) <- Troika sleigh ride: TCHAIKOVSKY
S'allontana per non innamorarsi -> Sento nel core: A.SCARLAT-
TI
Salomon symphonies / London symphonies -> Symphony, M. 93, D
major; M. 94, G major; M. 95, C minor; M. 96, D major; M.
97, C major; M. 98, B♭ major; M. 99, E♭ major; M. 100, G
major; M. 101, D major; M. 102, B♭ major; M. 103, E♭ major;
M. 104, D major: J.HAYDN
Salon Pitzelberger -> Monsieur Choufleuri restera chez lui
le...: OFFENBACH
Salut printemps <- Printemps, women's voices & orchestra: DE-
BUSSY
Salutatory overture -> Greetings overture: MIASKOVSKY
Salve morale e sprituale (Gloria) <- Gloria concertata: MON-
TEVERDI
Salve Regina, D. 379 / Hymne an die heilige Mutter Gottes ->
Deutsches Salve Regina, D. 379, F major: SCHUBERT
Salzburg symphonies -> Divertimento, K. 125a (136) D major;
K. 125b (137) B♭ major; K. 125c (138) F major: MOZART
San Antonio -> Il morto redivivo: CALDARA
San Francisco symphony -> Symphony, no. 8: HARRIS
Santa Genuinda, La <- L'innocenza difesa dall' inganno: A.
SCARLATTI
Sancte Paule apostole -> Motets, 8 part (Magnus sanctus Pau-
lus): PALESTRINA
Sarcasms -> Pieces, piano, op. 17: PROKOFIEV
Sarnia <- An island sequence: IRELAND
Sătaescă / Villageoise -> Suite, orchestra, no. 3, op. 27:
ENESCO

Satyrn in Arcadien, Die -> Der neumodische Liebhaber: TELE-
MANN

Sauvages de la Fürstemberg, Les -> Concertos comiques (No.
25): CORRETTE

Scandinavian suite -> Traumspiel-Suite: VLADIGEROV

Scapino <- Comedy overture: WALTON

Scène héroïque <- La révolution grecque: BERLIOZ

Scènes bohémiennes -> La jolie fille de Perth (Selections):
BIZET

Scènes de la csárda, no. 4, op. 32 <- Hejre Kati: HUBAY

Scènes mignonnes / Scènes musicales sur un thème connu de
F. Schubert -> Sehnsuchtswalzervariationen, piano: SCHU-
MANN

Scènes musicales sur un thème connu de F. Schubert / Scènes
mignonnes -> Sehnsuchtswalzervariationen, piano: SCHUMANN

Schatzgräber, Die -> Betrug durch Aberglauben: DITTERSDORF

Schatz-Walzer, orchestra <- Zigeunerbaron-Walzer: JOHANN
STRAUSS

Schelomo <- Hebrew rhapsody: BLOCH

Scherz, Der / The joke / Russian quartets / Jungfern-Quar-
tette / Maiden quartets -> Quartet, strings, no. 39, op.
33, no. 2, Eb major: J.HAYDN

Scherzo, band <- Over the pavements: IVES

Scherzo, piano, B minor <- Little trumpet piece: MENDELSSOHN

Scherzo, piano, no. 1, op. 20, B minor <- Le banquet infernal: CHOPIN

Scherzo, piano, 4 hands, winds, bells & violin <- All the
way around and back: IVES

Scherzo, piano & orchestra, op. 2 <- Burlesque: BARTÓK

Scherzo, string quartet <- Holding your own: IVES

Scherzo humoristique, piano <- The cat and the mouse: COP-
LAND

Schiavi per amore, Gli -> La gare generose: PAISIELLO

Schicksal und Treue / Der Berggeist -> Rübezahl: DANZI

Schicksal-Sinfonie / Fate symphony -> Symphony, no. 5, op.
67, C minor: BEETHOVEN

Schiffende, Die / Lied eines Liebenden -> Der Liebende, D.
207: SCHUBERT

Schiffers Nachtlied -> Lied eines Schiffers an die Dioskuren, D. 360: SCHUBERT

Schiffspatron, Der <- Der neue Gutsherr: DITTERSDORF

Schlaflied, D. 527 <- Abendlied / Schlummerlied: SCHUBERT

Schlage doch, gewünschte Stunde, S. 53 <- Trauermusik: J.S.
BACH

Schlittenfahrt, Die / The sleigh ride -> Deutsche Tänze, K.
605 (No. 3): MOZART

Schlummerlied / Abendlied -> Schlaflied, D. 527: SCHUBERT

Schlummerlieder -> Wiegenlieder-Walzer, orchestra: JOSEPH

STRAUSS
Schmücke dich, o liebe Seele / Leipzig chorales -> Chorale
  prelude, S. 654: J.S.BACH
Schöne Minka -> Air russe, op. 40: WEBER
Schöne Mullerin, Die -> Quartet, strings, no. 7, op. 192,
  no. 2: RAFF
Schöne Mullerin, Die <- Müllerlieder: SCHUBERT
Schöne Mullerin, Die (Das Wandern) <- Wanderschaft: SCHUBERT
Schönen Weiber von Georgien, Die -> Les Géorgiennes: OFFEN-
  BACH
Schöpfungsmesse / Creation mass / Missa solemnis -> Mass, H.
  XXII,13, Bb major: J.HAYDN
Schoolmaster, The / Der schulmeister -> Symphony, M. 55, Eb
  major: J.HAYDN
Schubert an sein Klavier / Seraphine an ihr Klavier -> An
  mein Klavier, D. 342: SCHUBERT
Schübler chorales -> Chorale prelude, S. 645; S, 646; S. 647;
  S. 648; S. 649; S. 650: J.S.BACH
Schulmeister, Der / The schoolmaster -> Symphony, M. 55, Eb
  major: J.HAYDN
Schulmeister mit seinen 2 Scholaren, Der <- Cantata comica:
  PAISIELLO
Schulwerk <- Educational music: HINDEMITH
Schumann variations -> Variationen über ein Thema von Robert
  Schumann, piano, op. 9; Variationen über ein Thema von Ro-
  bert Schumann, piano, 4 hands, op. 23: BRAHMS
Schumanniana <- Chants sans paroles: INDY
Schwanendreher, Der <- Concerto, viola: HINDEMITH
Schwanengesang / Unfinished quartet -> Quartet, strings, no.
  84, op. 103, Bb major: J.HAYDN
Schwanengesang-Sinfonie -> Symphony, K. 543, Eb major: MOZART
Schweiget stille, plaudert nicht, S. 211 <- Kaffee-Kantate /
  Coffee cantata: J.S.BACH
Schweizer-Sinfonie / Swiss symphony -> Symphony, string
  orchestra, no. 9, C minor: MENDELSSOHN
Schwergewicht <- Die Ehre der Nation: KRENEK
Scompagnata tortorella <- La tortorella: A.SCARLATTI
Scompigli domestici, Gli -> La moda: DITTERDORF
Scompigli domestici, I -> La moda: SALIERI
Scottish fantasy -> Fantasie unter freier Benutzung schott-
  ischer Volksmelodien, violin & orchestra, op. 46: BRUCH
Scottish symphony -> Symphony, no. 3, op. 56, A minor: MEN-
  DELSSOHN
Scuffiara, La <- La modista raggiratrice: PAISIELLO
Scythian suite, orchestra <- Ala and Lolly: PROKOFIEV
Sea symphony, A -> Symphony, no. 1: VAUGHAN WILLIAMS
Seasons, The / Die Jahreszeiten -> Symphony, no. 9, op. 143:
  SPOHR

Secrèt, Le -> Haydée: AUBER
See the kind indulgent gates <- Vauxhall songs: J.C.BACH
Seguidillas -> Suite española, piano, no. 1 (Castilla): AL-
  BÉNIZ
Sehnsucht / Artaserse -> Leiden der Trennung, D. 509: SCHU-
  BERT
Sehnsucht, D. 310 <- Lied der Mignon: SCHUBERT
Sehnsucht, D. 359 <- Lied der Mignon: SCHUBERT
Sehnsucht, D. 481 <- Lied der Mignon: SCHUBERT
Sehnsucht, D. 656 <- Lied der Mignon: SCHUBERT
Sehnsucht nach dem Frühlinge -> Komm lieber Mai: MOZART
Sehnsuchtswalzer / Trauerwalzer -> Originaltänze, piano, D.
  365 (No. 2): SCHUBERT
Sehnsuchtswalzervariationen, piano <- Scènes mignonnes /
  Scènes musicales sur un thème connu de F. Schubert: SCHU-
  MANN
Sei Lob und Ehr, S. 251 <- Trauungschoräle / Wedding cho-
  rales: J.S.BACH
Sei pur bella <- La bianca rosa: HÄNDEL
Sekelskifteskantaten -> Vid sekelskiftet: ALFVÉN
Seligen Augenblicke, Die -> Die Entzückung an Laura, D. 390;
  D. 577: SCHUBERT
Sendschreiben / Epistel -> Herrn Josef Spaun, D. 749: SCHU-
  BERT
Sentinelle, La <- L'astre de nuit: HUMMEL
Sento nel core <- S'allontana per non innamorarsi: A.SCAR-
  LATTI
Septet, op. 29 -> Suite, 3 clarinets & strings, op. 29:
  SCHÖNBERG
Septet, piano, winds & strings, op. 114, C major <- Grand
  military septet / Military septet: HUMMEL
Seraglio, Il -> Die Entführung aus dem Serail: MOZART
Séraphine <- Absente et présente: GRÉTRY
Seraphine an ihr Klavier / Schubert an sein Klavier -> An
  mein Klavier, D. 342: SCHUBERT
Serenade / Ständchen -> Kling leise mein Lied: LISZT
Serenade -> Symphonie pour petit orchestre, no. 3: MILHAUD
Serenade, K. 62a (100) D major <- Finalmusik: MOZART
Serenade, K. 167a (185) D major <- Finalmusik / Antretter
  serenade: MOZART
Serenade, K. 189b (203) D major <- Colloredo serenade: MOZART
Serenade, K. 239, D major <- Serenata notturna: MOZART
Serenade, K. 248b (250) D major <- Haffner serenade: MOZART
Serenade, K. 250a (101) F major <- Contredanse serenade: MO-
  ZART
Serenade, K. 320, D major <- Posthorn serenade: MOZART
Serenade, K. 370a (361) B♭ major <- Gran partita: MOZART
Serenade, K. 388, C minor <- Nachtmusique: MOZART

Serenade, K. 525, G major -> Eine kleine Nachtmusik: MOZART
Serenade, string orchestra, C major <- Nachtwächterbass-Se-
  renade / Night watchman's call serenade: BIBER
Serenade, string trio, op. 8, D major [arr.] <- Notturno,
  viola & piano, op. 42, D major: BEETHOVEN
Serenade after Plato's Symposium -> Symposium, after Plato:
  BERNSTEIN
Serenade quartet / Serenaden-Quartett / Quartet, strings,
  no. 18, op. 3, no. 5, F major: J.HAYDN -> Quartet, strings,
  op. 3, no. 5, F major: ROMAN HOFFSTETTER
Serenaden, Die <- Little cantata on romantic texts: HINDEMITH
Serenaden-Quartett / Serenade quartet / Quartet, strings,
  no. 18, op. 3, no. 5, F major: J.HAYDN -> Quartet, strings,
  op. 3, no. 5, F major: ROMAN HOFFSTETTER
Serenata -> Suite española, piano, no. 1 (Granada): ALBÉNIZ
Serenata a tre <- La ninfa e il pastore: VIVALDI
Serenata notturna -> Serenade, K. 239, D major: MOZART
Serestas (Modinha) <- Love song: VILLA-LOBOS
Serious song, string orchestra <- Lament for string orch-
  estra: FINE
Serment, Le <- Les faux-monnayeurs: AUBER
Serse <- Xerse: CAVALLI
Serse <- Xerxes: HÄNDEL
Servante au bon tabac, La -> Concertos comiques (No. 7):
  CORRETTE
Service sacré pour le samedi matin <- Office du samedi matin:
  MILHAUD
Servo padrone, Il <- L'amor perfetto: PICCINNI
Settimio / Il proscritto -> L'esule di Roma: DONIZETTI
Seufzer, D. 198 <- Die Nachtigall: SCHUBERT
Seven Czech dances, piano / Czech dances, piano -> Borová:
  MARTINŮ
Seven rituals of music -> Symphony, no. 11: COWELL
Seven tears -> Lachrimae: DOWLAND
Sevillanas -> Suite española, piano, no. 2 (Sevilla): ALBÉ-
  NIZ
Sextet, piano & woodwinds (Blues) <- Divertimento no. 2:
  MARTINŮ
Sextet, piano & woodwinds (Scherzo) <- Divertimento no. 1:
  MARTINŮ
Sextet, strings, op. 70 -> Souvenir de Florence: TCHAIKOVSKY
Shake-down song -> Las agachada: COPLAND
Shakespeare sketches -> The England of Elizabeth (Selec-
  tions; arr.): VAUGHAN WILLIAMS
Shakespeare songs -> Songs, op. 60: SIBELIUS
Shalimar <- Suite, piano, op. 177: HOVANESS
Sheep-shearing, The <- Florizel and Perdita: ARNE
Shepherd boy etude / Aeolian harp etude / Harp etude ->

Etude, piano, op. 25, no. 1, Ab major: CHOPIN
Shepherd's complaint, The -> Lieder ohne Worte, op. 67 (No.
    5): MENDELSSOHN
Short chorale mass / Windhager Messe -> Mass, alto, 2 horns
    & organ, C major: BRUCKNER
Short etudes -> Petites études: PEPIN
Short story <- Novelettes, piano [arr.]: GERSHWIN
Short symphony -> Symphony, no. 2 [1933]: COPLAND
Short symphony -> Symphony, no. 4: COWELL
Short symphony -> Symphony, no. 5, op. 170: HOVANESS
Siberian polonaise -> Polonaise, piano, op. 26, no. 2, Eb ma-
    jor: CHOPIN
Sicilian air -> Tre giorni son che Nina [arr.]: PERGOLESI
Sicilian usurper, The -> The history of King Richard II: PUR-
    CELL
Sicilien, Le <- L'amour peintre: LULLY
Side by side / Am schlummernden Strom -> Songs, op. 73 (We
    sat together): TCHAIKOVSKY
Side show -> Circus overture: SCHUMAN
Sieg der Schönheit <- Gensericus: TELEMANN
Sieg vom Helden Coburg, Der / The victory of the hero of Co-
    burg -> Kontretanz, K. 587: MOZART
Siège de Mégare, Le / Metamorphosen-Sinfonien / Ovid sympho-
    nies -> Symphony, K. 80: DITTERSDORF
Siège de Naumbourg, Le -> Les hussites: MÉHUL
Siege of Belgrade, The / Die Belagerung Belgrads / La bat-
    aille -> Kontretanz, K. 535: MOZART
Sielanka -> Mazurka, violin & piano, op. 12, no. 1, D major:
    WIENIAWSKI
Siface -> La Sofonisba: GLUCK
Signor Bruschino, Il <- Il figlio per azzardo: ROSSINI
Silent mass -> Organoeida ad missam lectam: KODÁLY
Silhouette <- Galilee: BERNSTEIN
Silvain <- Éraste et Lucinde: GRÉTRY
Silver pilgrimage -> Symphony, no. 15, op. 199: HOVANESS
Simple variations, piano -> Children's pieces, piano, op. 43,
    book 3: MIASKOVSKY
Sinfonia al Santo Sepolcro -> Concerto, string orchestra, R.
    169, B minor: VIVALDI
Sinfonia Antartica -> Symphony, no. 7: VAUGHAN WILLIAMS
Sinfonia Berchtolsgadensis / Toy symphony / Kindersinfonie:
    J.HAYDN -> Cassation, 2 horns, strings & toy instruments,
    C major (Selections): LEOPOLD MOZART
Sinfonia boreale -> Symphony, no. 8, op. 56: HOLMBOE
Sinfonia brevis -> Symphony, no. 3, op. 70: INDY
Sinfonia brevis -> Symphony, no. 8: MALIPIERO
Sinfonia de Antigona -> Symphony, no. 1: CHAVEZ
Sinfonia dell' ahimè -> Symphony, no. 9: MALIPIERO

Sinfonia della campane -> Symphony, no. 3: MALIPIERO
Sinfonia delle canzoni -> Symphony, no. 7: MALIPIERO
Sinfonia delle cornamuse -> Symphony, no. 11: MALIPIERO
Sinfonia elegiaca -> Symphony, no. 2: MALIPIERO
Sinfonia espansiva -> Symphony, no. 3, op. 27: NIELSEN
Sinfonia funebre, F minor <- Elegiac symphony: LOCATELLI
Sinfonia giocosa -> Symphony, no. 9, string orchestra: BA-
  DINGS
Sinfonia grave -> Symphony, no. 2: ROSENBERG
Sinfonia in memoriam -> Symphony, no. 4: MALIPIERO
Sinfonia india -> Symphony, no. 2: CHAVEZ
Sinfonia proletaria -> Llamados: CHAVEZ
Sinfonia romantica / Romantic symphony -> Symphony, no. 4:
  CHAVEZ
Sinfonia rustica -> Symphony, no. 3, op. 25: HOLMBOE
Sinfonia sacra -> Symphony, no. 5, op. 43: HANSON
Sinfonia sacra -> Symphony, no. 4, op. 29: HOLMBOE
Sinfonia semplice -> Symphony, no. 6: NIELSEN
Sinfonia semplice -> Symphony, no. 6: ROSENBERG
Sinfonia veneziana -> Symphony, D major [Veneziana]: SALIERI
Sinfonie capricieuse -> Symphony, no. 2, D major: BERWALD
Sinfonie naïve -> Symphony, no. 4, E♭ major: BERWALD
Sinfonie sérieuse -> Symphony, no. 1, G minor: BERWALD
Sinfonie singulière -> Symphony, no. 3, C major: BERWALD
Sinfonietta (Allegretto) <- Sokol fanfare: JANÁČEK
Sinfonietta, no. 1 <- A memoria de Mozart: VILLA-LOBOS
Sinfonietta, string orchestra <- A Brasileira / The Brazili-
  an: KŘENEK
Sinfonische Klangfiguren -> Symphony, no. 12: BADINGS
Sing unto God <- Wedding anthem for the Prince of Wales: HÄN-
  DEL
Singular pieces, piano, op. 44 (Nocturne) <- Cats on the roof:
  DOHNANYI
Sir Anthony Love <- The rambling lady: PURCELL
Sir Barnaby Wigg <- No wit like a woman's: PURCELL
Sir John in love <- Falstaff opera: VAUGHAN WILLIAMS
Sir Robert Sidney his galliard -> The Lord Viscount Lisle
  his galliard: DOWLAND
Sissy [Lisa] <- Lisa: KREISLER
Sketch to Viennese rhapsody -> Viennese rhapsodic fantasi-
  etta, violin & piano: KREISLER
Sketches based in Indian themes, string quartet <- Indian
  sketches: GRIFFES
Slåtter, piano, op. 72 <- Norwegian folk dances: GRIEG
Slava <- A political overture: BERNSTEIN
Slavonic mass / Festival mass -> Glagolitic mass: JANÁČEK
Slavonic quartet -> Quartet, strings, no. 3, op. 26: GLAZUNOV
Slavonic symphony -> Symphony, no. 1, op. 5, E major: GLAZU-

NOV

Sleep of sorrow -> Songs, op. 25 (Reconciliation): TCHAIKOVS-
KY

Sleep, son of peasants / A peasant's lullaby -> Cradle song:
MUSORGSKY

Sleeping beauty, The (Pas de deux; arr.) <- Bluebird: TCHAI-
KOVSKY

Sleigh ride, The / Die Schlittenfahrt -> Deutsche Tänze,
orchestra, K. 605 (No. 3): MOZART

Sly little fox, The <- The cunning little vixen: JANÁČEK

Smiling Venus <- Vauxhall songs: J.C.BACH

Snow maiden, The <- Spring tale: RIMSKY-KORSAKOV

Sönerna <- Cain and Abel: ROSENBERG

Sofonisba, La <- Siface: GLUCK

Soir, Le / La tempête -> Symphony, M. 8, G major: J.HAYDN

Soir de fête / Naila -> La source: DELIBES

Soirs transylvains / Transylvanian evenings -> Trio, strings,
no. 3, op. 41: LAJTHA

Sokol fanfara -> Sinfoniette (Allegretto): JANÁČEK

Sokol march -> Towards a new life: SUK

Soldier's call to the war, The -> Hark how the trumpet: HÄN-
DEL

Soldier's song, A <- A war song: ELGAR

Sole, Urania e Clio <- La muse Urania e Clio: A.SCARLATTI

Solemn march for the coronation of Alexander III / Coronation
march -> Festival coronation march: TCHAIKOVSKY

Solemn overture for the 20th anniversary of the October revo-
lution <- Triumpham overture: GLIÈRE

Soli, Les -> Symphony, harp, percussion & string orchestra,
op. 33: LAJTHA

Solitaires, Les <- Dans l'îsle de Cythère: COUPERIN

Solitude -> Songs, op. 73 (Again, as, before, alone): TCHAI-
KOVSKY

Sombrero de tres picos, El (Danza del molinero) <- Farruca:
FALLA

Some south-paw pitching! -> Study, piano, no. 21: IVES

Sommeil, Le -> Suite, string orchestra, B3, Bb major: TELEMANN

Son and stranger -> Die Heimkehr aus der Fremde: MENDELSSOHN

Sonata, flute & continuo, B.8,1, A minor <- Halle sonatas:
HÄNDEL

Sonata, flute & continuo, B.8,2, B minor <- Halle sonatas:
HÄNDEL

Sonata, flute & continuo, B.3,3, B minor <- Halle sonatas:
HÄNDEL

Sonata, flute & continuo, op. 2, no. 1, G major <- L'Henriette: BLAVET

Sonata, flute & continuo, op. 2, no. 2, D minor <- La vibray:
BLAVET

Sonata, flute & continuo, op. 2, no. 4, G minor <- La Lumagne:
  BLAVET
Sonata, flute & harpsichord, op. 13, no. 1, C major -> Il
  pastor fido (No. 1): VIVALDI
Sonata, flute & harpsichord, op. 13, no. 2, C major -> Il
  pastor fido (No. 2): VIVALDI
Sonata, flute & harpsichord, op. 13, no. 3, G major -> Il
  pastor fido (No. 3): VIVALDI
Sonata, flute & harpsichord, op. 13, no. 4, A major -> Il
  pastor fido (No. 4): VIVALDI
Sonata, flute & harpsichord, op. 13, no. 5, C major -> Il
  pastor fido (No. 5): VIVALDI
Sonata, flute & harpsichord, op. 13, no. 6, G minor -> Il
  pastor fido (No. 6): VIVALDI
Sonata, 2 flutes, op. 5, no. 1, G major <- Canonic sonatas:
  TELEMANN
Sonata, 2 flutes, op. 5, no. 2, D major <- Canonic sonatas:
  TELEMANN
Sonata, 2 flutes, op. 5, no. 3, A minor <- Canonic sonatas:
  TELEMANN
Sonata, 2 flutes, op. 5, no. 4, D minor <- Canonic sonatas:
  TELEMANN
Sonata, 2 flutes, op. 5, no. 5, A major <- Canonic sonatas:
  TELEMANN
Sonata, 2 flutes, op. 5, no. 6, A minor <- Canonic sonatas:
  TELEMANN
Sonata, harp, F major <- The lass of Richmond Hill: DUSSEK
Sonata, harpsichord, C major [ca. 1789] <- The feast of
  Apollo: J.C.BACH
Sonata, harpsichord, K. 8 (L. 488) G minor <- Bucolic sona-
  ta: D.SCARLATTI
Sonata, harpsichord, K. 9 (L. 413) D minor <- Pastoral sona-
  ta: D.SCARLATTI
Sonata, harpsichord, K. 20 (L. 375) E major <- Capriccio: D.
  SCARLATTI
Sonata, harpsichord, K. 30 (L. 499) G minor <- The cat's
  fugue / Il fuga del gatto: D.SCARLATTI
Sonata, harpsichord, K. 96 (L. 465) D major <- La caccia: D.
  SCARLATTI
Sonata, harpsichord, K. 159 (L. 104) C major <- La caccia:
  D.SCARLATTI
Sonata, harpsichord, K. 206 (L. 257) E major <- Les adieux
  sonata: D.SCARLATTI
Sonata, harpsichord, K. 213 (L. 108) D minor <- The lover:
  D.SCARLATTI
Sonata, harpsichord, K. 328 (L.s. 27) G major <- The bells /
  Les cloches: D.SCARLATTI
Sonata, harpsichord, K. 380 (L. 23) E major <- Cortège: D.

SCARLATTI

Sonata, harpsichord, K. 429 (L. 132) A major <- Barcarolle:
    D.SCARLATTI

Sonata, harpsichord, K. 430 (L. 463) D major <- Tempo di bal-
    lo: D.SCARLATTI

Sonata, harpsichord, K. 450 (L. 338) G minor <- Burlesca: D.
    SCARLATTI

Sonata, harpsichord, K. 487 (L. 205) C major <- Neapolitan
    folk dance: D.SCARLATTI

Sonata, harpsichord, W. 48, no. 1, F major <- Preussische
    Sonaten / Prussian sonatas: C.P.E.BACH

Sonata, harpsichord, W. 48, no. 2, Bb major <- Preussische
    Sonaten / Prussian sonatas: C.P.E.BACH

Sonata, harpsichord, W. 48, no. 3, E major <- Preussische
    Sonaten / Prussian sonatas: C.P.E.BACH

Sonata, harpsichord, W. 48, no. 4, C minor <- Preussische
    Sonaten / Prussian sonatas: C.P.E.BACH

Sonata, harpsichord, W. 48, no. 5, C major <- Preussische
    Sonaten / Prussian sonatas: C.P.E.BACH

Sonata, harpsichord, W. 48, no. 6, A major <- Preussische
    Sonaten / Prussian sonatas: C.P.E.BACH

Sonata, harpsichord, W. 49, no. 1, A minor <- Wurttemberg
    sonatas: C.P.E.BACH

Sonata, harpsichord, W. 49, no. 2, Ab major <- Wurttemberg
    sonatas: C.P.E.BACH

Sonata, harpsichord, W. 49, no. 3, E minor <- Wurttemberg
    sonatas: C.P.E.BACH

Sonata, harpsichord, W. 49, no. 4, Bb major <- Wurttemberg
    sonatas: C.P.E.BACH

Sonata, harpsichord, W. 49, no. 5, Eb major <- Wurttemberg
    sonatas: C.P.E.BACH

Sonata, harpsichord, W. 49, no. 6, B minor <- Wurttemberg
    sonatas: C.P.E.BACH

Sonata, harpsichord, W. 63, no. 1, C major <- Easy sonatas /
    Essay sonatas / probesonaten: C.P.E.BACH

Sonata, harpsichord, W. 63, no. 2, D minor <- Easy sonatas /
    Essay sonatas / Probesonaten: C.P.E.BACH

Sonata, harpsichord, W. 63, no. 3, A major <- Easy sonatas /
    Essay sonatas / Probesonaten: C.P.E.BACH

Sonata, harpsichord, W. 63, no. 4, B minor <- Easy sonatas /
    Essay sonatas / Probesonaten: C.P.E.BACH

Sonata, harpsichord, W. 63, no. 5, E major <- Easy sonatas /
    Essay sonatas / Probesonaten: C.P.E.BACH

Sonata, harpsichord, W. 63, no. 6, F minor <- Easy sonatas /
    Essay sonatas / Probesonaten: C.P.E.BACH

Sonata, organ, no. 2, op. 65, Ab major <- Fantasie-Sonate:
    RHEINBERGER

Sonata, organ, no. 3, op. 88, G major <- Pastoral-Sonate:

RHEINBERGER
Sonata, organ, no. 17, op. 181, B major <- Fantasie-Sonate:
RHEINBERGER
Sonata, organ, no. 20, op. 196, F major <- Zur Friedensfeier:
RHEINBERGER
Sonata, organ & orchestra, K. 263, C major <- Church sonatas
/ Kirchensonaten / Epistle sonatas / Festival sonatas: MO-
ZART
Sonata, organ & orchestra, K. 271e (278) C major <- Church
sonatas / Kirchensonaten / Epistle sonatas / Festival so-
natas: MOZART
Sonata, organ & orchestra, K. 317a (329) C major <- Church
sonatas / Kirchensonaten / Epistle sonatas / Festival sona-
tas: MOZART
Sonata, organ & string orchestra, K. 41h (67) E♭ major <-
Church sonatas / Kirchensonaten / Epistle sonatas / Festi-
val sonatas: MOZART
Sonata, organ & string orchestra, K. 41i (68) B♭ major <-
Church sonatas / Kirchensonaten / Epistle sonatas / Festi-
val sonatas: MOZART
Sonata, organ & string orchestra, K. 41k (69) D major <-
Church sonatas / Kirchensonaten / Epistle sonatas / Festi-
val sonatas: MOZART
Sonata, organ & string orchestra, K. 124a (144) D major <-
Church sonatas / Kirchensonaten / Epistle sonatas / Festi-
val sonatas: MOZART
Sonata, organ & string orchestra, K. 124b (145) F major <-
Church sonatas / Kirchensonaten / Epistle sonatas / Festi-
val sonatas: MOZART
Sonata, organ & string orchestra, K. 212, B♭ major <- Church
sonatas / Kirchensonaten / Epistle sonatas / Festival so-
natas: MOZART
Sonata, organ & string orchestra, K. 241, G major <- Church
sonatas / Kirchensonaten / Epistle sonatas / Festival sonatas: MOZART
Sonata, organ & string orchestra, K. 241a (224) F major <-
Church sonatas / Kirchensonaten / Epistle sonatas / Festival sonatas: MOZART
Sonata, organ & string orchestra, K. 241b (225) A major <-
Church sonatas / Kirchensonaten / Epistle sonatas / Festival sonatas: MOZART
Sonata, organ & string orchestra, K. 244, F major <- Church
sonatas / Kirchensonaten / Epistle sonatas / Festival sonatas: MOZART
Sonata, organ & string orchestra, K. 245, D major <- Church
sonatas / Kirchensonaten / Epistle sonatas / Festival sonatas: MOZART
Sonata, organ & string orchestra, K. 271d (274) G major <-

Church sonatas / Kirchensonaten / Epistle sonatas / Festi-
val sonatas: MOZART
Sonata, organ & string orchestra, K. 317c (328) C major <-
Church sonatas / Kirchensonaten / Epistle sonatas / Festi-
val sonatas: MOZART
Sonata, organ & string orchestra, K. 336d (336) C major <-
Church sonatas / Kirchensonaten / Epistle sonatas / Festi-
val sonatas: MOZART
Sonata, piano, A♭ major <- Album sonata: WAGNER
Sonata, piano, E♭ minor <- Z ulice / From the street / Sona-
ta I. X. 1905: JANÁČEK
Sonata, piano, D. 840, C major <- Reliquie / Unfinished so-
nata: SCHUBERT
Sonata, piano, K. 10, B♭ major <- London sonatas: MOZART
Sonata, piano, K. 11, G major <- London sonatas: MOZART
Sonata, piano, K. 12, A major <- London sonatas: MOZART
Sonata, piano, K. 13, F major <- London sonatas: MOZART
Sonata, piano, K. 14, C major <- London sonatas: MOZART
Sonata, piano, K. 15, B♭ major <- London sonatas: MOZART
Sonata, piano, K. 47, no. 1, E♭ major <- Kurfürstensonaten:
BEETHOVEN
Sonata, piano, K. 47, no. 2, F minor <- Kurfürstensonaten:
BEETHOVEN
Sonata, piano, K. 47, no. 3, D major <- Kurfürstensonaten:
BEETHOVEN
Sonata, piano, K. 51, C minor <- Eleonoren-Sonate: BEETHOVEN
Sonata, piano, K. 205 (284) D major <- Dürnitz sonata: MOZART
Sonata, piano, K. 284b (309) C major <- Cannabich sonata:
MOZART
Sonata, piano, K. 284c (311) D major <- Freysinger sonata:
MOZART
Sonata, piano, K. 300d (300) A minor <- Paris sonatas: MO-
ZART
Sonata, piano, K. 300h (330) C major <- Paris sonatas: MO-
ZART
Sonata, piano, K. 300i (331) A major <- Paris sonatas: MO-
ZART
Sonata, piano, K. 300i (331) A major (Rondo alla turca) <-
Turkish march: MOZART
Sonata, piano, K. 300k (332) F major <- Paris sonatas: MO-
ZART
Sonata, piano, K. 315c (333) B♭ major <- Paris sonatas: MO-
ZART
Sonata, piano, K. 576, D major <- Hunt sonata / Jagd-Sonate
/ Trumpet sonata: MOZART
Sonata, piano, no. 1 <- Sonata-fantasia: CHAVEZ
Sonata, piano, no. 1 <- Fantasy sonata: TIPPETT
Sonata, piano, no. 1, op. 28, D major <- Faust sonata: RACH-

MANINOFF
Sonata, piano, no. 1, op. 45, G minor / Tragic sonata -> Sonata tragica, piano: MACDOWELL
Sonata, piano, no. 1, op. 47, C major <- Symphonic sonata: RHEINBERGER
Sonata, piano, no. 2 <- Airplane sonata: ANTHEIL
Sonata, piano, no. 2 <- Concord sonata: IVES
Sonata, piano, no. 2 <- Guggenheim sonata: THOMSON
Sonata, piano, no. 2, op. 14, F minor <- Concert sans orchestre: SCHUMANN
Sonata, piano, no. 2, op. 14, F minor (Andantino de Clara Wieck) <- Variations on a theme by Clara Wieck: SCHUMANN
Sonata, piano, no. 2, op. 19, G# minor <- Sonata-fantasy: SKRIABIN
Sonata, piano, no. 2, op. 35, Bb minor <- Funeral march sonata: CHOPIN
Sonata, piano, no. 2, op. 50, G minor -> Sonata eroica, piano: MACDOWELL
Sonata, piano, no. 3 <- Death of machines: ANTHEIL
Sonata, piano, no. 3, op. 23, F# minor <- États d'ame: SKRIABIN
Sonata, piano, no. 3, op. 57 <- Norse sonata: MACDOWELL
Sonata, piano, no. 4 <- Jazz sonata: ANTHEIL
Sonata, piano, no. 4, op. 29, C minor <- From old notebooks: PROKOFIEV
Sonata, piano, no. 4, op. 59 <- Keltic sonata: MACDOWELL
Sonata, piano, no. 4, op. 184, F# minor <- Romantic sonata: RHEINBERGER
Sonata, piano, no. 6, op. 82, A major <- War sonatas: PROKOFIEV
Sonata, piano, no. 7, op. 64, F# major <- White mass: SKRIABIN
Sonata, piano, no. 7, op. 83, Bb major <- Stalingrad sonata / War sonatas: PROKOFIEV
Sonata, piano, no. 8, op. 13, C minor <- Pathétique sonata: BEETHOVEN
Sonata, piano, no. 8, op. 84, Bb major <- War sonatas: PROKOFIEV
Sonata, piano, no. 9, op. 68, F major <- Black mass: SKRIABIN
Sonata, piano, no. 12, op. 26, Ab major <- Funeral march sonata / Trauermarsch-Sonate: BEETHOVEN
Sonata, piano, no. 14, op. 27, C# minor <- Mondschein-Sonate / Moonlight sonata / Arbor sonata / Sunset sonata: BEETHOVEN
Sonata, piano, no. 15, op. 28, D major <- Pastoral sonata: BEETHOVEN
Sonata, piano, no. 17, op. 31, no. 2, D minor <- Tempest so-

nata / Sturm-Sonate / Recitativ sonata: BEETHOVEN
Sonata, piano, no. 18, op. 31, no. 3, E♭ major <- Hunt sona-
    ta / Jagd-Sonate: BEETHOVEN
Sonata, piano, no. 21, C major <- Esterházy sonatas: J.HAYDN
Sonata, piano, no. 21, op. 53, C major <- Waldstein sonata:
    BEETHOVEN
Sonata, piano, no. 22, E major <- Esterházy sonatas: J.HAYDN
Sonata, piano, no. 23, F major <- Esterházy sonatas: J.HAYDN
Sonata, piano, no. 23, op. 57, F minor < Appassionata: BEET-
    HOVEN
Sonata, piano, no. 24, D major <- Esterházy sonatas: J.HAYDN
Sonata, piano, no. 25, E♭ major <- Esterházy sonatas: J.HAYDN
Sonata, piano, no. 25, op. 79, G major <- Cuckoo sonata:
    BEETHOVEN
Sonata, piano, no. 26, A major <- Esterházy sonatas: J.HAYDN
Sonata, piano, no. 26, op. 81a, E major <- Les adieux sonata:
    BEETHOVEN
Sonata, piano, no. 29, op. 106, B♭ major <- Hammerklavier so-
    nata: BEETHOVEN
Sonata, piano, no. 49, E major <- Genzinger sonata: J.HAYDN
Sonata, piano, no. 50, C major <- London sonatas: J.HAYDN
Sonata, piano, no. 51, D major <- London sonatas: J.HAYDN
Sonata, piano, no. 52, E♭ major <- London sonatas: J.HAYDN
Sonata, piano, op. 16, D major <- La chasse: CLEMENTI
Sonata, piano, op. 25, no. 2, D major <- La matinée: DUSSEK
Sonata, piano, op. 37, G major <- Grand sonata: TCHAIKOVSKY
Sonata, piano, op. 44, E♭ major <- Les adieux / The farewell:
    DUSSEK
Sonata, piano, op. 50, no. 3, G minor <- Didone abbandonata:
    CLEMENTI
Sonata, piano, op. 61, F# minor <- Élégie harmonique sur la
    mort de Son Altesse Royale le prince Louis Ferdinand de
    Prusse: DUSSEK
Sonata, piano, op. 70, A♭ major <- Le retour a Paris: DUSSEK
Sonata, piano, op. 77, F minor <- L'invocation: DUSSEK
Sonata, piano, op. 175 -> Lake of Van sonata, piano: HOVANESS
Sonata, piano, op. 176 -> Madras sonata, piano, op. 176: HOVA-
    NESS
Sonata, piano, op. 191 -> Poseidon sonata, piano, op. 191:
    HOVANESS
Sonata, piano, op. 192 -> Bardo sonata, piano, op. 192: HOVA-
    NESS
Sonata, piano, 4 hands, C major <- Grande ouverture: DUSSEK
Sonata, piano, 4 hands, D. 812, C major <- Grand duo, op. 140:
    SCHUBERT
Sonata, recorder & continuo, B.156,1, B♭ major <- Fitzwilliam
    sonatas: HÄNDEL
Sonata, recorder & continuo, B.156,2, D minor <- Fitzwilliam

sonatas: HÄNDEL

Sonata, recorder & continuo, B.156,3, D minor <- Fitzwilliam
sonatas: HÄNDEL

Sonata, 8 trumpets, kettledrums & continuo <- Sonata St. Polycarpi: BIBER

Sonata, violin, op. 20, C major / Duo merveille -> Duet, 1
violin, C major: PAGANINI

Sonata, violin & continuo, D minor <- Sonata impetuosa: GEMI-
NIANI

Sonata, violin & continuo, G minor <- Devil's trill sonata /
Trillo del diavolo: TARTINI

Sonata, violin & continuo, G minor (Didone abbandonata) <-
Didone abbandonata: TARTINI

Sonata, violin & continuo (Bayerische Staatsbibliothek: Mus.
Ms. 4123) no. 1, D minor <- Biblical sonatas / Mystery sonatas / Rosary sonatas / Rosenkranz-Sonaten: BIBER

Sonata, violin & continuo (Bayerische Staatsbibliothek: Mus.
Ms. 4123) no. 2, A major <- Biblical sonatas / Mystery sonatas / Rosary sonatas / Rosenkranz-Sonaten: BIBER

Sonata, violin & continuo (Bayerische Staatsbibliothek: Mus.
Ms. 4123) no. 3, B minor <- Biblical sonatas / Mystery sonatas / Rosary sonatas / Rosenkranz-Sonaten: BIBER

Sonata, violin & continuo (Bayerische Staatsbibliothek: Mus.
Ms. 4123) no. 4, D minor <- Biblical sonatas / Mystery sonatas / Rosary sonatas / Rosenkranz-Sonaten: BIBER

Sonata, violin & continuo (Bayerische Staatsbibliothek: Mus.
Ms. 4123) no. 5, A major <- Biblical sonatas / Mystery sonatas / Rosary sonatas / Rosenkranz-Sonaten: BIBER

Sonata, violin & continuo (Bayerische Staatsbibliothek: Mus.
Ms. 4123) no. 6, C minor <- Biblical sonatas / Mystery sonatas / Rosary sonatas / Rosenkranz-Sonaten: BIBER

Sonata, violin & continuo (Bayerische Staatsbibliothek: Mus.
Ms. 4123) no. 7, F major <- Biblical sonatas / Mystery sonatas / Rosary sonatas / Rosenkranz-Sonaten: BIBER

Sonata, violin & continuo (Bayerische Staatsbibliothek: Mus.
Ms. 4123) no. 8, Bb major <- Biblical sonatas / Mystery sonatas / Rosary sonatas / Rosenkranz-Sonaten: BIBER

Sonata, violin & continuo (Bayerische Staatsbibliothek: Mus.
Ms. 4123) no. 9, A minor <- Biblical sonatas / Mystery sonatas / Rosary sonatas / Rosenkranz-Sonaten: BIBER

Sonata, violin & continuo (Bayerische Staatsbibliothek: Mus.
Ms. 4123) no. 10, G minor <- Biblical sonatas / Mystery sonatas / Rosary sonatas / Rosenkranz-Sonaten: BIBER

Sonata, violin & continuo (Bayerische Staatsbibliothek: Mus.
Ms. 4123) no. 11, G major <- Biblical sonatas / Mystery sonatas / Rosary sonatas / Rosenkranz-Sonaten: BIBER

Sonata, violin & continuo (Bayerische Staatsbibliothek: Mus.
Ms. 4123) no. 12, C major <- Biblical sonatas / Mystery so-

natas / Rosary sonatas / Rosenkranz-Sonaten: BIBER
Sonata, violin & continuo (Bayerische Staatsbibliothek: Mus.
  Ms. 4123) no. 13, D minor <- Biblical sonatas / Mystery so-
  natas / Rosary sonatas / Rosenkranz-Sonaten: BIBER
Sonata, violin & continuo (Bayerische Staatsbibliothek: Mus.
  Ms. 4123) no. 14, D major <- Biblical sonatas / Mystery so-
  natas / Rosary sonatas / Rosenkranz-Sonaten: BIBER
Sonata, violin & continuo (Bayerische Staatsbibliothek: Mus.
  Ms. 4123) no. 15, C major <- Biblical sonatas / Mystery so-
  natas / Rosary sonatas / Rosenkranz-Sonaten: BIBER
Sonata, violin & continuo (Bayerische Staatsbibliothek: Mus.
  Ms. 4123) no. 16, G minor <- Biblical sonatas / Mystery so-
  natas / Rosary sonatas / Rosenkranz-Sonaten: BIBER
Sonata, violin & continuo, op. 5, no. 6, C minor <- Le tomb-
  eau: LECLAIR
Sonata, violin & continuo, op. 5, no. 7, F minor <- Au tomb-
  eau: LOCATELLI
Sonata, violin & continuo, op. 5, no. 12, D minor <- La fol-
  lia: CORELLI
Sonata, violin & Continuo, R. 63, D minor <- La follia: VI-
  VALDI
Sonata, violin & harpsichord, op. 25, no. 4, E minor <- Les
  amusements d'Apollon: CORRETTE
Sonata, violin & harpsichord, op. 25, no. 5, D major <- Les
  jeux olympiques: CORRETTE
Sonata, violin & piano, D minor <- In memory of Garcia Lor-
  ca: POULENC
Sonata, violin & piano [1853] <- Frei aber einsam: SCHUMANN
Sonata, violin & piano, K. 26, E♭ major <- Weilburg sonatas:
  MOZART
Sonata, violin & piano, K. 27, G major <- Weilburg sonatas:
  MOZART
Sonata, violin & piano, K. 28, C major <- Weilburg sonatas:
  MOZART
Sonata, violin & piano, K. 29, D major <- Weilburg sonatas:
  MOZART
Sonata, violin & piano, K. 30, F major <- Weilburg sonatas:
  MOZART
Sonata, violin & piano, K. 31, B♭ major <- Weilburg sonatas:
  MOZART
Sonata, violin & piano, no. 1, op. 78, G major < Rain sonata
  / Regen-Sonate: BRAHMS
Sonata, violin & piano, no. 2 -> Poème mystique: BLOCH
Sonata, violin & piano, no. 2, op. 82 <- Sonata española /
  Spanish sonata: TURINA
Sonata, violin & piano, no. 2, op. 100, A major <- Meister-
  singer sonata / Thun sonata: BRAHMS
Sonata, violin & piano, no. 4 <- Children's day at the camp

meeting: IVES

Sonata, violin & piano, no. 4, op. 129, G minor <- Chromatische Sonate: RAFF

Sonata, violin & piano, no. 5, op. 24, F major <- Frühlings-
Sonate / Spring sonata: BEETHOVEN

Sonata, violin & piano, no. 7, op. 30, no. 2, C minor <-
Eroica sonata: BEETHOVEN

Sonata, violin & piano, no. 9, op. 47, A major <- Kreutzer
sonata: BEETHOVEN

Sonata, violin & piano, no. 10, op. 96, G major <- Cockcrow
sonata: BEETHOVEN

Sonata, 2 violins, viola & continuo, R. 130, Eb major <- Sonata al Santo Sepolcro: VIVALDI

Sonata, 3 violins, 2 viols & continuo, Bb major <- Die Bauernkirchfahrt / Die Pfauenkirchfahrt: BIBER

Sonata, violoncello & piano, D. 821, A minor <- Arpeggione
sonata: SCHUBERT

Sonata, violoncello & piano, no. 4, op. 102, no. 1, C major
<- Freie Sonate: BEETHOVEN

Sonata a preghiera con variazioni, violin & orchestra <-
Fantasy on the G-string / Moses fantasy: PAGANINI

Sonata al Santo Sepolcro -> Sonata, 2 violins, viola & continuo, R. 130, Eb major: VIVALDI

Sonata appassionata con variazioni -> Introduzione e variazioni sul tema Nel cor più non mi sento: PAGANINI

Sonata con variazioni, violin & orchestra <- Weigl variations: PAGANINI

Sonata eroica, piano <- Sonata, piano, no. 2, op. 50, G minor: MACDOWELL

Sonata española / Spanish sonata -> Sonata, violin & piano,
no. 2, op. 82: TURINA

Sonata impetuosa -> Sonata, violin & continuo, D minor: GEMI-
NIANI

Sonata 1.X.1905 / From the street / Z ulice -> Sonata, piano, Eb minor: JANÁČEK

Sonata representativa, violin & continuo, A major <- Animal
sonata: BIBER

Sonata St. Polycarpi -> Sonata, 8 trumpets, kettledrums &
continuo: BIBER

Sonata, tragica, piano <- Sonata, piano, no. 1, op. 45, G minor / Tragic sonata: MACDOWELL

Sonata-fantasia, piano -> Sonata, piano, no. 1: CHAVEZ

Sonata-fantasia, violin & piano, no. 1 <- Déséspérance: VIL-
LA-LOBOS

Sonata-fantasy -> Sonata, piano, no. 2, op. 19, G# minor:
SKRIABIN

Sonatas of four parts (No. 9) <- Golden sonata: PURCELL

Sonate écossaise -> Fantasia, piano, op. 28, F# minor: MEN-

DELSSOHN
Sonaten für die Jugend, op. 118 (No. 1) <- Kindersonate:
   SCHUMANN
Sonatina, piano [arr.] <- Transylvanian dances: BARTÓK
Sonatina, piano, no. 3 <- Sonatina ad usum infantis: BUSONI
Sonatina, piano, no. 4 <- Sonatina in diem nativitatis Chris-
   ti: BUSONI
Sonatina, piano, no. 5 <- Sonatina in signo Joannis Sebasti-
   ani magni: BUSONI
Sonatina, piano, no. 6 <- Chamber fantasy on Carmen / Kammer-
   Fantasie über Carmen / Sonatina super Carmen: BUSONI
Sonatina, violin & piano, op. 100, G major (Larghetto) <- In-
   dian canzonette / Indian lament: DVOŘÁK
Sonatina, wood-winds & brasses, no. 1, F major <- Aus der
   Werkstatt eines Invaliden / From an invalid's workshop: R.
   STRAUSS
Sonatina, wood-winds & brasses, no. 2, Eb major <- Fröhliche
   Werkstatt / Merry workshop: R.STRAUSS
Sonatina ad usum infantis -> Sonatina, piano, no. 3: BUSONI
Sonatina brevis in signo Joannis Sebastiani magni -> Sonati-
   na, piano, no. 5: BUSONI
Sonatina in diem nativitatis Christi -> Sonatina, piano, no.
   4: BUSONI
Sonatina super Carmen / Chamber fantasy on Carmen / Kammer-
   Fantasie über Carmen -> Sonatina, piano, no. 6: BUSONI
Song [E.E. Cummings] <- Poet's song: COPLAND
Song for our late Sovereign King Charles II -> If prayers
   and tears: PURCELL
Song of faith -> A magyarokhoz: KODÁLY
Song of Gruzia / Chanson géorgienne -> Songs, op. 4 (Oh never
   sing to me again): RACHMANINOFF
Song of praise, A -> Cantique de Jean Racine: FAURÉ
Song of Solomon -> Hebrew song: MUSORGSKY
Song of the flea <- Mephistopheles' serenade: MUSORGSKY
Song of the night / Lied der Nacht -> Symphony, no. 7: MAHLER
Song of the night / Le chant de nuit -> Symphony, no. 3, op.
   27: SZYMANOWSKI
Song of the old man / The harper's song -> Old man's song:
   MUSORGSKY
Song of the traveller -> Lieder ohne Worte, op. 85 (No. 6):
   MENDELSSOHN
Songs, op. 2 (The rose and the nightingale) <- Oriental song:
   RIMSKY-KORSAKOV
Songs, op. 4 (The drooping corn) <- Harvest of sorrow: RACH-
   MANINOFF
Songs, op. 4 (Oh, never sing to me again) <- Chanson géorgi-
   enne / Song of Gruzia: RACHMANINOFF
Songs, op. 6 <- Megkésett melódiák: KODÁLY

Songs, op. 6 (Not a word, O my friend) <- A summer love / Do not speak, beloved: TCHAIKOVSKY

Songs, op. 6 (Painfully and sweetly) <- What torment: TCHAIKOVSKY

Songs, op. 9 <- Poems of Verlaine: STRAVINSKY

Songs, op. 10 <- Chamber music: BARBER

Songs, op. 14 (Floods of spring) <- Spring waters: RACHMANINOFF

Songs, op. 21 (How fair this spot) <- Here beauty dwells: RACHMANINOFF

Songs, op. 25 (Reconciliation) <- Sleep of sorrow: TCHAIKOVSKY

Songs, op. 26 (Before my window) <- The cherry tree: RACHMANINOFF

Songs, op. 27 (To sleep) <- Invocation: TCHAIKOVSKY

Songs, op. 28 (The fearful minute) <- One small word / Sweet maid, answer me: TCHAIKOVSKY

Songs, op. 38 (Daisies; arr.) <- Album leaf: RACHMANINOFF

Songs, op. 38 (Don Juan's serenade) <- Spanish serenade: TCHAIKOVSKY

Songs, op. 38 (In the din of the ball) <- At the ball: TCHAIKOVSKY

Songs, op. 38 (Pimpinella) <- Florentine song: TCHAIKOVSKY

Songs, op. 47 (Was I not a little blade of grass?) <- The bride's complaint / La nouvelle mariée: TCHAIKOVSKY

Songs, op. 54 (A legend) <- Christ in his garden: TCHAIKOVSKY

Songs, op. 54 (Lullaby) <- My Lisochek: TCHAIKOVSKY

Songs, op. 54 (Lullaby in a storm) <- Winter: TCHAIKOVSKY

Songs, op. 54 (Spring) <- The grass grown green: TCHAIKOVSKY

Songs, op. 57 (On the golden cornfields) <- Remorse: TCHAIKOVSKY

Songs, op. 57 (Only you) <- All for you: TCHAIKOVSKY

Songs, op. 60 <- Shakespeare songs: SIBELIUS

Songs, op. 60 (While I wait) <- In the boat: GRIEG

Songs, op. 63 (I opened the window) <- New hopes / At the open window: TCHAIKOVSKY

Songs, op. 65 (Rondel) <- The charmer: TCHAIKOVSKY

Songs, op. 73 (Again, as before, alone) <- Solitude: TCHAIKOVSKY

Songs, op. 73 (In this moonlight) <- In this summer night / O thou moonlit night: TCHAIKOVSKY

Songs, op. 73 (We sat together) <- Side by side / Am schlummernden Strom: TCHAIKOVSKY

Songs from the Norwegian (Twilight fancies) <- Evening voices: DELIUS

Songs of a great war -> The cost: IRELAND

Songs of sundrie natures (Who made thee, Hob) <- A dialogue between two shepherds: BYRD

Sonnambula fantasy -> Fantaisie sur des motifs favoris de
   l'opéra La sonnambule de Bellini, piano: LISZT
Sonnenaufgang-Quartett / Sunrise quartet / Erdödy quartets
   -> Quartet, strings, no. 79, op. 76, no. 4, Bb major: J.
   HAYDN
Sonnenquartette / Sun quartets -> Quartet, strings, no. 32,
   op. 20, no. 1, Eb major; no. 33, op. 20, no. 2, C major;
   no. 34, op. 20, no. 3, G minor; no. 35, op. 20, no. 4, D
   major; no. 36, op. 20, no. 5, F minor; no. 37, op. 20, no.
   6, D major: J.HAYDN
Sonno, Il -> Questo silenzio: A.SCARLATTI
Sophonisba <- Hannibal's overthrow: PURCELL
Sopra un' eccelsa torre -> Il Nerone: STRADELLA
Sorrowful soul, The -> Lieder ohne Worte, op. 53 (No. 4):
   MENDELSSOHN
Sosi <- The forest of prophetic sound: HOVANESS
Sospetto, Il -> Concerto, violin & string orchestra, R.199,
   C minor: VIVALDI
Sospiro, Un -> Études de concert, piano (No. 3): LISZT
Souls of the righteous, The <- Funeral anthem: BOYCE
Source, La <- Naila / Soir de fête: DELIBES
Souvenir d'Amérique <- Yankee doodle: VIEUXTEMPS
Souvenir d'Andalousie -> Boléro: CHOPIN
Souvenir de Florence <- Sextet, strings, op. 70: TCHAIKOVSKY
Souvenir de Nizza <- Erinnerungen an Riga: JOHANN STRAUSS
Souvenir de Porto Rico <- Marche de gibaros: GOTTSCHALK
Souvenir d'une nuit d'été <- Spanish overture, no. 2 / Recu-
   erdos de Castilla: GLINKA
Souvenirs -> Espagne: ALBÉNIZ
Spanish friar, The <- The double discovery: PURCELL
Spanish overture, no. 1 / Capriccio brillante -> Jota arago-
   nesa, orchestra: GLINKA
Spanish overture, no. 2 / Recuerdos de Castilla -> Souvenir
   d'une nuit d'été: GLINKA
Spanish serenade -> Songs, op. 38 (Don Juan's serenade):
   TCHAIKOVSKY
Spanish sonata / Sonata española -> Sonata, violin & piano,
   no. 2, op. 82: TURINA
Sparrow mass / Spatzenmesse -> Missa brevis, K. 196b (220) C
   major: MOZART
Spatzenmesse / Sparrow mass -> Missa brevis, K. 196b (220) C
   major: MOZART
Spaur mass -> Missa brevis, K. 258, C major: MOZART
Spectre de la rose, Le -> Aufforderung zum tanz: WEBER
Spinnerlied / Spinning song / The bee's wedding -> Lieder
   ohne Worte, op. 67 (No. 4): MENDELSSOHN
Spinning song / Spinnerlied / The bee's wedding -> Lieder
   ohne Worte, op. 67 (No. 4): MENDELSSOHN

Spinning top, The / La toupie -> Jeux d'enfants (Impromptu):
BIZET
Spiritata, La -> Canzoni per sonare (No. 1): G.GABRIELI
Spiritus intelligentiae sanctus <- Pfingstoratorium / Whit-
sun oratorio: KŘENEK
Spitfire prelude -> The first of the few (Prelude and fugue):
WALTON
Sposa in contrasto, La / Il barone deluso -> I due baroni di
Rocca Azzurra: CIMAROSA
Sposalizio-Trauung / Geistliche Vermählungsmusik -> Ave Maria,
no. 3: LISZT
Sposo senza moglie, Lo -> I due supposti conti: CIMAROSA
Spring / La primavera / Concerto, op. 8, no. 1, E major ->
Il cimento dell' armonia e dell' inventione (No. 1): VIVAL-
DI
Spring cantata / Frühlingskantate -> Alles tönet, schallt
und singt: TELEMANN
Spring quartet / Frühlingsquartett / Haydn quartets -> Quar-
tet, strings, K. 387, G major: MOZART
Spring quintet / Frühlings-Quintett -> Quintet, strings, op.
88, F major: BRAHMS
Spring sonata / Frühlings-Sonate -> Sonata, violin & piano,
no. 5, op. 24, F major: BEETHOVEN
Spring song / Frühlingslied / Camberwell Green -> Lieder oh-
ne Worte, op. 62 (No. 6): MENDELSSOHN
Spring symphony / Frühlings-Sinfonie -> Symphony, no. 4, op.
60, Bb major: BEETHOVEN
Spring symphony / Le printemps -> Symphony, no. 4, op. 52:
LAJTHA
Spring symphony / Le printemps -> Symphonie pour petit orch-
estre, no. 1: MILHAUD
Spring symphony / Frühlings-Sinfonie -> Symphony, no. 1, op.
38, Bb major: SCHUMANN
Spring symphony / Frühlings-Symphonie -> Symphony, A major,
no. 4: STAMITZ
Spring tale -> The snow maiden: RIMSKY-KORSAKOV
Spring waters -> Songs, op. 14 (Floods of spring): RACHMANI-
NOFF
Sprüche <- Anthems, op. 79: MENDELSSOHN
Stabat mater, D. 383 <- Deutsches Stabat mater: SCHUBERT
Stadler quintet -> Quintet, clarinet & strings, K. 581, A ma-
jor: MOZART
Ständchen / Serenade -> Kling leise, mein Lied: LISZT
Ständchen / Ruhe -> Leise, leise lasst uns singen, D. 635:
SCHUBERT
Stalingrad sonata / War sonatas -> Sonata, piano, no. 7, op.
83, Bb major: PROKOFIEV
Stelle, perfide stelle <- Partenza: HÄNDEL

Sternen-Lieder -> Heine Lieder, 3. Heft: CASTELNUOVO-TEDESCO
Stiffelio <- Giuglielmo Wellingrode: VERDI
Still falls the rain <- Canticle III: BRITTEN
Stille Land, Das -> Das Grab, D. 569: SCHUBERT
Stimmungen (Studie) <- Hommage à Chopin: GRIEG
Stone flower, The (Suite) <- Gypsy fantasy: PROKOFIEV
Storm, The -> Tempest: TCHAIKOVSKY
Storm quintet / Sturm-Quintett -> Quintet, strings, op. 29,
  C major: BEETHOVEN
Stornelli e ballate -> Quartet, strings, no. 2: MALIPIERO
Strassburg concerto -> Concerto, violin, K. 218, D major:
  MOZART
Stravaganti, Gli -> Madama l'umorista: PAISIELLO
Stravaganza, La <- Concerto, op. 4, no. 1, B♭ major; no. 2,
  E minor; no. 3, G major; no. 4, A minor; no. 5, A major;
  no. 6, G minor; no. 7, C major; no. 8, D minor; no. 9, F
  major; no. 10, C minor; no. 11, D major; no. 12, G major:
  VIVALDI
Stravaganze d'amore, La <- Giulietta ed Armidoro: CIMAROSA
Streghe, Le <- Witches' dance: PAGANINI
Streit zwischen Phoebus und Pan, Der / The contest between
  Phoebus and Pan -> Geschwinde, geschwinde, ihr wirbelnden
  Winde, S. 201: J.S.BACH
Strophe von Schiller -> Die Götter Griechenlands, D. 677:
  SCHUBERT
Studien, pedal-piano, op. 56 <- Canonic etudes: SCHUMANN
Studien, piano, op. 35 <- Paganini studies / Paganini vari-
  ations: BRAHMS
Studien nach Capricen von Paganini, piano, op. 3 <- Paganini
  studies: SCHUMANN
Study, piano, no. 21 <- Some south-paw pitching: IVES
Study for ears or aural and mental exercise -> Varied air
  and variations: IVES
Study in thirds -> Etude, piano, op. 8, no. 10, D♭ major:
  SKRIABIN
Stücke, musical clock, H.XIX,6 <- Der Kaffeeklatsch: J.HAYDN
Stücke, musical clock, H.XIX,8 <- Der Wachtelschlag: J.HAYDN
Stücke, organ, op. 145 (Dankpsalm) <- Praise to the Lord:
  REGER
Stunde schlägt, Die <- Abschiedsgesang: BEETHOVEN
Sturm und Drang symphonies -> Symphony, M. 44, E minor; M.
  45, F# minor; M. 46, B major; M. 47, G major; M. 48, C ma-
  jor; M. 49, F minor: J.HAYDN
Sturm-Quintett / Storm quintet -> Quintet, strings, op. 29,
  C major: BEETHOVEN
Sturm-Sonate / Tempest sonata / Recitativ sonata -> Sonata,
  piano, no. 17, op. 31, no. 2, D minor: BEETHOVEN
Suicide de bigorneau, Le -> Deux sous de charbon: DELIBES

Süsse Hoffnung, wenn ich frage <- Die Hoffnung des Wieder-
sehens: TELEMANN
Suite, 3 clarinets & strings, op. 29 <- Septet, op. 29:
SCHÖNBERG
Suite, flute, no. 5 <- Wedding music: LUENING
Suite, flute & string orchestra, A minor <- Les plaisirs:
TELEMANN
Suite, harpsichord, S. 806, A major <- English suites: J.S.
BACH
Suite, harpsichord, S. 807, A minor <- English suites: J.S.
BACH
Suite, harpsichord, S. 808, G minor <- English suites: J.S.
BACH
Suite, harpsichord, S. 809, F major <- English suites: J.S.
BACH
Suite, harpsichord, S. 810, E minor <- English suites: J.S.
BACH
Suite, harpsichord, S. 811, D minor <- English suites: J.S.
BACH
Suite, harpsichord, S. 812, D minor <- French suites: J.S.
BACH
Suite, harpsichord, S. 813, C minor <- French suites: J.S.
BACH
Suite, harpsichord, S. 814, B minor <- French suites: J.S.
BACH
Suite, harpsichord, S. 815, E♭ major ← French suites: J.S.
BACH
Suite, harpsichord, S. 816, G major <- French suites: J.S.
BACH
Suite, harpsichord, S. 817, E major <- French suites: J.S.
BACH
Suite, harpsichord, 1st collection, no. 5, E major (Air) <-
Grobschmied-Variationen / The harmonious blacksmith: HÄN-
DEL
Suite, harpsichord, 2d collection, no. 2, G major <- Cha-
conne with 21 variations: HÄNDEL
Suite, ondes Martenot & piano <- Le chateau des papes
(Suite; arr.): MILHAUD
Suite, orchestra, C major <- Hamburger Ebb und Fluht / Water
music: TELEMANN
Suite, orchestra, D <- Suite for the birthday of Prince
Charles: TIPPETT
Suite, orchestra, Bll, B♭ major -> La bourse: TELEMANN
Suite, orchestra, Fll, F major <- Alster overture / A musi-
cal joke / Ein musikalischer Spass: TELEMANN
Suite, orchestra, no. 1 -> Pièces faciles, piano, 4 hands
[1917] (Selections; arr.): STRAVINSKY
Suite, orchestra, no. 1, op. 79b < Russian suite: BRUCH

Suite, orchestra, no. 2 -> Pièces faciles, piano, 4 hands
[1915;arr.]: STRAVINSKY
Suite, orchestra, no. 2, op. 34a <- Geharnischte Suite: BUSO-
NI
Suite, orchestra, no. 2, op. 48 <- Indian suite: MACDOWELL
Suite, orchestra, no. 2, op. 53, C major <- Suite caractéris-
tique: TCHAIKOVSKY
Suite, orchestra, no. 2, op. 89 <- Nordland-Suite / Swedish
suite: BRUCH
Suite, orchestra, no. 2, op. 194, F major <- Suite in ungar-
ischer Weise / Suite in the Hungarian manner: RAFF
Suite, orchestra, no. 3, op. 27 <- Sătaescă / Villageoise:
ENESCO
Suite, orchestra, no. 4, op. 61, G major <- Mozartiana:
TCHAIKOVSKY
Suite, orchestra, op. 39, D minor <- Czech suite: DVOŘÁK
Suite, orchestra, op. 110 -> Waltzes, orchestra, op. 110:
PROKOFIEV
Suite, orchestra, S. 1068, D major (Aria) <- Air on the G-
string / Aria of the fallen angels: J.S.BACH
Suite, piano, no. 1, op. 3 <- Suite dans le style ancien:
ENESCO
Suite, piano, no. 3, op. 18 <- Pièces impromptus: ENESCO
Suite, piano, op. 21, G major <- Festive march suite: SUK
Suite, piano, op. 26 -> 1922 suite, piano: HINDEMITH
Suite, piano, op. 98, A major <- American suite: DVOŘÁK
Suite, piano, op. 177 -> Shalimar: HOVANESS
Suite, piano, 4 hands, op. 18 <- Hungarian folk dances: WEI-
NER
Suite, 4 saxophones <- Canonic suite: CARTER
Suite, string orchestra, A5, A major <- Festliche Suite /
Festive suite: TELEMANN
Suite, string orchestra, B3, B♭ major <- Le sommeil: TELEMANN
Suite, string orchestra, B5, B♭ major <- Völker-Ouverture:
TELEMANN
Suite, string orchestra, B8, B♭ major <- Ouverture burlesque:
TELEMANN
Suite, string orchestra, C5, C major / La bouffonne -> Lust-
ige Suite, string orchestra: TELEMANN
Suite, string orchestra, D5, D major <- La galante: TELEMANN
Suite, string orchestra, D12, D major <- Perpetuum mobile:
TELEMANN
Suite, string orchestra, D13, D major <- La gaillarde: TELE-
MANN
Suite, string orchestra, e8, E minor <- L'omphale: TELEMANN
Suite, string orchestra, Es3, E♭ major <- La lyra: TELEMANN
Suite, string orchestra, F7, F major <- Ouverture à la pas-
torelle: TELEMANN

Suite, string orchestra, F10, F major <- Ouverture à la bur-
   lesque: TELEMANN
Suite, string orchestra, g1, G minor <- La musette: TELEMANN
Suite, string orchestra, g2, G minor <- La changeante: TELE-
   MANN
Suite, string orchestra, G2, G major <- La bizarre: TELEMANN
Suite, string orchestra, G8, G major <- La querelleuse: TE-
   LEMANN
Suite, string orchestra, G10, G major / Burlesque de Quix-
   otte -> Don Quichotte: TELEMANN
Suite, string orchestra, G12, G major <- Suite burlesque:
   TELEMANN
Suite, string orchestra, h3, B minor <- La prude: TELEMANN
Suite, trumpet & string orchestra, D8, D major <- La tromba:
   TELEMANN
Suite, trumpet, strings & continuo, D major <- Water piece:
   HÄNDEL
Suite, violin & piano, op. 73 -> Kirgiz suite, violin & pi-
   ano: HOVANESS
Suite, violin & piano, op. 103a, A minor <- Hausmusik / Vor-
   tragsstücke: REGER
Suite burlesque -> Suite, string orchestra, G12, G major:
   TELEMANN
Suite caractéristique -> Suite, orchestra, no. 2, op. 53, C
   major: TCHAIKOVSKY
Suite dans le style ancien -> Suite, piano, no. 1, op. 3:
   ENESCO
Suite española, piano, no. 1 (Asturias) <- Leyenda: ALBÉNIZ
Suite española, piano, no. 1 (Castilla) <- Seguidillas: AL-
   BÉNIZ
Suite española, piano, no. 1 (Granada) <- Serenata: ALBÉNIZ
Suite española, piano, no. 2 (Sevilla) <- Sevillanas: ALBÉ-
   NIZ
Suite for the birthday of Prince Charles -> Suite, orchestra,
   D: TIPPETT
Suite hébraïque -> Pièces hébraïques, viola & piano: BLOCH
Suite in älterer Form / Suite in the older form -> Quartet,
   strings, no. 6, op. 192, no. 1: RAFF
Suite in the Hungarian manner / Suite in ungarischer Weise
   -> Suite, orchestra, no. 2, op. 194, F major: RAFF
Suite in the older form / Suite in älterer Form -> Quartet,
   strings, no. 6, op. 192, no. 1: RAFF
Suite in ungarischer Weise / Suite in the Hungarian manner
   -> Suite, orchestra, no. 2, op. 194, F major: RAFF
Suite pastorale -> Pièces pittoresques, piano (Selections;
   arr.): CHABRIER
Suite populaire espagnole -> Canciones populares españolas:
   FALLA

Suite symphonique <- Impressions of Paris / Paris suite:
  IBERT
Suite symphonique, no. 2 <- Protée: MILHAUD
Suite Transylvanie / Transylvanian suite -> Quartet, strings,
  no. 10, op. 58: LAJTHA
Suleika, D. 717 <- Westwind: SCHUBERT
Suleika, D. 720 <- Ostwind / Glückliches Geheimnis: SCHUBERT
Sumé Pater patrium -> Symphony, no. 10: VILLA-LOBOS
Summer / L'estate / Concerto, op. 8, no. 2, B♭ major -> Il
  cimento dell' armonia e dell' inventione (No. 2): VIVALDI
Summer day suite, orchestra <- Music for children: PROKOFIEV
Summer love, A / Do not speak, beloved -> Songs, op. 6 (Not
  a word, O my friend): TCHAIKOVSKY
Summer night -> The duenna (Suite): PROKOFIEV
Sun and the moon, The / The origins of the Amazon -> Lenda
  amerindia (Erosão): VILLA-LOBOS
Sun quartets / Sonnenquartette -> Quartet, strings, no. 32,
  op. 20, no. 1, E♭ major; no. 33, op. 20, no. 2, C major;
  no. 34, op. 20, no. 3, G minor; no. 35, op. 20, no. 4, D
  major; no. 36, op. 20, no. 5, F minor; no. 37, op. 20, no.
  6, D major: J.HAYDN
Sun was sunk, The <- The poor shepherd: HÄNDEL
Sunday afternoon music <- The young pioneers: COPLAND
Sunrise quartet / Sonnenaufgang-Quartett / Erdödy quartets
  -> Quartet, strings, no. 79, op. 76, no. 4, B♭ major: J.
  HAYDN
Sunset sonata / Mondschein-Sonate / Moonlight sonata / Arbor
  sonata -> Sonata, piano, no. 14, op. 27, no. 2, C# minor:
  BEETHOVEN
Suonata con variazioni, violin & orchestra <- Variations on
  a theme by Joseph Weigl: PAGANINI
Suor Angelica <- Il trittico: PUCCINI
Suppliantes d'eschyle <- Hiketides: XENAKIS
Surprise box, The / Vitrina encantada -> Caixinha de boas
  festas: VILLA-LOBOS
Surprise symphony / Paukenschlagsymphonie / Salomon sympho-
  nies / London symphonies -> Symphony, M. 94, G major: J.
  HAYDN
Swedish rhapsody, orchestra, no. 1, op. 19 <- Midsommervaka:
  ALFVÉN
Swedish rhapsody, orchestra, no. 2, op. 24 <- Uppsalarapso-
  di: ALFVÉN
Swedish rhapsody, orchestra, no. 3, op. 48 <- Dalarapsodi /
  Dalecartian rhapsody: ALFVÉN
Swedish suite / Nordland-Suite -> Suite, orchestra, no. 2,
  op. 89: BRUCH
Sweet maid answer me / One small word -> Songs, op. 28 (The
  fearful minute): TCHAIKOVSKY

Sweet remembrance -> Lieder ohne Worte, op. 19 (No. 1): MEN-
DELSSOHN

Swiss symphony / Schweizer-Sinfonie -> Symphony, string orchestra, no. 9, C minor: MENDELSSOHN

Sylphe des Friedens, Der -> Ridenta la calma: MOZART

Sylphen, D. 341 <- Die Elfenkönigin: SCHUBERT

Sylphes supposés, Les -> Isabelle et Gertrude: GRÉTRY

Sylphides, Les -> Works, piano (Selections; arr.): CHOPIN

Sylvan rhapsody -> Earth's call: IRELAND

Sylvia <- Le nymphe de Diane: DELIBES

Symphatie, La -> Acanthe et Céphise: RAMEAU

Symphonia serena (Rather fast) <- Geschwindmarsch: HINDEMITH

Symphoniae sacrae <- Sacred concertos: SCHÜTZ

Symphonic elegy, A -> Farewell to pioneers: HARRIS

Symphonic sonata -> Sonata, piano, no. 1, op. 47, C major:
RHEINBERGER

Symphonic studies / Études symphoniques -> Études en forme
de variations, piano, op. 13: SCHUMANN

Symphonie cévenole -> Symphonie sur un chant montagard français: INDY

Symphonie dramatique / Dramatic symphony -> Symphony, no. 4,
op. 95, D minor: RUBINSTEIN

Symphonie gothique / Gothic symphony -> Symphony, organ, no.
9, op. 70: WIDOR

Symphonie italienne / Italian symphony -> Symphony, no. 1:
INDY

Symphonie liturgique / Liturgic symphony -> Symphony, no. 3:
HONEGGER

Symphonie marine -> Symphony, no. 1: IBERT

Symphonie pour petit orchestre, no. 1 <- Le printemps /
Spring symphony: MILHAUD

Symphonie pour petit orchestre, no. 2 <- Pastorale: MILHAUD

Symphonie pour petit orchestre, no. 3 <- Serenade: MILHAUD

Symphonie rhodanienne -> Symphony, no. 8, D: MILHAUD

Symphonie romane / Roman symphony -> Symphony, organ, no. 10,
op. 73: WIDOR

Symphonie romantique / Romantic symphony -> Symphony, no. 11:
MILHAUD

Symphonie rurale / Rural symphony -> Symphony, no. 12: MILHAUD

Symphonie sur un chant montagnard français <- Symphonie cévenole: INDY

Symphonie zu Dantes Divina commedia <- Dante symphony: LISZT

Symphony, A major, no. 4 < Spring symphony / Frühlings-Symphonie: STAMITZ

Symphony, C major [ca. 1822]: FRIEDRICH WITT <- Jena symphony: BEETHOVEN

Symphony, D major [Veneziana] <- Sinfonia veneziana: SALIERI

Symphony, D minor <- Nullte Symphonie: BRUCKNER
Symphony, D minor <- Youthful symphony: RACHMANINOFF
Symphony, F major <- Urbs Roma: SAINT-SAËNS
Symphony, G major, no. 16: LEOPOLD MOZART <- Neue Lambacher-
  Sinfonie: WOLFGANG AMADEUS MOZART
Symphony, G minor <- Unfinished symphony / Zwickau symphony:
  SCHUMANN
Symphony, D. 417, C minor < Tragic symphony: SCHUBERT
Symphony, D. 589, C major <- Little C major symphony: SCHU-
  BERT
Symphony, D. 759, B minor <- Unfinished symphony / Unvollen-
  dete Sinfonie: SCHUBERT
Symphony, D. 944, C major <- Gastein symphony / Great C major
  symphony: SCHUBERT
Symphony, G. 506, D minor <- La casa del diavolo: BOCCHERINI
Symphony, K. 42a (76) F major <- Lambacher Sinfonie: MOZART
Symphony, K. 48, B♭ major <- Im Postzug: DITTERSDORF
Symphony, K. 73 <- Les quatre ages du monde / Metamorphosen-
  Sinfonien / Ovid symphonies: DITTERSDORF
Symphony, K. 74 <- La chûte de Phaèton / Metamorphosen-Sin-
  fonien / Ovid symphonies: DITTERSDORF
Symphony, K. 75 <- Actéon changé en cerf / Metamorphosen-
  Sinfonien / Ovid symphonies: DITTERSDORF
Symphony, K. 76 <- Andromède sauvée par persée / Metamorpho-
  sen-Sinfonien / Ovid symphonies: DITTERSDORF
Symphony, K. 77 <- Phinée avec ses amis changés en rochers /
  Metamorphosen-Sinfonien / Ovid symphonies: DITTERSDORF
Symphony, K. 78 <- Les paysans changés en grenouilles / Me-
  tamorphosen-Sinfonien / Ovid symphonies: DITTERSDORF
Symphony, K. 79 <- Jason qui enlève la toison d'or / Meta-
  morphosen-Sinfonien / Ovid symphonies: DITTERSDORF
Symphony, K. 80 <- Le siege de Mégare / Metamorphosen-Sinfo-
  nien / Ovid symphonies: DITTERSDORF
Symphony, K. 81 <- Hercule changé en dieu / Metamorphosen-
  Sinfonien / Ovid symphonies: DITTERSDORF
Symphony, K. 82 <- Orphée et Euridice / Metamorphosen-Sinfo-
  nien / Ovid symphonies: DITTERSDORF
Symphony, K. 83 <- Midas élu pour Juge entre Pan et Apollon
  / Metamorphosen-Sinfonien / Ovid symphonies: DITTERSDORF
Symphony, K. 84 <- Ajax et Ulisse qui se dis putent les arm-
  es d'Achille / Metamorphosen-Sinfonien / Ovid symphonies:
  DITTERSDORF
Symphony, K. 94, D major <- Carnaval symphony: DITTERSDORF
Symphony, K. 135, D major -> Lucio Silla (Overture): MOZART
Symphony, K. 173dB (183) G minor <- Little G minor symphony:
  MOZART
Symphony, K. 300a (297) D major <- Paris symphony: MOZART
Symphony, K. 318, G major <- Italian overture: MOZART

Symphony, K. 385, D major <- Haffner symphony: MOZART
Symphony, K. 425, C major <- Linz symphony: MOZART
Symphony, K. 504, D major <- Prague symphony: MOZART
Symphony, K. 543, Eb major <- Schwanengesang-Sinfonie: MOZART
Symphony, K. 550, G minor <- Great G minor symphony: MOZART
Symphony, K. 551, C major <- Jupiter symphony: MOZART
Symphony, M. 1, D major <- Morzin symphonies: J.HAYDN
Symphony, M. 2, C major <- Morzin symphonies: J.HAYDN
Symphony, M. 6, D major <- Le matin: J.HAYDN
Symphony, M. 7, C major <- Le midi: J.HAYDN
Symphony, M. 8, G major <- Le soir / La tempète: J.HAYDN
Symphony, M. 10, D major <- Morzin symphonies: J.HAYDN
Symphony, M. 13, D major <- Jupiter symphony: J.HAYDN
Symphony, M. 15, D major <- Morzin symphonies: J.HAYDN
Symphony, M. 18, G major <- Morzin symphonies: J.HAYDN
Symphony, M. 22, Eb major <- The philosopher: J.HAYDN
Symphony, M. 26, D minor <- Christmas symphony / Weihnachts-
  symphonie / Lamentatione: J.HAYDN
Symphony, M. 27, G major <- Bruckenthal symphony: J.HAYDN
Symphony, M. 30, C major <- Alleluia symphony: J.HAYDN
Symphony, M. 31, D major <- Hornsignal-Sinfonie / Auf dem An-
  stand: J.HAYDN
Symphony, M. 37, C major <- Morzin symphonies: J.HAYDN
Symphony, M. 38, C major <- Echo symphony: J.HAYDN
Symphony, M. 43, Eb major <- Mercury symphony: J.HAYDN
Symphony, M. 44, E minor <- Funeral symphony / Trauer-sympho-
  nie / Sturm und Drang symphonies: J.HAYDN
Symphony, M. 45, F# minor <- Abschieds-Symphonie / Farewell
  symphony / Sturm und Drang symphonies: J.HAYDN
Symphony, M. 47, G major <- Palindrom-Sinfonie / Sturm und
  Drang symphonies: J.HAYDN
Symphony, M. 48, C major <- Maria Theresa symphony / Sturm
  und Drang symphonies: J.HAYDN
Symphony, M. 49, F minor <- La passione / Sturm und Drang
  symphonies: J.HAYDN
Symphony, M. 53, D major <- L'impériale: J.HAYDN
Symphony, M. 53 (1st movement) <- Festino overture: J.HAYDN
Symphony, M. 55, Eb major <- The schoolmaster / Der Schul-
  meister: J.HAYDN
Symphony, M. 59, A major <- Feuersymphonie / Fire symphony:
  J.HAYDN
Symphony, M. 60, C major <- Il distratto: J.HAYDN
Symphony, M. 63, C major <- La Roxolane: J.HAYDN
Symphony, M. 64, A major <- Tempora mutantur: J.HAYDN
Symphony, M. 69, C major <- Laudon symphony: J.HAYDN
Symphony, M. 73, D major <- La chasse: J.HAYDN
Symphony, M. 82, C major <- The bear / L'ours / Paris sympho-
  nies: J.HAYDN

Symphony, M. 83, G minor <- The hen / La poule / Paris sym-
phonies: J.HAYDN
Symphony, M. 84, E♭ major <- Paris symphonies: J.HAYDN
Symphony, M. 85, B♭ major <- La reine / Paris symphonies: J.
HAYDN
Symphony, M. 86, D major <- Paris symphonies: J.HAYDN
Symphony, M. 87, A major <- Paris symphonies: J.HAYDN
Symphony, M. 92, G major <- Oxford symphony: J.HAYDN
Symphony, M. 93, D major <- Salomon symphonies / London sym-
phonies: J.HAYDN
Symphony, M. 94, G major <- Paukenschlag-Symphonie / Surprise
symphony / Salomon symphonies / London symphonies: J.HAYDN
Symphony, M. 95, C minor <- Salomon symphonies / London sym-
phonies: J.HAYDN
Symphony, M. 96, D major <- The miracle / Salomon symphonies
/ London symphonies: J.HAYDN
Symphony, M. 97, C major <- Salomon symphonies / London sym-
phonies: J.HAYDN
Symphony, M. 98, B♭ major <- Salomon symphonies / London sym-
phonies: J.HAYDN
Symphony, M. 99, E♭ major <- Salomon symphonies / London sym-
phonies: J.HAYDN
Symphony, M. 100, D major <- Military symphony / Salomon sym-
phonies / London symphonies: J.HAYDN
Symphony, M. 101, D major <- Clock symphony / Die Uhr / Sal-
omon symphonies / London symphonies: J.HAYDN
Symphony, M. 102, B♭ major <- Salomon symphonies / London
symphonies: J.HAYDN
Symphony, M. 103, E♭ major <- Drum-roll symphony / Pauken-
wirbel-Symphonie / Salomon symphonies / London symphonies:
J.HAYDN
Symphony, M. 104, D major <- London symphony / Salomon sym-
phonies / London symphonies: J.HAYDN
Symphony, no. 1 <- Zingareska: ANTHEIL
Symphony, no. 1 -> Jeremiah: BERNSTEIN
Symphony, no. 1 <- Sinfonia de Antigona: CHAVEZ
Symphony, no. 1 -> La nuit des tropiques: GOTTSCHALK
Symphony, no. 1 <- 1933 symphony: HARRIS
Symphony, no. 1 <- Boston symphony: HONEGGER
Symphony, no. 1 <- Symphonie marine: IBERT
Symphony, no. 1 <- Italian symphony / Symphonie italienne:
IBERT
Symphony, no. 1 <- Proletarians, unite: KABALEVSKY
Symphony, no. 1 <- Choreographic symphony: SCHUMAN
Symphony, no. 1 <- A sea symphony: VAUGHAN WILLIAMS
Symphony, no. 1 <- O imprevisto: VILLA-LOBOS
Symphony, no. 1 [1924] <- Organ symphony: COPLAND
Symphony, no. 1, B♭ major <- Music in London: BOYCE

Symphony, no. 1, D major <- Titan symphony: MAHLER
Symphony, no. 1, G major <- Sinfonie sérieuse: BERWALD
Symphony, no. 1, op. 3, C minor <- The bells of Zlonice:
  DVOŘÁK
Symphony, no. 1, op. 5, C minor <- On Sjølund's fair plains:
  GADE
Symphony, no. 1, op. 5, E major <- Slavonic symphony: GLAZU-
  NOV
Symphony, no. 1, op. 10 -> Wallenstein: RHEINBERGER
Symphony, no. 1, op. 13, G minor <- Winter dreams: TCHAIKOVSKY
Symphony, no. 1, op. 17, no. 2 <- Exile symphony: HOVANESS
Symphony, no. 1, op. 21, E minor <- Nordic symphony: HANSON
Symphony, no. 1, op. 25, D major -> Classical symphony: PRO-
  KOFIEV
Symphony, no. 1, op. 38, B♭ major <- Frühlings-Sinfonie /
  Spring symphony: SCHUMANN
Symphony, no. 1, op. 96, D major <- Aus das Vaterland: RAFF
Symphony, no. 2 <- American symphony: ANTHEIL
Symphony, no. 2 -> The age of anxiety: BERNSTEIN
Symphony, no. 2 <- Sinfonia india: CHAVEZ
Symphony, no. 2 <- Anthropos: COWELL
Symphony, no. 2 <- A Montevideo: GOTTSCHALK
Symphony, no. 2 <- Bostoniana: IBERT
Symphony, no. 2 <- Bell symphony: KHACHATURIAN
Symphony, no. 2 <- Sinfonia elegiaca: MALIPIERO
Symphony, no. 2 <- Sinfonia grave: ROSENBERG
Symphony, no. 2 <- Ascensão: VILLA-LOBOS
Symphony, no. 2 [1933] <- Short symphony: COPLAND
Symphony, no. 2, C minor <- Auferstehungs-Symphonie / Resur-
  rection symphony: MAHLER
Symphony, no. 2, D major <- Sinfonie capricieuse: BERWALD
Symphony, no. 2, G major <- London symphony: VAUGHAN WILLIAMS
Symphony, no. 2, op. 9 -> Antar: RIMSKY-KORSAKOV
Symphony, op. 14 <- October symphony / To October: SHOSTAKO-
  VICH
Symphony, no. 2, op. 16 <- The four temperaments: NIELSEN
Symphony, no. 2, op. 17, C minor <- Little Russian symphony
  / Ukrainian symphony: TCHAIKOVSKY
Symphony, no. 2, op. 27, C minor <- Asrael / Angel of death:
  SUK
Symphony, op. 2, op. 30 <- Romantic symphony: HANSON
Symphony, no. 2, op. 42, C major <- Océan: RUBINSTEIN
Symphony, no. 2, op. 46, C major <- An die Freunde: PFITZNER
Symphony, no. 2, op. 52, B♭ major -> Lobgesang: MENDELSSOHN
Symphony, no. 2, op. 132 <- Mysterious mountain: HOVANESS
Symphony, no. 3 <- Northern symphony: BAX
Symphony, no. 3 -> Kaddish: BERNSTEIN
Symphony, no. 3 <- Gaelic symphony: COWELL

Symphony, no. 3 <- Three mysteries: CRESTON
Symphony, no. 3 <- Liturgic symphony / Symphonie liturgique:
  HONEGGER
Symphony, no. 3 <- The camp meeting: IVES
Symphony, no. 3 <- Symphony-poem: KHACHATURIAN
Symphony, no. 3 <- Sinfonia della campane: MALIPIERO
Symphony, no. 3 <- Hymnus Ambrosianus / Ambrosian hymn: MIL-
  HAUD
Symphony, no. 3 <- Quasars: PEPIN
Symphony, no. 3 <- The four ages of man / De fyra tidsåldar-
  na: ROSENBERG
Symphony, no. 3 <- Pastoral symphony: VAUGHAN WILLIAMS
Symphony, no. 3 <- A guerra: VILLA-LOBOS
Symphony, no. 3, A minor <- Unfinished symphony: BORODIN
Symphony, no. 3, C major <- Sinfonie singulière: BERWALD
Symphony, no. 3, D minor <- Wagner symphony: BRUCKNER
Symphony, no. 3, G major <- Great national symphony: CLEMENTI
Symphony, no. 3, op. 20 <- First of May / May Day symphony:
  SHOSTAKOVICH
Symphony, no. 3, op. 25 <- Sinfonia rustica: HOLMBOE
Symphony, no. 3, op. 27 <- Sinfonia espansiva: NIELSEN
Symphony, no. 3, op. 27 <- Le chant de nuit / Son of the
  night: SZYMANOWSKI
Symphony, no. 3, op. 29, D major <- Polish symphony: TCHAI-
  KOVSKY
Symphony, no. 3, op. 42, B minor <- Ilya Murometz: GLIÈRE
Symphony, no. 3, op. 43, C minor-major <- Divine poem: SKRIA-
  BIN
Symphony, no. 3, op. 44, C minor <- Fiery angel / Flaming
  angel: PROKOFIEV
Symphony, no. 3, op. 55, E♭ major <- Eroica symphony / Hero-
  ic symphony: BEETHOVEN
Symphony, no. 3, op. 56, A minor <- Scottish symphony: MEN-
  DELSSOHN
Symphony, no. 3, op. 70 <- Sinfonia brevis: INDY
Symphony, no. 3, op. 78, C minor <- Organ symphony: SAINT-
  SAËNS
Symphony, no. 3, op. 97, E♭ major <- Rhenish symphony: SCHU-
  MANN
Symphony, no. 3, op. 118 <- Dante symphony / Vita nuova: HU-
  BAY
Symphony, no. 3, op. 153, F major <- Im Walde: RAFF
Symphony, no. 4 <- 1942 symphony: ANTHEIL
Symphony, no. 4 <- Romantic symphony / Sinfonia romantica:
  CHAVEZ
Symphony, no. 4 <- Short symphony: COWELL
Symphony, no. 4 <- Folksong symphony: HARRIS
Symphony, no. 4 <- Deliciae Basilienses: HONEGGER

Symphony, no. 4 <- Sinfonia in memoriam: MALIPIERO
Symphony, no. 4 <- 1848 symphony: MILHAUD
Symphony, no. 4 <- Johannis uppenbarelse / The revelation of
    St.John: ROSENBERG
Symphony, no. 4 <- A vitória: VILLA-LOBOS
Symphony, no. 4, E♭ major <- Sinfonie naïve: BERWALD
Symphony, no. 4, E♭ major <- Romantic symphony: BRUCKNER
Symphony, no. 4, op. 29 <- Sinfonia sacra: HOLMBOE
Symphony, no. 4, op. 29 <- The inextinguishable: NIELSEN
Symphony, no. 4, op. 39, C minor <- Från havsbandet: ALFVÉN
Symphony, no. 4, op. 52 <- Le printemps / Spring symphony:
    LAJTHA
Symphony, no. 4, op. 60, B♭ major <- Frühlings-Sinfonie /
    Spring symphony: BEETHOVEN
Symphony, no. 4, op. 86 <- Die Weihe der Töne: SPOHR
Symphony, no. 4, op. 90, A major <- Italian symphony: MEN-
    DELSSOHN
Symphony, no. 4, op. 95, D minor <- Dramatic symphony / Sym-
    phonie dramatique: RUBINSTEIN
Symphony, no. 4, op. 119 <- Petöfi symphony: HUBAY
Symphony, no. 5 <- Joyous symphony: ANTHEIL
Symphony, no. 5 <- Di tre re: HONEGGER
Symphony, no. 5 <- Hortulanus / The keeper of the garden /
    Örtagårmästaren: ROSENBERG
Symphony, no. 5 <- A paz: VILLA-LOBOS
Symphony, no. 5, B♭ major <- Tragic symphony: BRUCKNER
Symphony, no. 5, C# minor <- The giant: MAHLER
Symphony, no. 5, op. 43 <- Sinfonia sacra: HANSON
Symphony, no. 5, op. 67, C minor <- Schicksalssinfonie / Fate
    symphony: BEETHOVEN
Symphony, no. 5, op. 107, D minor <- Reformation symphony:
    MENDELSSOHN
Symphony, no. 5, op. 107, G minor <- Russian symphony: RUBIN-
    STEIN
Symphony, no. 5, op. 170 <- Short symphony: HOVANESS
Symphony, no. 5, op. 177, E major < Lenore: RAFF
Symphony, no. 6 <- After Delacroix: ANTHEIL
Symphony, no. 6 <- Psalm symphony: BADINGS
Symphony, no. 6 <- Gettysburg symphony: HARRIS
Symphony, no. 6 <- Fantaisies symphoniques: MARTINŮ
Symphony, no. 6 <- Sinfonia semplice: NIELSEN
Symphony, no. 6 <- Sinfonia semplice: ROSENBERG
Symphony, no. 6 <- Montanhas do Brasil: VILLA-LOBOS
Symphony, no. 6, A major <- Philosophic symphony: BRUCKNER
Symphony, no. 6, A minor <- Tragic symphony: MAHLER
Symphony, no. 6, op. 68, F major <- Pastoral symphony: BEET-
    HOVEN
Symphony, no. 6, op. 74, B minor <- Pathétique symphony:

TCHAIKOVSKY
Symphony, no. 6, op. 116, G major <- Historische Sinfonie:
SPOHR
Symphony, no. 6, op. 173 <- Celestial gate: HOVANESS
Symphony, no. 6, op. 189, D minor <- Gelebt, gestrebt, ge-
litten: RAFF
Symphony, no. 7 <- Louisville symphony: BADINGS
Symphony, no. 7 <- Song of the night / Lied der Nacht: MAHLER
Symphony, no. 7 <- Sinfonia delle canzoni: MALIPIERO
Symphony, no. 7 <- Sinfonia antartica: VAUGHAN WILLIAMS
Symphony, no. 7 <- Odisséia da paz: VILLA-LOBOS
Symphony, no. 7, E major <- Lyric symphony: BRUCKNER
Symphony, no. 7, op. 60 <- Leningrad symphony: SHOSTAKOVICH
Symphony, no. 7, op. 63 <- L'automne: LAJTHA
Symphony, no. 7, op. 77, F major <- Pastoral symphony: GLAZU-
NOV
Symphony, no. 7, op. 92, A major <- Dance symphony: BEETHOVEN
Symphony, no. 7, op. 121 <- Irdisches und Göttliches im Men-
schenleben / Double symphony: SPOHR
Symphony, no. 7, op. 201, Bb major <- In dem Alpen: RAFF
Symphony, no. 7, band, op. 178 <- Nanga Parvat: HOVANESS
Symphony, no. 8 <- Hannover symphony: BADINGS
Symphony, no. 8 <- Choral symphony: COWELL
Symphony, no. 8 <- San Francisco symphony: HARRIS
Symphony, no. 8 <- Sinfonia brevis: MALIPIERO
Symphony, no. 8 <- In cadidum: ROSENBERG
Symphony, no. 8, C minor <- Apocalyptic symphony: BRUCKNER
Symphony, no. 8, D <- Symphonie rhodanienne: MILHAUD
Symphony, no. 8, Eb major <- Symphony of a thousand: MAHLER
Symphony, no. 8, op. 56 <- Sinfonia boreale: HOLMBOE
Symphony, no. 8, op. 88, G major <- English symphony: DVOŘÁK
Symphony, no. 8, op. 179 <- Arjuna: HOVANESS
Symphony, no. 8, op. 205, A major <- Frühlingsklänge: RAFF
Symphony, no. 9 <- Sinfonia dell' ahimè: MALIPIERO
Symphony, no. 9 <- The Ardeatine caves / Les fosses Ardea-
tine: SCHUMAN
Symphony, no. 9, D minor <- Unfinished symphony: BRUCKNER
Symphony, no. 9, op. 95, E minor <- From the New world / New
World symphony: DVOŘÁK
Symphony, no. 9, op. 125, D minor <- Choral symphony: BEET-
HOVEN
Symphony, no. 9, op. 125, D minor (Presto) <- Ode an die
Freude / Ode to joy: BEETHOVEN
Symphony, no. 9, op. 125, D minor (Presto; arr.) <- The Euro-
pean anthem / L'hymne européen: BEETHOVEN
Symphony, no. 9, op. 143 <- Die Jahreszeiten / The seasons:
SPOHR
Symphony, no. 9, op. 208, E minor <- Im Sommer: RAFF

Symphony, no. 9, string orchestra <- Sinfonia giocosa: BAD-
INGS
Symphony, no. 10 <- Abraham Lincoln symphony: HARRIS
Symphony, no. 10 <- Atropo: MALIPIERO
Symphony, no. 10 <- American muse: SCHUMAN
Symphony, no. 10 <- Sumé Pater patrium: VILLA-LOBOS
Symphony, no. 10, op. 213, F minor <- Zur Herbstzeit: RAFF
Symphony, no. 11 <- Seven rituals of music: COWELL
Symphony, no. 11 <- Sinfonia delle cornamuse: MALIPIERO
Symphony, no. 11 <- Romantic symphony / Symphonie romantique:
MILHAUD
Symphony, no. 11, op. 103 <- 1905 symphony / The year 1905:
SHOSTAKOVICH
Symphony, no. 11, op. 186 <- All men are brothers: HOVANESS
Symphony, no. 11, op. 214, A minor <- Der Winter: RAFF
Symphony, no. 12 <- Sinfonische Klangfiguren: BADINGS
Symphony, no. 12 <- Father Marquette symphony / Père Marqu-
ette symphony: HARRIS
Symphony, no. 12 <- Symphonie rurale / Rural symphony: MIL-
HAUD
Symphony, no. 12, op. 35,G minor <- Collective farm symphony:
MIASKOVSKY
Symphony, no. 12, op. 112 <- 1917 symphony / The year 1917 /
To the memory of Lenin: SHOSTAKOVICH
Symphony, no. 12, op. 188 <- Choral symphony: HOVANESS
Symphony, no. 13 <- Madras symphony: COWELL
Symphony, no. 13 <- Bicentennial symphony 1776: HARRIS
Symphony, no. 13, D major <- Turkish suite / Zaïre: M.HAYDN
Symphony, no. 13, op. 113 <- Babi Yar symphony: SHOSTAKOVICH
Symphony, no. 14, band, op. 194 <- Ararat: HOVANESS
Symphony, no. 15 <- Thesis: COWELL
Symphony, no. 15, op. 199 <- Silver pilgrimage: HOVANESS
Symphony, no. 16 <- Icelandic symphony: COWELL
Symphony, no. 17 <- Lancaster symphony: COWELL
Symphony, no. 18, op. 204 <- Circe: HOVANESS
Symphony, no. 19, op. 217 <- Vishnu: HOVANESS
Symphony, no. 20, band, op. 223 <- Three journeys to a holy
mountain: HOVANESS
Symphony, no. 21, op. 234 <- Etchmiadzin symphony: HOVANESS
Symphony, no. 22, op. 236 <- City of light: HOVANESS
Symphony, no. 23, band, op. 249 <- Ani: HOVANESS
Symphony, no. 24, op. 273 <- Majuun: HOVANESS
Symphony, no. 25, op. 275 <- Odysseus symphony: HOVANESS
Symphony, no. 51, Bb major <- La confidenza: M.HAYDN
Symphony, op. 4, no. 2, D major <- Pastoral symphony: STAMITZ
Symphony, op. 6, no. 7, D major <- Der Reiter: STAMITZ
Symphony, op. 9, no. 2, Eb major (Andante) <- La celeste: J.
C.BACH

Symphony, op. 18, no. 2, B♭ major <- Lucio Silla overture: J. C.BACH

Symphony, op. 26, E♭ major <- Ländliche Hochzeit / Rustic wedding symphony: GOLDMARK

Symphony, op. 44, G major <- Kleine Symphonie / Little symphony: PFITZNER

Symphony, op. 65, no. 2 -> Avak [Symphony]: HOVANESS

Symphony, op. 118, no. 4 -> Dance symphony, op. 118, no. 4: HOVANESS

Symphony, op. 180 -> Saint Vartan symphony: HOVANESS

Symphony, band <- West Point symphony: HARRIS

Symphony, harp, percussion & string orchestra, op. 33 <- Les soli: LAJTHA

Symphony, organ, no. 9, op. 70 <- Gothic symphony / Symphonie gothique: WIDOR

Symphony, organ, no. 10, op. 73 <- Symphonie romane / Roman symphony: WIDOR

Symphony, string orchestra, C major -> L'incoronazione di Dario (Sinfonia): VIVALDI

Symphony, string orchestra, no. 9, C minor <- Schweizer-Sinfonie / Swiss symphony: MENDELSSOHN

Symphony, string orchestra, W.182, no. 2, B♭ major <- Hamburg symphonies: C.P.E.BACH

Symphony, string orchestra, W.182, no. 3, C major <- Hamburg symphonies: C.P.E.BACH

Symphony, string orchestra, W.182, no. 4, A major <- Hamburg symphonies: C.P.E.BACH

Symphony, string orchestra, W.182, no. 5, B minor <- Hamburg symphonies: C.P.E.BACH

Symphony of a thousand -> Symphony, no. 8, E♭ major: MAHLER

Symphony-poem -> Symphony, no. 3: KHACHATURIAN

Symposium after Plato <- Serenade after Plato's Symposium: BERNSTEIN

Syncopations etude -> Etude, piano, op. 25, no. 4, A minor: CHOPIN

T.S. Eliot in memoriam -> Introitus: STRAVINSKY

Tabarro, Il <- Il trittico: PUCCINI

Tabescere me fecit -> Mirabilia testimonia tua: COUPERIN

Tabulatura nova (Warum betrübst du dich) <- Variations on Warum betrübst du dich, mein Herz: SCHEIDT

Tänze, orchestra, K. 17 <- Mödlinger Tänze / Viennese dances: BEETHOVEN

Tänze, 2 violins & double bass, K. 15 <- Ländlerische Tänze: BEETHOVEN

Take-offs, orchestra <- Cartoons: IVES

Take-offs, piano (Rough and ready et al) <- The jumping frog: IVES

Tale of Tsar Saltan, The -> Tsar Saltan: RIMSKY-KORSAKOV
Talens lyriques, Les -> Les fêtes d'Hébé: RAMEAU
Tales of our countryside <- Irish legends: COWELL
Talin <- Concerto, viola & string orchestra, op. 93: HOVANESS
Tamara -> King Kojata: BAX
Tamerlano <- Bajazet: VIVALDI
Tango español, piano, A minor -> Danses espagnoles, piano,
   op. 164 (Tango): ALBÉNIZ
Tante Toureleroutte, La -> Concertos comiques (No. 11): COR-
   RETTE
Tantum ergo, D. 461 <- An das Vaterland: SCHUBERT
Tantum ergo, D. 730 <- Die deutsche Eiche: SCHUBERT
Tanzvariationen / Dance variations -> Variationen über das
   Lied Zeg knezelte wilde gij dansen, orchestra: BADINGS
Tarantelle -> Lieder ohne Worte, op. 102 (No. 3): MENDELSSOHN
Tarantelle styrienne -> Danse, piano: DEBUSSY
Tarare <- Axur, re D'Ormus: SALIERI
Tavern song / Merrymaking -> Mulató gajd: KODÁLY
Te Deum <- Prague Te Deum: CALDARA
Te Deum, Bb major <- Chandos Te Deum: HÄNDEL
Te Deum, D major <- Caroline Te Deum: HÄNDEL
Telemacco, Il <- L'isola di Circe: GLUCK
Telemann variations -> Variationen und Fuge über ein Thema
   von Telemann, piano: REGER
Télémaque <- Fragments des modernes: CAMPRA
Tell me, some pitying angel <- The blessed Virgin's expostu-
   lation: PURCELL
Tell me, where is fancy bred <- Fancy: KODÁLY
Temora -> Der Abend, D. 221: SCHUBERT
Tempest <- The storm: TCHAIKOVSKY
Tempest sonata / Sturm-Sonate / Recitativ sonata -> Sonata,
   piano, no. 17, op. 31, no. 2, D minor: BEETHOVEN
Tempestà, La -> No, non turbarti: BEETHOVEN
Tempestà di mare, La -> Il cimento dell' armonia e dell' in-
   ventione (No. 5); Concerto, flute, R. 433, F major; Con-
   certo, orchestra, R. 570, F major: VIVALDI
Tempête, La / Le soir -> Symphony, M. 8, G major: J.HAYDN
Tempo il ballo -> Sonata, harpsichord, K. 430 (L.463) D ma-
   jor: D.SCARLATTI
Tempora mutantur -> Symphony, M. 64, A major: J.HAYDN
Tender virgins shun deceivers <- Vauxhall songs: J.C.BACH
Tendre Nanette, La -> Pièces de clavecin, 1. livre, 1. ordre
   (La fleurie): COUPERIN
Ternengewinnst, Der <- Der gedemütigte Stolz: DITTERSDORF
Terra è liberata, La -> Apollo e Dafne: HÄNDEL
Terzetto concertante -> Trio, violin violoncello & guitar,
   op. 66, D major: PAGANINI
Texten intuitiver Musik für kommende Zeiten -> Für kommende

Zeiten: STOCKHAUSEN
Thanksgiving, A -> The Lord bee thanked: DOWLAND
That's for remembrance -> Rosemary: ELGAR
Theaterprobe, Die -> L'abbé de l'Attaignant: DANZI
Theme and variations, accordion & orchestra <- Concerto, accordion & orchestra: HARRIS
Theme and variations, harp / Variations, harp -> Pastorale, theme and variations, harp, B. 161, G minor: HÄNDEL
Theme and variations, piano & string orchestra -> The four temperaments: HINDEMITH
Thème varié sur le nom Abegg, piano, no. 1 <- Abegg variations: SCHUMANN
Theodosius <- The force of love: ARNE
Theodosius <- The force of love: PURCELL
There is a lane <- Widmung: IVES
Theresienmesse -> Mass, H.XXII,12, B♭ major: J.HAYDN
Thesis -> Symphony, no. 15: COWELL
They are there <- Fighting for the people's new free world / A war song march: IVES
This day <- Christmas cantata: VAUGHAN WILLIAMS
This is the day <- Wedding anthem for Princess Anne: HÄNDEL
Thomas and Sally <- The sailor's return: ARNE
Three journeys to a holy mountain -> Symphony, no. 20, band, op. 223: HOVANESS
Three mysteries -> Symphony, no. 3: CRESTON
Three places in New England <- A New England symphony: IVES
Three-quarter blues <- Irish waltz: GERSHWIN
Threni <- Lamentationes Jeremiae prophetae: STRAVINSKY
Threnody for the victims of Hiroshima -> To the victims of Hiroshima: PENDERECKI
Thun sonata / Meistersinger sonata -> Sonata, violin & piano, no. 2, op. 100, A major: BRAHMS
Thunderstorm, The / Das Donnerwetter -> Kontretanz, K. 534: MOZART
Tiefes Leid -> Im Jänner 1817, D. 876: SCHUBERT
Tigrane <- L'egual impegno d'amore e di fede: A.SCARLATTI
Tigrane, Il -> La virtù trionfante dell' amore e dell' odio: VIVALDI
Timide, Le <- Le nouveau séducteur: AUBER
Timon of Athens overture -> Trumpet sonata, no. 2: PURCELL
Tiranna, La -> Quartet, strings, G. 223, G major: BOCCHERINI
Tiridate, Il <- La verità nell' inganno [1717]: CALDARA
Titan symphony -> Symphony, no. 1, D major: MAHLER
Titus -> La clemenza di Tito: MOZART
To be sung of a summer night on the water [arr.] <- Aquarelles: DELIUS
To October / October symphony -> Symphony, no. 2, op. 14, C major: SHOSTAKOVICH

To the forest / Pilgrim's song -> Songs, op. 47 (I bless
you, forests): TCHAIKOVSKY
To the memory of Lenin / The year 1917 / 1917 symphony ->
Symphony, no. 12, op. 112: SHOSTAKOVICH
To the victims of Hiroshima <- Threnody for the victims of
Hiroshima: PENDERECKI
Toast to Stalin <- Hail to Stalin: PROKOFIEV
Tod und das Mädchen, Der / Death and the maiden -> Quartet,
strings, D. 810, D minor: SCHUBERT
Todeskuss -> Todesmusik, D. 758: SCHUBERT
Todesmusik, D. 758 <- Todeskuss: SCHUBERT
Tolomeo e Alessandro <- La corona disprezzata: A.SCARLATTI
Tom Sawyer <- Mark twain overture: ANTHEIL
Tom Thumb the Great -> Opera of operas: ARNE
Tombeau, Le -> Sonata, violin & continuo, op. 5, no. 6, C mi-
nor: LECLAIR
Tombeau de claude Debussy, Le / In memory of Debussy -> Ho-
menajes (A C. Debussy): FALLA
Tondichtungen nach Arnold Böcklin <- Böcklin suite: REGER
Torrent -> Etude, piano, op. 10, no. 4, C# minor: CHOPIN
Tortorella, La -> Scompagnata tortorella: A.SCARLATTI
Tost quartets -> Quartet, strings, no. 58, op. 54, no. 1, G
major; no. 59, op. 54, no. 2, C major; no. 60, op. 54, no.
3, F major; no. 61, op. 55, no. 1, A major; no. 62, op.
55, no. 2, F minor; no. 63, op. 55, no. 3, Bb major; no.
64, op. 64, no. 1, C major; no. 65, op. 64, no. 2, B mi-
nor; no. 66, op. 64, no. 3, Bb major; no. 67, op. 64, no.
4, G major; no. 68, op. 64, no. 5, D major; no. 69, op.
64, no. 6, Eb major: J.HAYDN
Totengesang der Frauen und Mädchen / Funeral song -> Coro-
nach, D. 836: SCHUBERT
Totengräberweise, D. 869 <- An der Bahre: SCHUBERT
Totenmarsch -> Grablied auf einen Soldaten, D. 454: SCHUBERT
Toupie, La / The spinning top -> Jeux d'enfants (Impromptu):
BIZET
Touriere, La -> Concertos comiques (No. 18): CORRETTE
Tout n'est qu'images fugitives <- Karnevalslied: WAGNER
Towards a new life <- Sokol march: SUK
Toy, A -> Alman, keyboard instrument, H. 34: GIBBONS
Toy, A / Adieu coranto -> Coranto, keyboard instrument, H. 40:
GIBBONS
Toy symphony / Kindersinfonie / Sinfonia Berchtolsgadensis:
J.HAYDN -> Cassation, 2 horns, strings & toy instruments,
C major (Selections): LEOPOLD MOZART
Traci amanti, I <- Gli turchi amanti: CIMAROSA
Tragic overture -> Estrella de Soria (Overture): BERWALD
Tragic overture / Dramatic overture -> Alfred (Overture):
DVOŘÁK

Tragic polonaise -> Polonaise, piano, op. 44, F# minor: CHO-
PIN
Tragic sonata / Sonata, piano, no. 1, op. 45, G minor -> So-
nata tragica, piano: MACDOWELL
Tragic symphony -> Symphony, no. 5, B♭ major: BRUCKNER
Tragic symphony -> Symphony, no. 6, A minor: MAHLER
Tragic symphony -> Symphony, D. 417, C minor: SCHUBERT
Transatlantic <- The people's choice: ANTHEIL
Transcendental etudes -> Études d'exécution transcendante,
piano: LISZT
Transylvanian dances -> Sonatina, piano [arr.]: BARTÓK
Transylvanian evenings / Soirs transylvains -> Trio, strings,
no. 3, op. 41: LAJTHA
Transylvanian suite / Suite Transylvanie -> Quartet, strings,
no. 10, op. 58: LAJTHA
Trapeze -> Divertissement, orchestra, op. 43 [arr.]; Quintet,
oboe, clarinet & strings, op. 39 [arr.]: PROKOFIEV
Trapp-Polka -> Maskenzug: JOHANN STRAUSS
Trattenimenti armonici per camera, op. 6 (No. 11) <- St. Mark
concerto: ALBINONI
Trauer-Kantate / Funeral cantata -> Du aber, Daniel, gehe
hin: TELEMANN
Trauermarsch / Funeral march -> Lieder ohne Worte, op. 62
(No. 3): MENDELSSOHN
Trauermarsch / Funeral march, op. 40 -> Grande marche, piano,
4 hands, D. 819, no. 5: SCHUBERT
Trauermarsch-Sonate / Funeral march sonata -> Sonata, piano,
no. 12, op. 26, A♭ major: BEETHOVEN
Trauermusik -> Schlage doch, gewünschte Stunde, S. 53: J.S.
BACH
Trauer-Ode / Funeral ode -> Lass Fürstin, lass noch einen
Strahl, S. 198: J.S.BACH
Trauer-Symphonie / Funeral symphony -> Symphony, M. 44, E mi-
nor: J.HAYDN
Trauerwalzer -> Waltz, piano, 4 hands, op. 39, no. 15, A♭ ma-
jor: BRAHMS
Trauerwalzer / Sehnsuchtswalzer -> Originaltänze, piano, D.
365 (No. 2): SCHUBERT
Traum, Der -> Ein närrischer Traum: M.HAYDN
Traum-Quartett / Dream quartet / Preussische Quartette / Prus-
sian quartets -> Quartet, strings, no. 49, op. 50, no. 5, F
major: J.HAYDN
Traumspiel-Suite <- Scandinavian suite: VLADIGEROV
Trauungschoräle / Wedding chorales -> Was Gott tut, ist wohl-
getan, S. 250; Sei Lob und Ehr, S. 251; Nun danket den Her-
re Gott, S. 252: J.S.BACH
Trauungskantate / Hochzeitskantate / Wedding cantata -> Der
Herr denket an uns, S. 196: J.S.BACH

Tre burle, Le -> Falstaff: SALIERI
Tre giorni son che Nina <- Nina: PERGOLESI
Tre giorni son che Nina [arr.] <- Sicilian air: PERGOLESI
Tregian's ground -> Hugh Aston's ground: BYRD
Tremolo caprice -> Caprice, violin, op. 1, no. 6, G major:
    PAGANINI
Tremolo etude -> Grandes études de Paganini, piano (Mo. 1):
    LISZT
Trésor supposé, Le <- Le danger d'écouter aux portes: MÉHUL
Treubruch -> Der Zwerg, D. 771: SCHUBERT
Triangle concerto -> Concerto, piano, no. 1, Eb major: LISZT
Trillo del diavolo / Devil's trill sonata -> Sonata, violin
    & continuo, G minor: TARTINI
Trinity mass / Missa trinitatis -> Mass, K. 167, C major:
    MOZART
Trinklied, D. 183 <- Freundschaft und Wein: SCHUBERT
Trio, flute, viola & harps -> Elegiac trio: BAX
Trio, flutes & violoncello, H.IV,1, C major [arr.] <- Little
    symphony: J.HAYDN
Trio, piano & strings, H.XV,25, G major <- Gypsy trio / Zi-
    geunertrio: J.HAYDN
Trio, piano & strings, no. 1 <- Pièces brèves, violin, vio-
    loncello & piano: MARTINŮ
Trio, piano, & strings, no. 1, A minor <- Phantasie trio:
    IRELAND
Trio, piano & strings, no. 2, op. 67, E minor <- In memory
    of I.I. Sollertinsky: SHOSTAKOVICH
Trio, piano & strings, no. 3, C major <- Grand trio: MARTINŮ
Trio, piano & strings, no. 4, op. 70, no. 1, D major <- Geis-
    tertrio / Ghost trio: BEETHOVEN
Trio, piano & strings, no. 4, op. 90, E minor <- Dumky trio:
    DVOŘÁK
Trio, piano & strings, no. 6, op. 97, Bb major <- Archduke
    trio / Erzherzog-Trio: BEETHOVEN
Trio, piano & strings, op. 22, no. 3, C major <- La chasse:
    CLEMENTI
Trio, piano & strings, op. 35a, no. 3, D major <- La chasse:
    CLEMENTI
Trio, piano & strings, op. 50, A minor <- In memory of a
    great artist: TCHAIKOVSKY
Trio, piano, clarinet & viola, K. 498, Eb major <- Kegel-
    statt trio: MOZART
Trio, piano, clarinet & violoncello, op. 11, Bb major <-
    Gassenhauer trio: BEETHOVEN
Trio, strings, no. 3, op. 41 <- Soirs transylvains / Tran-
    sylvanian evenings: LAJTHA
Trio, violin, violoncello & guitar, op. 66, D major <- Ter-
    cetto concertante: PAGANINI

Trio, violins & violoncello, H.V,C4, C major <- Weinzierler
    trios: J.HAYDN
Trio, violins & violoncello, H.V,D3, D major <- Weinzierler
    trios: J.HAYDN
Trio, violins & violoncello, H.V,D4, D major <- Weinzierler
    trios: J.HAYDN
Trio, violins & violoncello, H.V,Es9, Eb major <-Weinzierler
    trios: J.HAYDN
Triomphe d'Alcide, Le -> Alceste: LULLY
Trionfo dell' onestà -> Cupido e onestà: A.SCARLATTI
Trionfo della gratia, Il <- La conversione di Maddalena: A.
    SCARLATTI
Trionfo della virtù, Il -> Amore e virtù: A.SCARLATTI
Trio-sonata, op. 2, no. 3, F major <- Dresden trio sonatas:
    HÄNDEL
Trio-sonata, op. 2, no. 8, G minor <- Dresden trio sonatas:
    HÄNDEL
Trio-sonata, op. 2, no. 9, E major <- Dresden trio sonatas:
    HÄNDEL
Trio-sonata, flutes & continuo, op. 5, no. 5, D minor <-
    Christmas sonata: LOCATELLI
Trio-sonata, violin, viola da gamba & continuo, F major <-
    Darmstädter Trio: TELEMANN
Trio-sonata, violins & continuo, W. 161, no. 1, C minor <-
    Conversation sonata: C.P.E.BACH
Trip to Syria, A <- Assyrian dance: GRIFFES
Triple concerto -> Concerto, flute, violin, harpsichord &
    string orchestra, S. 1044, A minor: J.S.BACH
Triple concerto -> Concerto, violin, violoncello & piano, op.
    56, C major: BEETHOVEN
Tristesse / Grief / L'intimité -> Etude, piano, op. 10, no.
    3, E major: CHOPIN
Trittico, Il -> Gianni Scicchi; Suor Angelica; Il tabarro:
    PUCCINI
Triumph der Unschuld, Der / La vestale -> La innocenza gius-
    tificata: GLUCK
Triumph of chastity, The -> La licorne: IBERT
Triumphal chant / Folk song / Volkslied -> Lieder ohne Worte,
    op. 53 (No. 5): MENDELSSOHN
Triumphal overture -> Solemn overture for the 20th anniver-
    sary of the October revolution: GLIÈRE
Triumphal symphony -> Festive symphony: SMETANA
Trockne Blumen-Variationen / Dried flowers variations -> In-
    troduction et variations sur un thème original, flute & pi-
    ano, D. 802, E minor: SCHUBERT
Troika sleigh ride -> Les saisons (Novembre): TCHAIKOVSKY
Trois exilés, Les <- Chant national: FRANCK
Trois veuves, Les -> Pièces de clavecin, 2. livre, 9. ordre

(Le petit-denil): COUPERIN
Tromb-al-Cazar <- Les criminels dramatiques: OFFENBACH
Tromba, La -> Suite, trumpet & string orchestra, D8, D major:
    TELEMANN
Trompette et tambour / Trumpet and drum -> Jeux d'enfants
    (Marche): BIZET
Trost, D. 97 <- An Elisa: SCHUBERT
Troubadour à la belle étoile, Le -> Il trovatore in carica-
    tura: DONIZETTI
Trout quintet / Forellen-Quintet -> Quintet, piano & strings,
    D. 667, A major: SCHUBERT
Trovatore in caricatura, Il <- Le troubadour à la belle éto-
    ile: DONIZETTI
Trumpet and drum / Trompette et tambour -> Jeux d'enfants
    (Marche): BIZET
Trumpet overture -> Overture, op. 101, C major: MENDELSSOHN
Trumpet sonata / Hunt sonata / Jagd-Sonate -> Sonata, piano,
    K. 576, D major: MOZART
Trumpet sonata, no. 2 <- Timon of Athens overture: PURCELL
Trumpet tune, harpsichord, Z. 678, C major <- Cebell / The
    cibell: PURCELL
Tryst <- In fountain court: IRELAND
Tsar Saltan <- The tale of Tsar Saltan: RIMSKY-KORSAKOV
Tscherkessen-Marsch / Marche des Gardes a Cheval -> Russisch-
    er Marsch, orchestra: JOHANN STRAUSS
Tu lumen, tu splendor patris <- Elevation motet: DEPRÈS
Turandot (Overture) <- Overtura chinesa, op. 37 / Chinese o-
    verture: WEBER
Turchi amanti, Gli -> I traci amanti: CIMAROSA
Turkish concerto -> Concerto, violin, K. 219, A major: MOZART
Turkish march -> Sonata, piano, K. 300i (331) A major (Rondo
    alla turca): MOZART
Turkish march -> March, orchestra, Ab major: MUSORGSKY
Turkish suite / Zaïre -> Symphony, no. 13, D major: M.HAYDN
Tuteur dupé, Le -> L'arbre enchanté: GLUCK
Tutto è illusione nel mondo -> Le metamorfosi di Pasquale:
    SPONTINI
Tutto il mal non vien per nocere <- Dal male il bene: A.SCAR-
    LATTI
Two contemplations / Contemplations -> The unanswered ques-
    tion; Central Park in the dark: IVES
Two Sosias, The -> Amphytrion: PURCELL
Two-four waltz -> Waltz, piano, op. 42, Ab major: CHOPIN
Tyran corrigé, le -> Euphrosine: MÉHUL
Tyrannic love <- The royal martyr: PURCELL
Tyrannie détruite, La -> Doria: MÉHUL
Tyrolean dances -> Deutsche Tänze und Ecossaisen, piano, D.
    783: SCHUBERT

Tzaikerk <- Evening song: HOVANESS

Uccelliera, L' -> Quintet, violins, viola & violoncellos,
  G. 276, D major: BOCCHERINI
Uhr, Die / Clock symphony / Salomon symphonies / London sym-
  phonies -> Symphony, M. 101, D major: J.HAYDN
Uirapuru <- The enchanted bird: VILLA-LOBOS
Ukko the firemaker -> The origin of fire: SIBELIUS
Ukrainian symphony / Little Russian symphony -> Symphony, no.
  2, op. 17, C minor: TCHAIKOVSKY
Unanswered question, The <- Contemplations / Two contempla-
  tions: IVES
Under Blanik <- Rustic march: SUK
Undertow (Selections) <- Choreographic episodes: SCHUMAN
Undine (Selections) <- Wedding music: HENZE
Unfinished mass -> Mass, Eb major: JANÁČEK
Unfinished quartet / Schwanengesang -> Quartet, strings, no.
  84, op. 103, Bb major: J.HAYDN
Unfinished sonata / Reliquie -> Sonata, piano, D. 840, C ma-
  jor: SCHUBERT
Unfinished symphony -> Symphony, no. 3, A minor: BORODIN
Unfinished symphony -> Symphony, no. 9, D minor: BRUCKNER
Unfinished symphony / Unvollendete Sinfonie -> Symphony, D.
  759, B minor: SCHUBERT
Unfinished symphony / Zwickau symphony -> Symphony, G minor:
  SCHUMANN
Ungaria-Kantate <- Hungaria, 1848: LISZT
Ungarische Melodien / Hungarian melodies -> Divertissement à
  l'hongroise, piano, 4 hands, D. 818, G minor: SCHUBERT
Ungarischer Sturm-Marsch, piano <- Marche hongroise / Hung-
  arian march: LISZT
Ungarisches Weihnachtslied / Hungarian Christmas song ->
  Pastorale, piano: DOHNÁNYI
Ungleiche Heirat, Die -> Pimpinone: TELEMANN
Unglückliche, Der / Der Fremdling -> Der Wanderer, D. 489:
  SCHUBERT
Unglückliche Liebe -> Als Luise die Briefe ihres ungetreuen
  Liebhabers verbrannte: MOZART
Unhappy lovers, The -> As Celia's fatal arrows: HÄNDEL
United quartet -> Quartet, strings, no. 4: COWELL
Universitetskantaten -> Kantat vid Uppsala universitets 450-
  års-jubileum: ALFVÉN
Unschuld, Kleinod reiner Seelen -> Lobet Gott in seinen Rei-
  chen, S. 11 (Jesu, deine Gnadenblicke): J.S.BACH
Unter Donner und Blitz <- Donner und Blitz-Polka: JOHANN
  STRAUSS
Unverhofft kommt oft -> Das Findelkind: BENDA
Unvollendete Sinfonie / Unfinished symphony -> Symphony, D.

759, B minor: SCHUBERT
Upon Westminster Bridge <- London: CASTELNUOVO-TEDESCO
Uppsalarapsodi -> Swedish rhapsody, orchestra, no. 2, op. 24:
    ALFVÉN
Ur -> Bendita sabedovia: VILLA-LOBOS
Urania -> Uraniens Flucht, D. 554: SCHUBERT
Uraniens Flucht, D. 554 <- Urania: SCHUBERT
Urbi et orbi <- Benediction papale: LISZT
Urbs Roma -> Symphony, F major: SAINT-SAËNS
Usurpato prepotenza, L' -> Don Coribaldi: DITTERSDORF
Ut mi re <- Hexachord fantasias: BYRD
Ut re mi <- Hexachord fantasias: BYRD
Utrecht Jubilate -> Utrecht Te Deum (O be joyful): HÄNDEL
Utrecht Te Deum (O be joyful) <- Utrecht Jubilate: HÄNDEL

Vahakn, no. 5 <- Artinis: HOVANESS
Valse <- Pas de fleurs: DELIBES
Valse caprice, piano & strings, op. 76 -> Wedding cake:
    SAINT-SAËNS
Valse chantée -> Je te veux: SATIE
Valse de concert -> Waltz, piano, no. 4, Bb major: BALAKIREV
Valse de l'adieu / Farewell waltz -> Waltz, piano, op. 69,
    no. 1, A major: CHOPIN
Valse-musette, 2 pianos -> L'embarquement pour Cythère: POU-
    LENC
Valses brillantes, op. 34 -> Waltzes, piano, op. 34, no. 1-3:
    CHOPIN
Vanità delusa, La <- Il mercato di Malmantile: CIMAROSA
Vardar <- Bulgarian rhapsody, op. 16: VLADIGEROV
Variantes -> Berceuse, piano, op. 57, Db major: CHOPIN
Variationen über das Lied Zeg kwezelke wilde gij dansen,
    orchestra <- Dance variations / Tanzvariationen: BADINGS
Variationen über das Motiv von Bach, piano <- Variations on
    Weinen, Klagen, Sorgen, Zagen: LISZT
Variationen über die Arie Ich schlief, da träumte mir <- As
    I slept, I dreamt / Ich schlief, da träumte mir: QUANTZ
Variationen über ein Menüett von Duport, piano, K. 573 <-
    Duport variations: MOZART
Variationen über ein Menüett von J.C. Fischer, piano, K. 189a
    (179) <- Fischer variations: MOZART
Variationen über ein Thema von Händel, piano, op. 24 <- Hän-
    del variations: BRAHMS
Variationen über ein Thema von Haydn, orchestra <- Haydn va-
    riations: BRAHMS
Variationen über ein Thema von Robert Schumann, piano, op. 9
    <- Schumann variations: BRAHMS
Variationen über ein Thema von Robert Schumann, piano, 4
    hands, op. 23 <- Schumann variations: BRAHMS

Variationen und Fuge über einen divergierenden c-moll-Drei-
  klang -> Quartet, strings, no. 5: BLACHER
Variationen über Ich bin der Schneider Kakadu, piano trio,
  op. 121a <- Kakadu variations: BEETHOVEN
Variationen und Fuge, piano, op. 22, C minor <- Chopin vari-
  ations: BUSONI
Variationen und Fuge über ein lustiges Thema von J.A. Hiller,
  orchestra, op. 100 <- Hiller variations: REGER
Variationen und Fuge über ein Thema von Bach, piano <- Bach
  variations: REGER
Variationen und Fuge über ein Thema von Beethoven, 2 pianos
  <- Beethoven variations: REGER
Variationen und Fuge über ein Thema von Mozart, 2 pianos <-
  Mozart variations: REGER
Variationen und Fuge über ein Thema von Telemann, piano <-
  Telemann variations: REGER
Variations, harp / Theme and variations, harp -> Pastorale,
  theme and variations, harp, B. 161, G minor: HÀNDEL
Variations, oboe & band <- Variations on a romance by Glinka
  / Glinka variations: RIMSKY-KORSAKOV
Variations, orchestra <- Improvisations, orchestra: BAX
Variations, orchestra <- Aldous Huxley in memoriam: STRAVIN-
  SKY
Variations, piano [arr.] <- Orchestral variations: COPLAND
Variations, piano, H.XVII,2, A major <- Arietta con variazi-
  oni, A major: J.HAYDN
Variations, piano, H.XVII,6, F minor <- Un piccolo diverti-
  mento: J.HAYDN
Variations, piano, op. 35, Eb major <- Eroica variations:
  BEETHOVEN
Variations, piano, op. 35 <- Glinka variations / Variations
  on a theme by Glinka: LIADOV
Variations, piano, op. posth., E major <- Hexameron varia-
  tions: CHOPIN
Variations and fugue on a theme of Purcell -> The young per-
  son's guide to the orchestra: BRITTEN
Variations on a Hungarian folksong, orchestra <- Peacock va-
  riations / Felszállott a páva: KODÁLY
Variations on a rococo theme, violoncello & orchestra <- Ro-
  coco variations: TCHAIKOVSKY
Variations on a romance by Glinka / Glinka variations -> Va-
  riations, oboe & band: RIMSKY-KORSAKOV
Variations on a theme by Clara Wieck -> Sonata, piano, no. 2,
  op. 14, F minor (Andantino de Clara Wieck): SCHUMANN
Variations on a theme by Corelli -> L'arte dell' arco: TARTINI
Variations on a theme by Hindemith, orchestra <- Hindemith
  variations: WALTON
Variations on a theme by Joseph Weigl -> Suonata con variazi-

oni, violin & orchestra: PAGANINI
Variations on an old English nurser song -> A frog went a-
   courting: HINDEMITH
Variations on an old slave song -> Appalachia: DELIUS
Variations on an original theme, orchestra <- Enigma varia-
   tions: ELGAR
Variations on God save the King -> Variazioni sull' inno
   Heil dir im Siegeskranz, violin & orchestra: PAGANINI
Variations on La folie d'Espagne -> Les folies d'Espagne: C.
   P.E.BACH
Variations on The last rose of summer -> Variations sur un
   air favori irlandais: KUHLAU
Variations on Warum betrübst du dich, mein Herz -> Tabula-
   tura nova (Warum betrübst du dich): SCHEIDT
Variations on Weinen, Klagen, Sorgen, Zagen -> Variationen
   über das Motiv von Bach, piano: LISZT
Variations sur des thèmes de Lully -> Les amant magnifiques:
   JOLIVET
Variations sur l'air de ballet de Castor et Pollux, piano <-
   Vogler variations: WEBER
Variations sur un air favori irlandais <- Variations on The
   last rose of summer: KUHLAU
Variations sur un nocturne de Chopin, piano <- Chopin varia-
   tions: SCHUMANN
Variations sur un thème de Beethoven, 2 pianos, op. 35 <-
   Beethoven variations: SAINT-SAËNS
Variations sur un thème de Paganini, violin & orchestra <-
   Paganini variations: YSAŸE
Variazioni sul' inno Heil dir im Siegeskranz, violin & orch-
   estra <- Variations on God save the King: PAGANINI
Varied air and variations <- Study #2 for ears or aural and
   mental exercise: IVES
Vårsång <- Maj: ALFVÉN
Vasco de Gama -> L'Africaine: MEYERBEER
Vaticini di pace <- Christmas cantata: CALDARA
Vaudeville -> Faisons du temps: COUPERIN
Vauxhall songs -> By my sighs; Cruel Stephon; Come, Colin;
   Ah, why shou'd love; In this shady blest retreat; Smiling
   Venus; Tender virgins shun deceivers; Lovely yet ungrate-
   ful swain; Midst silent shades; Ah seek to know; Would you
   a female heart inspire; Cease awhile, ye winds; Farewell,
   ye soft scenes; See the kind indulgent gates: J.C.BACH
Vedette, Die -> Die vierjährige Posten: SCHUBERT
Vega, La <- The Alhambra: ALBÉNIZ
Venere e Adone -> Il giardino di amore: A.SCARLATTI
Venetian gondola song / Venezianisches Gondellied -> Lieder
   ohne Worte, op. 19 (No. 6); op. 30 (No. 6); op. 62 (No. 5):
   MENDELSSOHN

Venezianisches Gondellied / Venetian gondola song -> Lieder
ohne Worte, op. 19 (No. 6); op. 30 (No. 6); op. 62 (No. 5):
MENDELSSOHN
Vengeance de l'amour, La -> Daphnis et Pandrose: MÉHUL
Veni, veni Emmanuel <- Ádventi ének: KODÁLY
Veni, veni, sponsa Christi <- Motet de Ste. Suzanne: COUPERIN
Vent de l'Esprit, Le -> Messe de la Pentecôte (Sortie): MES-
SIAEN
Vent du soir <- L'horrible festin: OFFENBACH
Vêpres siciliennes, Les <- Giovanna de Guzman: VERDI
Veränderungen über einen Walzer, piano, D. 718, C minor <-
Diabelli variations: SCHUBERT
Veränderungen über einen Walzer von A. Diabelli, piano, op.
120 <- Diabelli variations: BEETHOVEN
Vergine del sole, La <- Idalide: CIMAROSA
Vergiss mein nicht <- Antwort auf die Frage eines Mädchens:
J. HAYDN
Vergissmeinnicht, D. 792 <- Blumenballade: SCHUBERT
Vergnügte Pleissen Stadt, S. 216 <- Hochzeits-Kantate / Wed-
ding cantata: J.S.BACH
Verità nell' inganno, La [1717] -> Il Tiridate: CALDARA
Verità nell' inganno, La [1727] <- Arsinoe: CALDARA
Verklärung, D. 59 <- Dying Christian to his soul: SCHUBERT
Verschworenen, Die <- Der häusliche Krieg: SCHUBERT
Vert-vert -> Kakadu-Quadrille: JOHANN STRAUSS
Vesper mass <- Evening service, op. 37 / The vigil: RACHMA-
NINOFF
Vestale, La / Der Triumph der Unschuld -> La innocenza gius-
tificata: GLUCK
Viaggio a Reims, Il <- L'albergo del giglio d'oro: ROSSINI
Vibray, La -> Sonata, flute & continuo, op. 2, no. 2, D mi-
nor: BLAVET
Victoria! Christo resurgenti <- Motet pour le jour de Pâques:
COUPERIN
Victory of the hero of Coburg, The / Der Sieg vom Helden Co-
burg / La bataille -> Kontretanz, K. 587: MOZART
Vid sekelskiftet <- Sekelskifteskantaten: ALFVÉN
Vidapura <- Missa oratorio: VILLA-LOBOS
Vielka -> Ein Feldlager in Schlesien: MEYERBEER
Vienna life / Wiener Leben -> Wiener Blut-Walzer, orchestra:
JOHANN STRAUSS
Viennese dances / Mödlinger TAnze -> Tänze, orchestra, K. 17:
BEETHOVEN
Viennese quartets / Wiener Quartette / Austrian quartets /
Osterreichische Quartette -> Quartet, strings, K. 168, F
major; K. 169, A major; K. 170, C major; K. 171, E♭ major;
K. 172, B♭ major; K. 173, D minor: MOZART
Viennese rhapsodic fantasietta, violin & piano <- Sketch to

Viennese rhapsody: KREISLER
Viennese sonatinas / Wiener Sonatinen / Wiener Serenaden ->
  Divertimento, K. 439b (Anh. 229, 229a) no. 1, B♭ major: no.
  2, B♭ major; no. 3, B♭ major; no. 4, B♭ major; no. 5, B♭
  major: MOZART
Vierge le vivace et le bel aujourd'hui, Le -> Pli selon pli
  (Improvisation sur Mallarmé, no. 1): BOULEZ
Vierjährige Posten, Die <- Die Vedette: SCHUBERT
Vigil, The / Evening service, op. 37 -> Vesper mass: RACHMA-
  NINOFF
Viking battle-song -> Mircath: BAX
Villageoise / Sătaescă -> Suite, orchestra, no. 3, op. 27:
  ENESCO
Villageoises <- Petites pièces enfantines: POULENC
Villana riconosciuta, La <- La pastorella riconosciuta; La
  villanella rapita: CIMAROSA
Villanella rapita, la -> La villana riconosciuta: CIMAROSA
Villeggiatura, La -> L'apparenza inganna: CIMAROSA
Viola, D. 786 <- Blumenballade: SCHUBERT
Violence of love, The -> The rival sisters: PURCELL
Virtù trionfante dell' amore e dell' odio, La <- Il tigrane:
  VIVALDI
Virtuous wife, The <- Good luck at last: PURCELL
Vishnu -> Symphony, no. 19, op. 217: HOVANESS
Vision, The / Fleecy cloud -> Lieder ohne Worte, op. 53
  (No. 2): MENDELSSOHN
Vita nuova / Dante symphony -> Symphony, no. 3, op. 118: HU-
  BAY
Vitória, A -> Symphony, no. 4: VILLA-LOBOS
Vitrina encantada / The surprise box -> Caixinha de boas fes-
  tas: VILLA-LOBOS
Viva la mamma -> Le convenienze e le inconvenienze teatrali:
  DONIZETTI
Vive le roy <- Fanfare / Royal fanfare: DEPRÈS
V'la c'que c'est qu'd'aller aux bois -> Concertos comiques
  (No. 16): CORRETTE
Vocalise / Habanera / Pièce en forme de habanera -> Vocalise
  en form d'habanera: RAVEL
Vocalise en forme d'habanera <- Habanera / Vocalise / Pièce
  en forme de habanera: RAVEL
Voces intimae <- Quartet, strings, op. 56, D minor: SIBELIUS
Völker-Ouvertüre -> Suite, string orchestra, B5, B♭ major:
  TELEMANN
Vogelquartett / Bird quartet / Russian quartets / Jungfern-
  Quartette / Maiden quartets -> Quartet, strings, no. 40,
  op. 33, no. 3, C major: J.HAYDN
Vogler variations -> Variations sur l'air de ballet de Castor
  et Pollux: WEBER

Voices of freedom <- Battle hymn of the Republic: FINE
Volkslied / Folk song / Triumphal chant -> Lieder ohne Wor-
   te, op. 53 (No. 5): MENDELSSOHN
Vollmondnacht -> Mondenschein, D. 875: SCHUBERT
Vom Fels zum Meer <- Deutscher Siegesmarsch: LISZT
Vom Himmel hoch, da komm ich her, S. 769 -> Einige kanoni-
   sche Veränderungen, organ, S. 769: J.S.BACH
Vom künftigen Alter -> Greisengesang, D. 778: SCHUBERT
Von Gott will ich nicht lassen / Leipzig chorales -> Chorale
   prelude, S. 658: J.S.BACH
Von Ida, D. 228 <- Agnes: SCHUBERT
Vor deinen Thron tret ich / Wenn wir in höchsten Nöten sein
   / Leipzig chorales -> Chorale prelude, S. 668: J.S.BACH
Vortragsstücke / Hausmusik -> Suite, violin & piano, op.
   103a, A minor: REGER
Vote for names <- Election songs: IVES
Voyage au Mont-Bernard, Le -> Élisa: CHERUBINI

Wachet auf, ruft uns die Stimme / Schübler chorales ->
   Chorale prelude, S. 645: J.S.BACH
Wachtelschlag, Der -> Stücke, musical clock, H.XIX,8: J.
   HAYDN
Wagner symphony -> Symphony, no. 3, D minor: BRUCKNER
Waisenhausmesse / Orphanage mass -> Mass, K. 47a (139) C mi-
   nor: MOZART
Waldesnacht -> Im Walde, D. 708: SCHUBERT
Waldstein sonata -> Sonata, piano, no. 21, op. 53, C major:
   BEETHOVEN
Wallenstein <- Symphony, no. 1, op. 10: RHEINBERGER
Wallfahrtsarie / Lunz -> Abschied, D. 475: SCHUBERT
Walpurgisnacht -> Die erste Walpurgisnacht: MENDELSSOHN
Waltz, piano, no. 4, B♭ major <- Valse de concert: BALAKIREV
Waltz, piano, op. 18, E♭ major <- Invitation to the waltz /
   Grande valse brillante: CHOPIN
Waltz, piano, op. 34, no. 3, F major <- Cat waltz: CHOPIN
Waltz, piano, op. 42, A♭ major: Two-four waltz: CHOPIN
Waltz, piano, op. 64, no. 1, D♭ major <- Dog waltz / Minute
   waltz: CHOPIN
Waltz, piano, op. 69, no. 1, A♭ major <- L' adieu / Farewell
   waltz / Valse de l'adieu: CHOPIN
Waltz, piano, 4 hands, op. 39, no. 15, A♭ major <- Trauer-
   walzer: BRAHMS
Waltzes, orchestra, op. 110 <- Suite, orchestra, op. 110:
   PROKOFIEV
Waltzes, piano, D. 146 <- Letzte Walzer: SCHUBERT
Waltzes, piano, op. 34, no. 1-3 <- Valses brillantes: CHOPIN
Wanderer, The -> Lieder ohne Worte, op. 30 (No. 4): MENDELS-
   SOHN

Wanderer, Der, D. 489 <- Der Fremdling / Der Unglückliche:
  SCHUBERT
Wanderer-Fantasie -> Fantasia, piano, D. 760, C major: SCHU-
  BERT
Wanderlied -> Gedichte, op. 35 (Wanderlust): SCHUMANN
Wanderschaft -> Die schöne Müllerin (Das Wandern): SCHUBERT
War sonatas -> Sonata, piano, no. 6, op. 82, A major; no. 7,
  op. 83, Bb major; no. 8, op. 84, Bb major: PROKOFIEV
War song, A -> A soldier's song: ELGAR
War song march, A / Fighting for the people's new free world
  -> They are there: IVES
Was Gott tut ist wohlgetan, S. 250 <- Trauungschoräle / Wed-
  ding chorales: J.S.BACH
Was mir behagt, S. 208 <- Birthday cantata / Geburtstagskan-
  tate / Jagdkantate / Hunting cantata: J.S.BACH
Washington at Trenton -> McKonkey's Ferry: ANTHEIL
Wasps, The (Suite) <- Aristophanic suite: VAUGHAN WILLIAMS
Wassermann, Der <- The water goblin: DVOŘÁK
Wasserträger, Der / The water carrier -> Les deux journées:
  CHERUBINI
Water carrier, The / Der Wasserträger -> Les deux journées:
  CHERUBINI
Water goblin, The -> Der Wassermann: DVOŘÁK
Water music / Hamburger Ebb und Fluht -> Suite, orchestra, C
  major: TELEMANN
Water piece -> Suite, trumpet, strings & continuo, D major:
  HÄNDEL
Wedding anthem -> The King shall rejoice: BOYCE
Wedding anthem -> Beati omnes qui timent Dominum: PURCELL
Wedding anthem for Princess Anne -> This is the day: HÄNDEL
Wedding anthem for the Prince of Wales -> Sing unto God:
  HANDEL
Wedding cake <- Valse-caprice, piano & strings, op. 76: SAINT-
  SAËNS
Wedding cantata / Hochzeitskantate / Trauungskantate -> Der
  Herr denket an uns, S. 196: J.S.BACH
Wedding cantata / Hochzeitskantate -> Dem Gerechten muss das
  Licht, S. 195; Weichet nur, betrübte Schatten, S. 202; O
  holder Tag, S. 210; Vergnügte Pleissen Stadt, S. 216: J.S.
  BACH
Wedding chorales / Trauungschoräle -> Was Gott tut is wohl-
  getan, S. 250; Sei Lob und Ehr, S. 251; Nun danket den
  Herre Gott, S. 252: J.S.BACH
Wedding music -> Undine (Selections): HENZE
Wedding music -> Suite, flute, no. 5: LUENING
Wedge fugue / Great E minor prelude -> Prelude and fugue,
  organ, S. 548, E minor: J.S.BACH
Wehmut, Die, D. 404 <- Herbstnacht: SCHUBERT

Weiberfreund, Der, D. 271 <- The inconstant: SCHUBERT
Weichet nur, betrübte Schatten, S. 202 <- Hochzeitskantate
  / Wedding cantata: J.S.BACH
Weigl variations -> Sonata con variazioni, violin & orches-
  tra: PAGANINI
Weihe der Töne, Die -> Symphony, no. 4, op. 86: SPOHR
Weihnachtshistorie / The Christmas story / Christmas orato-
  rio -> Historia von der Geburt Jesu Christi: SCHÜTZ
Weihnachtskantate / Christmas cantata -> Christen, ätzet
  diesen Tag, S. 63: J.S.BACH
Weihnachtskantate / Christmas cantata -> Ehre sei Gott in
  der Höhe: TELEMANN
Weihnachtslied -> O heilige Nacht: LISZT
Weihnachtslied -> Lieder, op. 80 (Sehnsucht): WEBER
Weihnachtssymphonie / Christmas symphony / Lamentatione ->
  Symphony, M. 26, D minor: J.HAYDN
Weilburg sonatas -> Sonata, violin & piano, K. 26, E♭ major;
  K. 27, G major; K. 28, C major; K. 29, D major; K. 30, F
  major; K. 31, B♭ major: MOZART
Weinzierler trios -> Divertimento, H.II,33, F major; Diver-
  timento, H.II,38, A major; Trio, violins & violoncello, H.
  V,C4, C major; H.V,D3, D major; H.V,D4, D major; H.V,Es9,
  E♭ major: J.HAYDN
Welcome to all the pleasures <- Ode for Saint Cecilia's Day
  [1683]: PURCELL
Welcome, welcome glorious morn <- Ode for Queen Mary's
  birthday [1691]: PURCELL
Wellingtons Sieg <- Battle symphony: BEETHOVEN
Wenn wir in höchsten Nöten sein / Vor deinen Thron tret ich
  / Leipzig chorales -> Chorale prelude, S. 668: J.S.BACH
Wer kauft Liebesgötter?, D. 261 <- Liebesgötter auf dem
  Markte: SCHUBERT
Wer nur den lieben Gott lässt walten / Schübler chorales ->
  Chorale prelude, S. 647: J.S.BACH
Wesendonk songs -> Gedichte von Mathilde Wesendonk: WAGNER
West Point symphony -> Symphony, band: HARRIS
Westwind -> Suleika, D. 717: SCHUBERT
What torment -> Songs, op. 6 (Painfully and sweetly): TCHAI-
  KOVSKY
When Johnny comes marching home <- An American overture:
  HARRIS
When lilacs last in the door-yard bloom'd <- American requi-
  em / Fliederrequiem / A requiem for those we love: HINDE-
  MITH
Where righteous doth say <- The humble complaint of a sin-
  ner: DOWLAND
While Phoebus us'd to dwell <- The noble famous Queen: BYRD
While Thirsis, wrapt in downy sleep <- A pastoral coronation

song: PURCELL
Whimsies / Fancies, piano, op. 25 -> Bizarreries: MIASKOVSKY
White mass -> Sonata, piano, no. 7, op. 64, F# major: SKRIA-
    BIN
Whitsun oratorio / Pfingstoratorium -> Spiritus intelligen-
    tiae sanctus: KRENEK
Why, why are all the muses mute? (Selections) <- King James
    II suite: PURCELL
Widmung -> There is a lane: IVES
Wie ist dein Name so gross <- Donnerode / Ode to thunder:
    TELEMANN
Wiegenlied -> Aus der Kinderzeit (Schlummerlied): WOLF
Wiegenlieder-Walzer, orchestra <- Schlummerlieder: JOSEPH
    STRAUSS
Wiener Blut-Walzer, orchestra <- Wiener Leben / Vienna life:
    JOHANN STRAUSS
Wiener Frauen <- Der Klavierstimmer: LEHÁR
Wiener Frauen-Walzer, orchestra <- Les dames de St. Péters-
    bourgh: JOHANN STRAUSS
Wiener Kinder-Walzer, orchestra <- Heimatskinder: JOSEPH
    STRAUSS
Wiener Leben / Vienna life -> Wiener Blut-Walzer, orchestra:
    JOHANN STRAUSS
Wiener Quartette / Viennese quartets / Austrian quartets /
    Osterreichische Quartette -> Quartet, strings, K. 168, F
    major; K. 169, A major; K. 170, C major; K. 171, E♭ major;
    K. 172, B♭ major; K. 173, D minor: MOZART
Wiener Serenaden / Wiener Sonatinen / Viennese sonatinas ->
    Divertimento, K. 439b (Anh. 229, 229a) no. 1, B♭ major;
    no. 2, B♭ major; no. 3, B♭ major; no. 4, B♭ major; no. 5,
    D major: MOZART
Wiener Sonatinen / Viennese sonatinas / Wiener Serenaden ->
    Divertimento, K. 439b (Anh. 229, 229a) no. 1, B♭ major; no.
    2, B♭ major; no. 3, B♭ major; no. 4, B♭ major; no. 5, D ma-
    jor: MOZART
Wildbacher Ländler -> Ländler, violin, D. 374: SCHUBERT
Wilde Rosen <- Chrysanthemum-Walzer: LEHÁR
William Will <- Election songs: IVES
Wilson's wild <- Wolsey's wilde: BYRD
Wind-band mass / Harmoniemesse -> Mass, H.XXII,14, B♭ major:
    J.HAYDN
Windhager Messe / Short chorale mass -> Mass, alto, 2 horns
    & organ, C major: BRUCKNER
Winter, Der -> Symphony, no. 11, op. 214, A minor: RAFF
Winter -> Songs, op. 54 (Lullaby in a storm): TCHAIKOVSKY
Winter / L'inverno / Concerto, op. 8, no. 4, F minor -> Il
    cimento dell' armonia e dell' inventione (No. 4): VIVALDI
Winter bonfire, op. 122 <- Winter holiday / Children's suite:

PROKOFIEV

Winter dreams -> Symphony, no. 1, op. 13, G minor: TCHAIKOV-
SKY

Winter holiday / Children's suite -> Winter bonfire, op. 122:
PROKOFIEV

Winter wind etude -> Etude, piano, op. 25, no. 11, A minor: CHO-
PIN

Wintertag, Der, D.984 <- Geburtstagslied: SCHUBERT

Wirt und Gast <- Aus Scherz ernst / Die beiden Kalifen / Alimelek: MEYERBEER

Witches' dance -> Le streghe: PAGANINI

Witches' minuet / Hexenmenüett -> Quartet, strings, no. 77,
op. 76, no. 2, D minor (Minuet): J.HAYDN

Without repose -> Lieder ohne Worte, op. 30 (No. 2): MENDELS-
SOHN

Wives's excuse, The <- Cuckolds make themselves: PURCELL

Wo die Citronen blüh'n <- Bella Italia: JOHANN STRAUSS

Wo die Lerche singt -> A pacsirta: LEHÁR

Wo soll ich fliehen hin / Schübler chorales -> Chorale prelude, S. 646: J.S.BACH

Wolsey's wilde -> Wilson's wild: BYRD

Woman once in the night, A -> The Richmond heiress: PURCELL

Works (Selections; arr.) <- Birthday offering: GLAZUNOV

Works (Selections; arr.) <- Graduation ball: JOHANN STRAUSS

Works, piano (Selections; arr.) <- Les sylphides: CHOPIN

Would you a female heart inspire <- Vauxhall songs: J.C.BACH

Württemberg sonatas -> Sonata, harpsichord, W. 49, no. 1, A
minor; W. 49, no. 2, A♭ major; W. 49, no. 3, E minor; W.
49, no. 4, B♭ major; W. 49, no. 5, E♭ major; W. 49, no. 6,
B minor: C.P.E.BACH

Wut über den verlorenen Groschen, Der / Rage over the lost
penny -> Rondo a capriccio, piano, op. 129, G major: BEET-
HOVEN

Xerse -> Serse: CAVALLI

Xerxes -> Serse: HÄNDEL

Yankee doodle -> Souvenir d'Amérique: VIEUXTEMPS

Yarema's song -> On the Dnieper: MUSORGSKY

Year 1905, The / 1905 symphony -> Symphony, no. 11, op. 103:
SHOSTAKOVICH

Year 1917, The / 1917 symphony / To the memory of Lenin ->
Symphony, no. 12, op. 112: SHOSTAKOVICH

Yorck'scher Marsch / Landwehrmarsch -> March, band, K. 18, F
major: BEETHOVEN

Young person's guide to the orchestra, The <- Variations and
fugue on a theme by Purcell: BRITTEN

Young pioneers, The -> Sunday afternoon music: COPLAND

Young Thirsis' fate ye hills and groves deplore <- Elegy on
 the death of Thomas Farmer: PURCELL
Youth concerto -> Concerto, piano, no. 3, op. 50: KABALEVSKY
Youthful symphony -> Symphony, D minor: RACHMANINOFF

Z ulice / From the street / Sonata 1.X.1905 -> Sonata, pi-
 ano, E♭ minor: JANACEK
Zärtliche Liebe -> Ich liebe dich: BEETHOVEN
Zaïre / Turkish suite -> Symphony, no. 13, D major: M.HAYDN
Zampogna -> Concerto, recorder, oboe & continuo, C major:
 BOISMORTIER
Zanetta <- Jouer avec le feu: AUBER
Zarathustra -> Also sprach Zarathustra: R.STRAUSS
Zartik Parkim <- Concerto, piano, op. 177: HOVANESS
Zauberharfe (Overture), Die <- Rosamunde overture: SCHUBERT
Zeit, die Tag und Jahre macht, Die, S. 134a <- Gratulations-
 Kantate: J.S.BACH
Zeitlose, Die <- Reconnaissance: JOHANN STRAUSS
Zelmar <- L'asyle: GRÉTRY
Zelmira, La <- La marina del Granatello: PAISIELLO
Zéphire <- Les nymphes de Diane: RAMEAU
Zerline <- La corbeille d'oranges: AUBER
Zigeunerbaron-Walzer -> Schatz-Walzer, orchestra: JOHANN
 STRAUSS
Zigeuner-Trio / Gypsy trio -> Trio, piano & strings, H.XV,
 25, G major: J.HAYDN
Zingareska -> Symphony, no. 1: ANTHEIL
Zoraide, La -> Ricciardo e Zoraide: ROSSINI
Zum Abendsegen -> Lord, have mercy upon us: MENDELSSOHN
Zum Feste der Dreieinigkeit <- 0 beata et benedicta: MENDELS-
 SOHN
Zur Friedensfeier -> Sonata, organ, no. 20, op. 196, F major:
 RHEINBERGER
Zur Herbstzeit -> Symphony, no. 10, op. 213, F minor: RAFF
Zur Namensfeier / Namensfeier Ouvertüre -> Overture, op.115,
 C major: BEETHOVEN
Zur Trauerfeier -> Myrthen (Zum Schluss; arr.): SCHUMANN
Zwerg, Der, D. 771 <- Treubruch: SCHUBERT
Zwickau symphony / Unfinished symphony -> Symphony, G minor:
 SCHUMANN

List of Composers

Adam, de la Halle, ca. 1235-ca. 1288

Albéniz, Isaac, 1860-1909

x Alfvén, Hugo, 1872-1960

x Antheil, George, 1900-1959

Arne, Thomas Augustine, 1710-1778

x Auber, Daniel François, 1782-1871

Bach, Carl Philipp Emanuel, 1714-1788

Bach, Johann Christian, 1735-1782.

Bach, Johann Sebastian, 1685-1750

? Badings, Henk, 1906-

Balakirev, Milii Alekseevich, 1837-1910

Barber, Samuel, 1910-1981

Bartók, Béla, 1881-1945

Bax, ~~Sir~~ Arnold, 1883-1953

Beethoven, Ludwig van, 1770-1827

Benda, Jiri Antonin, 1722-1795

Berg, Alban, 1885-1935

Berlioz, Hector, 1803-1869

Bernstein, Leonard, 1918-

Berwald, Franz, 1796-1868

Biber, Heinrich Ignaz Franz, 1644-1704

Bizet, Georges, 1838-1875

Blacher, Boris, 1903-1975

Blavet, Michel, 1700-1768

Bloch, Ernest, 1880-1959

Blow, John, d. 1708

Boccherini, Luigi, 1743-1805

Boieldieu, François Adrien, 1775-1834

Boismortier, Joseph Bodin de, 1689-1755

Borodin, ~~Alexander~~ Aleksandr Porfirevich, 1833-1887

Boulez, Pierre, 1925-

Boyce, William, 1710-1779

Brahms, Johannes, 1833-1897

Britten, Benjamin, 1913-1976

Bruch, Max, 1838-1920

Bruckner, Anton, 1824-1896

Byrd, William, 1542 or 3-1623

Caldara, Antonio, 1670-1736

Campra, André, 1660-1744

Carissimi, Giacomo, 1605-1674

Carter, Elliott, 1908-

Castelnuovo-Tedesco, Mario, 1895-1968

Cavalli, Pier Francesco, 1602-1676

Chabrier, Emmanuel, 1841-1894

Chavez, Carlos, 1899-1978

Cherubini, Luigi, 1760-1842

Chopin, Frédéric, 1810-1849

Cimarosa, Domenico, 1749-1801

Clementi, Muzio, 1752-1832

Copland, Aaron, 1900-

Corelli, Arcangelo, 1653-1713

Corrette, Michel, 1709-1795

Couperin, François, 1668-1733

Cowell, Henry, 1897-1965

Creston, Paul, 1906-

Danzi, Franz, 1763-1826

Debussy, Claude, 1862-1918

Delibes, Léo, 1836-1891

Delius, Frederick, 1862-1934

Deprès, Josquin, d. 1521

Dittersdorf, Karl, 1739-1799

Dohnányi, Erno, 1877-1960

Dowland, John, 1563-1626

Dufay, Guillaume, d. 1474

Dussek, Johann Ladislaus, 1760–1812

Dvořák, Antonín, 1841–1904

Elgar, Sir Edward, 1857–1934

Enesco, Georges, 1881–1955

Fauré, Gabriel, 1845–1924

Fibich, Zdeněk, 1850–1900

Fine, Irving, 1914–1962

Françaix, Jean, 1912–

Franck, César, 1822–1890

Frescobaldi, Girolamo, 1583–1643

Fux, Johann Joseph, 1660–1741

Gabrieli, Andrea, ca. 1510–1586

Gabrieli, Giovanni, 1557–1612

Gade, Niels, 1817–1890

Geminiani, Francesco, 1687–1762

Gershwin, George, 1886–1937

Gibbons, Orlando, 1583–1625

Ginastera, Alberto, 1916–

Glazunov, Alexander, 1865–1936

Glière, Reinhold, 1875–1956

Glinka, Mikhail Ivanovich, 1804–1857

Gluck, Christoph Willibald, 1714–1787

Goldmark, Karl, 1830–1915

Gottschalk, Louis Moreau, 1829–1869

Gounod, Charles, 1818–1893

Granados, Enrique, 1867–1916

Grétry, André, 1741–1813

Grieg, Edvard, 1843–1907

Griffes, Charles Tomlinson, 1884–1920

Händel, Georg Friedrich, 1685–1759

Hanson, Howard, 1896–1981

Harris, Roy, 1898–1979

Haydn, Joseph, 1732–1809

Haydn, Michael, 1737–1806

Henze, Hans Werner, 1926–

Hindemith, Paul, 1895–1963

Holmboe, Vagn, 1909–

Honegger, Arthur, 1892–1955

Hubay, Jenö, 1858–1937

Hummel, Johann Nepomuk, 1778–1837

Ibert, Jacques, 1890–1962

Indy, Vincent d', 1851–1931

Ireland, John, 1879–1962

Ives, Charles, 1874–1954

Janáček, Leoš, 1854–1928

Jolivet, André, 1905–1974

Kabalevsky, Dmitri, 1904–

Khachaturian, Aram, 1903–1978

Kodály, Zoltán, 1882–1967

Kreisler, Fritz, 1875–1962

Křenek, Ernst, 1900–

Kuhnau, Johann, 1660–1722

Lajtha, László, 1892–1963

Lalo, Edouard, 1823–1892

Lassus, Orland de, d. 1594

Lechner, Leonard, d. 1606

Leclair, Jean Marie, 1697–1764

Lehár, Ferenc, 1870–1948

Leo, Leonardo, 1694–1744

Ligeti, György, 1923–

Liszt, Franz, 1811–1886

Locatelli, Pietro, 1695–1764

Luening, Otto, 1900–

Lully, Jean Baptiste, 1632–1687

MacDowell, Edward, 1861–1908

Mahler, Gustav, 1860–1911

Malipiero, Gian Francesco, 1882–1973

Manfredini, Francesco, 1684–1762

Martin, Frank, 1890–1974

Martinů, Bohuslav, 1890–1959

Méhul, Étienne, 1763–1817

Mendelssohn, Felix, 1809–1847

Meyerbeer, Giacomo, 1791–1864

Miaskovsky, Nikolai, 1881–1950

Milhaud, Darius, 1892–1974

Monteverdi, Claudio, 1567–1643

Mozart, Wolfgang Amadeus, 1756–1791

Musorgsky, Modest, 1839–1881

Nielsen, Carl, 1865–1931

Offenbach, Jacques, 1819–1880

Paganini, Nicolò, 1782–1840

Paisiello, Giovanni, 1740–1816

Palestrina, Giovanni, 1525?–1594

Penderecki, Krzysztof, 1933–

Pepin, Clermont, 1926–

Pergolesi, Giovanni Battista, 1710–1736

Pfitzner, Hans, 1869–1949

Piccinni, Niccolò, 1728–1800

Poulenc, Francis, 1899–1963

Prokofiev, Sergei, 1891–1953

Puccini, Giacomo, 1858–1924

Purcell, Henry, 1658 or 9–1695

Quantz, Johann Joachim, 1697–1773

Rachmaninoff, Sergei, 1873–1943

Raff, Joachim, 1822–1882

Rameau, Jean Philippe, 1683–1764

Ravel, Maurice, 1875–1937

Reger, Max, 1873–1916

Respighi, Ottorino, 1873–1936

Rheinberger, Joseph, 1839–1901

Rimsky-Korsakov, Nikolai, 1844–1908

Rosenberg, Hilding, 1892–

Rossini, Gioacchino, 1792–1868

Rubinstein, Anton, 1830–1894

Saint-Saëns, Camille, 1835–1921

Salieri, Antonio, 1750–1825

Satie, Erik, 1866–1925

Scarlatti, Alessandro, 1660–1725

Scarlatti, Domenico, 1685–1757

Scheidt, Samuel, 1587–1654

Schönberg, Arnold, 1874–1951

Schubert, Franz, 1797–1828

Schütz, Heinrich, 1585–1672

Schuman, William, 1910–

Schumann, Robert, 1810–1856

Shostakovich, Dmitri, 1906–1975

Sibelius, Jean, 1865–1957

Skriabin, Alexander, 1872–1915

Smetana, Bedřich, 1824–1884

Spohr, Louis, 1784–1859

Spontini, Gasparo, 1774–1851

Stamitz, Johann, 1717–1757

Stockhausen, Karlheinz, 1928–

Stradella, Alessandro, 1644–1682

Strauss, Johann, 1825–1899

Strauss, Joseph, 1827–1870

Strauss, Richard, 1864–1949

Stravinsky, Igor, 1882–1971

Suk, Josef, 1874-1935

Swelinck, Jan Pietersz., 1562-1621

Szymanowski, Karol, 1882-1937

Tartini, Giuseppe, 1692-1770

Tchaikovsky, Piotr Ilich, 1840-1893

Telemann, Georg Philipp, 1681-1767

Thomson, Virgil, 1896-

Tippett, Sir Michael, 1905-

Tomkins, Thomas, 1572-1656

Torelli, Giuseppe, 1658-1709

Turina, Joaquín, 1882-1949

Vaughan Williams, Ralph, 1872-1958

Verdi, Giuseppe, 1813-1901

Victoria, Tomás Luis de, ca. 1540-1611

Vieuxtemps, Henri, 1820-1881

Villa-Lobos, Heitor, 1887-1959

Vivaldi, Antonio, 1678-1741

Vladigerov, Pancho, 1899-

Wagner, Richard, 1813-1883

Waldteufel, Emil, 1837-1915

Walton, Sir William, 1902-1983

Weber, Karl Maria von, 1786-1826

Weill, Kurt, 1900-1950

Weiner, Leó, 1885-1960

Widor, Charles Marie, 1844-1937

Wieniawski, Henri, 1835-1880

Wolf, Hugo, 1860-1903

Xenakis, Iannis, 1922-

Ysaÿe, Eugène, 1858-1931

Key to Catalogue Numbers

BACH, Carl Philipp Emanuel
  W. numbers refer to Alfred Wotquenne, Thematisches Verzeichnis, 1964

BACH, Johann Sebastian
  S. numbers refer to Wolfgang Schmieder, Thematisches Verzeichnis, 1950

BEETHOVEN, Ludwig van
  K. numbers refer to Georg Kinsky, Thematisches Verzeichnis,
  1955

BOCCHERINI, Luigi
  G. numbers refer Yves Gérard, Thematic catalogue, 1969

BYRD, William
  MB numbers refer to the complete keyboard works, edited by
  Alan Brown in Musica Britannica, v. 27-28, 1969-1971

DITTERSDORF, Karl
  K. numbers refer to Karl Krebs, Dittersdorfiana, 1972

FUX, Johann Joseph
  K. numbers refer to Ludwig Köchel, Johann Joseph Fux, 1872

GIBBONS, Orlando
  H. numbers refer to Gerald Hendrie, The keyboard works of
  Orlando Gibbons, 1962

HÄNDEL, Georg Friedrich
  B. numbers refer to A. Craig Bell, Chronologicalt thematic
  catalogue, 1972

HAYDN, Joseph
  H. numbers refer to Anthony van Hoboken, Thematisches Ver-
  zeichnis, 1957-1978
  M. numbers refer to Eusebius Mandyczewski, Joseph Haydns
  Werke, 1922

MOZART, Wolfgang Amadeus
  K. numbers refer to Ludwig Köchel, Thematisches Verzeichnis, 6th ed., 1964

PURCELL, Henry
  Z. numbers refer to Franklin B. Zimmermann, An analytical
  catalogue of Purcell's music, 1963

SCARLATTI, Domenico
  K. numbers refer to Ralph Kirkpatrick, Thematisches Verzeichnis, 1972
  L. numbers in parentheses refer to A. Longo, Opere complete
  per clavicembalo, 1906-1908

SCHUBERT, Franz
  D. numbers refer to Otto Erich Deutsch, Thematisches Ver-

zeichnis, 2d ed., 1978

SWELINCK, Jan Pietersz.
L. numbers refer to Gustav Leonhardt, ed., Fantasias and toccatas, 1968

TELEMANN, Georg Philipp
The source for numbering of his overtures (orchestral suites) is Adolf Hoffmann, Die Orchestersuiten Georg Philipp Telemanns, 1969

TOMKINS, Thomas
T. numbers refer to the keyboard music of Tomkins, ed. by Stephen Tuttle, Musica Britannica, v. 5

VIVALDI, Antonio
R. numbers refer to Peter Ryom, Verzeichnis der Werke Antonio Vivaldis, 1971

Principal Sources

Baillie, Laureen, ed.
  The catalogue of printed music in the British Library to
  1980. London, K.G. Saur, 1981-

Berkowitz, Freda Pastor
  Popular titles and subtitles of musical compositions. 2d
  ed. Metuchen, N.J., The Scarecrow Press, 1975

Bielefelder Katalog
  Katalog der Schallplatten klassischer Musik. Bielefeld,
  Bielefelder Verlagsanstalt, 1953-

Blom, Eric, ed.
  Grove's dictionary of music and musicians, 5th ed. London, Macmillan, 1954

Blume, Friedrich, ed.
  Musik in der Gegenwart und Geschichte. Kassel, Bärenrei-
  ter-Verlag, 1959-1979

Clough, F.F., comp.
  The world's encyclopaedia of recorded music. London, Sidg-
  wick and Jackson, 1952-1957

Diapason
  Catalogue général des disques microsillons. Paris, Diapa-
  son-Microsillon, 1955-

Gatti, Guido M., ed.
  La musica; enciclopedia storia. Torino, Unione Tipografi-
  co-Editrice Torinese, 1968

Gatti, Guido M., ed.
  La musica; dizionario. Torino, Unione Tipografico-Editri-
  ce Torinese, 1968

The Gramophone
  Long playing classical record catalogue. Kenton, General
  Gramophone Publications Ltd., 1954-

The Gramophone Shop Encyclopedia of Recorded Music
  New York, The Gramophone Shop, 1936,1942,1948

The Gramophone Shop Encyclopedia of Recorded Music. Third ed.
  Westport, Conn., Greenwood Press, 1970

Hodgson, Julian
  Musical titles in translation; a checklist of musical compositions. London, Clive Bingley, 1976

Library of Congress
  The National Union Catalog of the Library of Congress; music and phonorecords. Ann Arbor, Mich., J.W. Edwards,
  1957-

New York Public Library (Reference Department)
  Dictionary catalog of the music collection. Boston, G.K.
  Hall, 1964-1973

New York Public Library (Rodgers and Hammerstein Archives of
Recorded Sound)
  Dictionary catalog of the Rodgers and Hammerstein Archives
  of Recorded Sound. Boston, G.K. Hall, 1981

Olmstead, Elizabeth H., ed.
  Music Library Association catalog of cards for printed music 1953-1972. Totona, N.J., Rowman and Littlefield, 1974

Pazdirek, Franz
  Universal-Handbuch der Musikliteratur aller Zeiten und
  Völker. Hilversum, Frits Knelf, 1967

Ranson, P., comp.
  ...by any other name...; a guide to the popular names and
  nicknames of classical music, 5th ed. Newcastle upon Tyne,
  Northern Regional Library System; Central Library, 1984

Sadie, Stanley, ed.
  The new Grove dictionary of music and musicians. London,
  Macmillan Publishers Ltd., 1980

Schwann Long Playing Record Catalog
  Boston, W. Schwann, 1949-

University of Toronto
  Card catalogues of the Edward Johnson Music Library

University of Toronto
  Phonodisc collection of the Sam Sniderman Archives in the
  Edward Johnson Music Library

ABOUT THE COMPILER

Steven G. Pallay is Records Librarian at Edward Johnson Music Library,
University of Toronto, Canada. He is the author of *ENUFFF!!—The Jaundiced
Ruminations of an Irascible Cat* (fiction), and *Cross Index Guide to Operas* (in
process).